Shariah, Society and Stratification

The **ISEAS – Yusof Ishak Institute** (formerly Institute of Southeast Asian Studies) is an autonomous organization established in 1968. It is a regional centre dedicated to the study of socio-political, security, and economic trends and developments in Southeast Asia and its wider geostrategic and economic environment. The Institute's research programmes are grouped under Regional Economic Studies (RES), Regional Strategic and Political Studies (RSPS), and Regional Social and Cultural Studies (RSCS). The Institute is also home to the ASEAN Studies Centre (ASC), the Singapore APEC Study Centre and the Temasek History Research Centre (THRC).

ISEAS Publishing, an established academic press, has issued more than 2,000 books and journals. It is the largest scholarly publisher of research about Southeast Asia from within the region. ISEAS Publishing works with many other academic and trade publishers and distributors to disseminate important research and analyses from and about Southeast Asia to the rest of the world.

Shariah, Society and Stratification

Muslim Lifestyles in Southeast Asia

Edited by
Norshahril Saat • Sharifah Afra Alatas

YUSOF ISHAK
INSTITUTE

First published in Singapore in 2024 by
ISEAS Publishing
30 Heng Mui Keng Terrace
Singapore 119614
E-mail: publish@iseas.edu.sg
Website: http://bookshop.iseas.edu.sg

All rights reserved. No part of this publication may be reproduced, stored in a retrieval system, or transmitted in any form or by any means, electronic, mechanical, photocopying, recording or otherwise, without the prior permission of the ISEAS – Yusof Ishak Institute.

© 2024 ISEAS – Yusof Ishak Institute, Singapore

The responsibility for facts and opinions in this publication rests exclusively with the authors and their interpretations do not necessarily reflect the views or the policy of the publisher or its supporters.

ISEAS Library Cataloguing-in-Publication Data

Name(s): Norshahril Saat, editor. | Alatas, Sharifah Afra, editor.
Title: Shariah, society and stratification : Muslim lifestyles in Southeast Asia / edited by Norshahril Saat and Sharifah Afra Alatas.
Description: Singapore : ISEAS – Yusof Ishak Institute, 2024. | Includes bibliographical references and index.
Identifiers: ISBN 9789815104943 (soft cover) | ISBN 9789815104950 (PDF) | ISBN 9789815104967 (epub)
Subjects: LCSH: Islam—Southeast Asia—Customs and practices. | Social structure—Religious aspects—Islam. | Muslims—Southeast Asia—Social life and customs.
Classification: LCC BP173.63 S53

Cover design by Lee Meng Hui
Index compiled by Raffaie Nahar
Typeset by Superskill Graphics Pte Ltd
Printed in Singapore by Markono Print Media Pte Ltd

Contents

About the Contributors   vii

1. Introduction   1
   Norshahril Saat and Sharifah Afra Alatas

PART I: DRIVERS AND PROCESSES

2. Marketing Religious Piety: Halal Products Forged and Disputed   9
   Faegheh Shirazi

3. Evolution of the Halal Industry and Lifestyle   27
   Mohammad Hashim Kamali

4. Drivers of Shariah-Compliant Lifestyle in Indonesia: Majelis Ulama Indonesia (MUI)   46
   Syafiq Hasyim

5. The Emergence of Islamic Finance and Its Impact on the Lives of Muslims in Thailand   62
   Tawat Noipom

PART II: SOCIALIZATION OF LIFESTYLE AND NEOLIBERAL CAPITALISM

6. Shariah Compliance and Impact on Reading Culture in Malaysia   81
   Azhar Ibrahim

7. Finding Soulmate through Halal Means: Online Ta'aruf among Indonesian Muslim Youth   96
   Wahyudi Akmaliah

8. Halal Lifestyle and the Everyday Politics of the Muslim Non-State Actors in Brunei   115
   Siti Mazidah Mohamad

9. Spirituality and Commodity: Drivers of Shariah Tourism
in Singapore 130
Norshahril Saat

10. Marketing an "Islamic Lifestyle" in Singapore: The Case of
Islamic-Inspired Products in Kampong Gelam 149
Sharifah Afra Alatas and Nadirah Norruddin

11. Branding Islam in Singapore: Between Representation and
Commodification 174
Sheikh Mohamad Farouq and Nailul Farah Mohd Masbur

12. Thai Muslim Women's Negotiation with Sharia through
Food and Clothing 199
Amporn Marddent

Index 219

The Contributors

Amporn Marddent is Assistant Professor in the Faculty of Sociology and Anthropology, Thammasat University, Thailand.

Azhar Ibrahim is Senior Lecturer at the Department of Malay Studies, National University of Singapore.

Faegheh Shirazi is Professor Emeritus at the Department of Middle Eastern Studies, College of Liberal Arts, the University of Texas at Austin.

Mohammad Hashim Kamali is Very Distinguished Fellow of the International Institute of Advanced Islamic Studies, Malaysia.

Nadirah Norruddin was formerly Research Officer in the Regional Social and Cultural Studies Programme, ISEAS – Yusof Ishak Institute, Singapore.

Nailul Farah Mohd Masbur is Research Analyst at the Centre for Research on Islamic and Malay Affairs (RIMA), Singapore.

Norshahril Saat is Senior Fellow and Coordinator of the Regional Social and Cultural Studies Programme, ISEAS – Yusof Ishak Institute, Singapore.

Sharifah Afra Alatas is Research Officer in the Regional Social and Cultural Studies Programme, ISEAS – Yusof Ishak Institute, Singapore.

Sheikh Mohamad Farouq Abdul Fareez was Senior Research Analyst at the Centre for Research on Islamic and Malay Affairs (RIMA), Singapore.

Siti Mazidah Mohamad is Assistant Professor in the Geography, Environment and Development Studies Programme and Director of the Centre for Advanced Research (CARe), Universiti Brunei Darussalam.

Syafiq Hasyim is Visiting Fellow in the Indonesia Studies Programme, ISEAS – Yusof Ishak Institute, and Lecturer and Director of Library and Culture at the Indonesian International Islamic University (IIIU), Jakarta.

Tawat Noipom is Assistant Professor at Prince of Songkla University, Thailand.

Wahyudi Akmaliah is a PhD candidate in the Department of Malay Studies, National University of Singapore.

1

INTRODUCTION

Norshahril Saat and Sharifah Afra Alatas

Three Malay bachelors had a long day at work. They gathered at one of their colleagues' workplaces and started their journey back to their house, by foot. Along the way, they discussed ways to reward themselves for the hard day's work. One suggested dining out, but the rest disagreed, preferring to cook. So, they stopped halfway and bought a live chicken from a Chinese seller by the roadside. This was how business was conducted in the 1950s in Singapore. "Two katis, so three ringgits!" said the seller. The three men agreed to share the purchase. They carried the living chicken all the way home. Upon arriving, they were greeted by a man called Nyong who was sweeping the compounds of the village. The man teased the bachelors, "So who would cook for you?" Despite being unmarried, the men replied that they were trained to cook, and requested Nyong to slaughter the chicken.

That was the opening scene of the movie *Bujang Lapok*, one of the well-known P. Ramlee comedies. While the film shared the struggles of young bachelors in pre-independent Singapore, scenes like this also encapsulate the lifestyle before the Islamic resurgence movement in the 1970s. Imagine how different the three bachelors would behave today. They could drop by a supermarket, choose slaughtered chickens from the freezer, and they could choose which part of it rather than purchasing the whole chicken. Being good Muslims, they can verify its halalness by looking at the halal logo indicated on the packaging, without needing to pass it to another Muslim to slaughter the chicken. The identity of the chicken owner is also unknown as the chicken might have been slaughtered at the slaughterhouse.

While once it was not uncommon for Muslims to patronize halal poultry without halal certification (because it did not yet exist), it is now almost unthinkable. A halal certificate symbolizes that the meat at a given supermarket is permitted for consumption, while the meat without such certification is deemed prohibited. The meat would have undergone a thorough process to meet halal standards.

The halal industry in Southeast Asia has been growing since the 1980s. It is a by-product of the Islamic resurgence (some referred to this period as Islamic revivalism or *dakwah* movement) which swept across the region in the 1970s and 1980s, witnessing the importation of ideologies from the Middle East such as Salafi-Wahhabism from Saudi Arabia, Shi'ism's *vilayet-e-faqeh* inspired by the 1979 Iranian Revolution, and the *tarbiyah* movement adapted from the Muslim Brotherhood in Egypt. Though competing with one another, these ideologies shared the common goal of establishing an Islamic socio-political order as an alternative to a Western order. Southeast Asia became the hotbed of Islamic resurgence, with groups championing a dogmatic ideology which emphasized "Islam as a way of life". Members of these groups, known as Islamists, were active on campus and in urban centres. At the same time, the emerging Muslim middle classes in Malaysia, Indonesia and Singapore provided the demand for halal consumer goods and the intellectual drive behind these movements. In the initial phases, the movement sought to focus attention on building Islamic states and implement shariah laws. Such demands were not realized after those in charge of the states refused to budge, so Islamists focused their attention more on developing shariah-compliant societies while grappling with development and modernity.

From the 1980s to the early 2000s, Islamic resurgence has manifested in aspirations for a "shariah-compliant" modernity. This aspiration for shariah compliance has resulted in institutional formations such as Islamic banks and increased religiosity in matters of identity formation. This process includes the increased donning of headscarves by Muslim women and the desire for greater forms of Islamic education. So too is the increasing demand and supply of halal consumer goods and services. Today, a shariah-compliant lifestyle has become so dominant that questioning it would be deemed un-Islamic, and critics would be easily brushed off as "liberal" Muslims. Beyond establishing Islamic financial systems and requiring halal certification for food and beverages, segments of the community now call for halal labels for non-consumable products such as paint, plastic bags, detergents, facial products, and electronics. Even the tourism sector is distinguished between shariah-compliant and non-shariah-compliant. Thus, with its penetration into various aspects of society, economics, and personal life, it has become difficult to reverse the emergence—and even institutionalization—of a shariah-compliant or halal lifestyle. It is therefore worth exploring the consequences of the emergence of such a lifestyle, and its similarities and differences with the calls for an all-encompassing Islamic lifestyle made in the 1970s and 1980s.

In today's context, halal lifestyle and consumption cannot be reversed to pre-resurgence levels. One could no longer question the process. A society captured in the *Bujang Lapok* scene described earlier would be unimaginable today; in fact, many of the portrayals of Malay society in the films created in the 1950s to 1970s would be deemed to be not conforming to Islamic standards.

Objectives of this Book

Shariah, Society and Stratification: Muslim Lifestyles in Southeast Asia examines the impact of Islamic resurgence in Southeast Asia five decades on. It compares five maritime Southeast Asian countries: Brunei, Indonesia, Malaysia, Singapore and Thailand. It focuses on what/who are the drivers of shariah-compliant business and certification; the extent to which Muslim societies embrace a shariah-compliant lifestyle whether through entertainment, literature, fashion, tourism, or food; and the prospects of a shariah-compliant lifestyle in the digital age.

In addressing these points, this volume has three objectives: (1) to identify specific trends in halal demand and consumption in Brunei, Indonesia, Malaysia, Singapore and Thailand. Such trends could include consumption patterns of traditional halal products such as food and drink, as well as non-traditional halal products and services, such as literature, banking, online dating, and tourism; (2) to identify the political, social, economic and religious forces behind these trends. It will examine the organizations, policies and actors who drive these trends. It will also look at how technology and social media influence consumption patterns among different age groups and socio-economic classes; and (3) to discuss the potential consequences of these trends.

To meet these objectives, the chapters are organized in two parts: Part I looks at the drivers and processes behind greater adherence to a shariah-compliant or halal lifestyle. Faegheh Shirazi (Chapter 2) focuses on an expanding global Muslim consumer market and how businesses' use of halal certification is more about commercial profit rather than honouring religious practice and faith. In the process, the chapter exposes how there have been goods fraudulently labelled as halal to take advantage of Muslim spending power. Chapter 3 by Mohammad Hashim Kamali looks at the emergence of halal industries and lifestyles in Southeast Asia in general, and Malaysia in particular. It provides an overview of the growth of industries such as halal fashion, cosmetics, dating and matchmaking in the region, while looking at halal standards, certification, industrial parks and pharmaceuticals in Malaysia. The chapter concludes that there has been much enthusiasm for the growth of various halal industries, whether from consumers, producers, or the state, and that more effort should be made to realize Malaysia's successful transition to a halal economy.

Moving on to Indonesia, Syafiq Hasyim (Chapter 4) looks at the role of Islamic organizations in promoting a shariah-compliant lifestyle. More specifically, it discusses how the Indonesian Council of Ulama (Majelis Ulama Indonesia, MUI), through its issuing of *fatwa* (legal opinions) has been successful in promoting "shariahtization through lifestyle". In doing so, the chapter illustrates how a shariah-compliant lifestyle in the aspects of food and finance, for example, is more palatable to the Indonesian public than other organizations' calls for an Islamic state. To close this section, Tawat Noipom in Chapter 5 traces the growth of the Islamic finance industry in Thailand and its impact on Muslims there. An analysis of its growth reveals that while Islamic finance has been beneficial for Thai Muslims, the industry has become more commercialized and no longer focuses as much on religious requirements as opposed to commercial goals. Consequently, the chapter suggests that such commercialization might be the only way for Thai Muslims to keep the industry alive and preserve a part of their Muslim identity.

Part II then looks at specific case studies in the region and examines how there has been a socialization of a shariah-compliant or "Islamic lifestyle", influenced by the forces of neoliberal capitalism. Azhar Ibrahim (Chapter 6) examines the impact of shariah-compliance on reading culture in Malaysia. In doing so, he focuses on the calls for "Sastera Islam" (Islamic Literature) and how such calls have produced more exclusivist literature. In the process, there is a rejection of literature that emphasizes the values already entrenched in Malay literature, such as humanism, pluralism and multiculturalism. Focusing on a more private aspect of life, in Chapter 7, Wahyudi Akmaliah discusses the emergence of online halal dating among Muslim youth in Indonesia and how this has been fuelled by the rise to prominence of new religious authorities in the country, large-scale digitalization, and the global phenomenon of halal online matchmaking among Muslims.

Siti Mazidah Mohamad in Chapter 8 then looks at the case of Brunei and how non-state actors such as micro-celebrities, influencers, and ordinary youth participate in everyday halal activism on digital media. In discussing their digital presence, she argues that the everyday surveillance and moral policing of Muslims' everyday lives is illustrative of shariah-compliant use of social media which serves to reinforce the hegemonic practices of the country's religious authority. In Chapter 9, Norshahril Saat brings readers worldwide and discusses how shariah compliance has affected tourism. Looking at the case of Singapore, he argues that the rise of the Muslim middle class, combined with the forces of Islamic resurgence, have contributed to the growth of shariah-compliant tourism. However, while shariah-compliant tour packages may fulfil Muslim travellers' needs, they tend to lack a holistic approach and are superficial in cherishing Islamic principles, at the same time giving little regard to inequality, environmental concerns and good standards.

Sharifah Afra Alatas and Nadirah Norruddin (Chapter 10) continue on the topic of the Muslim middle class and how the growth in popularity of Islamic-inspired products is illustrative of a moulding of an "Islamic lifestyle". Their discussion raises questions about how the commodification of religion and conspicuous consumption may affect expressions of religiosity or undermine the spiritual value of important religious symbols. In Chapter 11, Sheikh Mohamad Farouq and Nailul Farah Mohd Masbur also examine the commodification of religion in Singapore, arguing that the forces of neoliberalism and Islamophobia have allowed market actors to capitalize on Muslim piety for commercial gains. In doing so, they look at three case studies of paid partnerships between Singaporean Muslim micro-celebrities and business corporations, demonstrating how the aforementioned forces interact with a Muslim's sense of piety. Finally, Amporn Marddent (Chapter 12) examines how Muslim women in Thailand negotiate the shariah and halal requirements through their entrepreneurial activities. In studying women who own small food businesses, she illustrates how their religious identities influence their business practices and the provision of halal goods and services.

Book's Limitations

The editors of this volume declare at the outset the limitations of compiling a book on evolving trends. First, it is impossible to cover all ASEAN countries in an edited volume. Even though we have limited the scope of the book to maritime Southeast Asian countries, we are unable to include Muslims in the Philippines due to space constraints. This is not to imply that the countries not covered in this book are less important. As this is the first book discussing a relatively understudied subject matter, we hope countries left out in this volume will be covered in subsequent books, once scholarship on this area develops. To be sure, Muslim societies are also grappling with pressures from other parts of the region, as well as globally, to meet prescribed standards of shariah that did not exist in the past.

Second, the authors in this volume too have different views regarding the status of shariahtization. Some are more sympathetic compared to others, as they grapple with the data presented to them. Ultimately, as editors, we allow for differences of opinion, as long as writers are not promoting exclusivist or radical ideas, such as promoting the Islamization of societies at the expense of minority rights. Southeast Asian societies cherish diversity, and multiculturalism remains the crux of their national identities. More importantly, the contributors' standpoint is backed by extensive data and case studies from fieldwork. All authors acknowledged that there was a significant change in how Muslims expressed their identity before the Islamic resurgence (in the 1970s) and thereafter. None of the authors pass judgements of lifestyles before that period as un-Islamic or not conforming to Islamic teachings.

The chapters in this volume cover a range of issues over selected Southeast Asian countries. This does not mean that issues highlighted in one case study do not occur in another. The book can be treated as a conversation starter, and it is worth to cover other countries in depth in future.

Acknowledgements

This volume would not have been possible without the support and help of a number of individuals. We wish to thank the Islamic Religious Council of Singapore (Muis) for providing us with a grant to work on this project. The editors wish to express our gratitude to Mr Choi Shing Kwok, Director and Chief Executive Officer of the ISEAS – Yusof Ishak Institute, and Dr Terence Chong, Senior Director, Research Division and Deputy Chief Executive Officer, for their continuous support of the project, Ng Kok Kiong, Director, Publishing Division, and editor Rahilah Yusuf for all their hard work in stringing this volume together, as in the past ISEAS publications on similar themes. We also wish to thank ISEAS research officers and assistants for their hard work: Tay Jun Pin, Siti Suhaila Mohd Harith, Rebecca Neo, and Hasyir Hamid.

Part I
DRIVERS AND PROCESSES

2

MARKETING RELIGIOUS PIETY
Halal Products Forged and Disputed

Faegheh Shirazi

Introduction

This chapter addresses important issues relating to the halal certification of Islamic products within a thriving and expanding consumer market, including approximately two billion Muslims, accounting for 25 per cent of the world population. The discussion focuses on the fraudulent marketing of halal products in addition to several examples of disputed products that do not have a universal halal certification agreement among the Muslim *ulama* (religious scholars) in different parts of the world or even within the same nation. According to a global halal food market report: "The global halal food market size is expected to grow from $1,134.14 billion in 2021 to $1,290.35 billion in 2022 at a compound annual growth rate (CAGR) of 13.8 per cent. The global halal foods market size is expected to grow to $2,228.63 billion in 2026 at a CAGR of 14.6 per cent" (The Business Research Company 2023). This figure applies only to food products, not halal hygienic, pharmaceutical, cosmetic products, and services.

Southeast Asia, with a large Muslim population, is one of the most important halal food markets. Halal products are sought and consumed by a majority of the Muslim population in this region of the world. One big issue is the circulation of non-halal food in the market. This issue is not limited to imported food from outside the nations but within several ASEAN countries that do not have halal certification licenses.

Since the 11 September 2001 terrorist attacks (commonly known as 9/11) against the United States, Western nations, particularly the American public, have been increasingly curious about and frequently baffled by the politics, culture, and religious precepts of Islam. Islam and Muslims are discussed in the media regularly, scapegoated for failures in governmental policies such as immigration, and used by politicians as wedge issues to score cheap political points in election years. Information technology and the Internet opened the door to the commercialization of Islam. A new demand for halal consumer goods and services emerged where no demand previously existed, resulting in a wide range of halal products, from beach balls and cosmetics to bathing suits, toothbrushes and socks, to service industries like hospitals, banking and vacations marketed under the auspices of Islam, blessed by the watchful eyes of ayatollahs, *ulama*, and muftis. The commercialization of Islamic piety today often involves a certification process that is less about faith and more about the commercial business of generating profits. These profit-driven products exploit the rise of a new Islamic economic paradigm not specifically created with the objective of honouring religious practice and sentiment solely, but rather for business purposes. In these markets, some of these products are halal, while others are fraudulently labelled halal (Shirazi 2016).

Goods and services are packaged today to appeal exclusively to Muslims—particularly to devout practitioners for whom conspicuous piety is important. Some of the products labelled halal are mundane, such as socks, a plastic comb or a toothbrush. Such products do not require halal certification except for reasons of piety and otherwise as an inducement for sales. In recent years we also have witnessed how technology and media, such as the Internet and television, are used by self-promoting individuals masquerading as spiritual guides and gurus to appeal to the younger generation of Muslims, offering sermons and disseminating the teachings of Allah quite different from the traditional *ulama*. These Muslim "pop" preachers are one of the new trends in several Islamic nations with many followers. For example, as noted by Hoesterey (2012):

> In contemporary Indonesia, a new generation of Muslim pop preachers and self-help gurus tap into, and trade on, the symbolic and economic capital of Islam, science, and media technologies. Through television sermons and elaborate PowerPoint presentations, these pop preachers and self-help gurus summon the Prophet Muhammad's life and teachings in ways that resonate with the civic concerns, consumerist desires, and aspirational piety of the Muslim middle classes (p. 38).

This young generation, such as those mentioned in contemporary Indonesia above, represents a large segment of halal lifestyle followers who desire a contemporary lifestyle that also includes a pious path. This trend is also evident in other Muslim-majority nations. This younger generation is well educated and well spoken, and most of them dress in secular (Western) attire. The pop preacher's audience is middle-class educated and generally populates the Arab world (ibid.).

For those Muslims whose concern is maintaining a wholesome dietary regimen, some useful technologies exist that contribute positively to food science technology and aid in identifying cheating producers. Many packaged products labelled as halal in the areas of hygiene, pharmacy and cosmetics qualify for kosher, vegan and vegetarian lifestyles. A halal—or kosher—packaged product containing no alcohol or animal products presents an attractive choice for vegan and vegetarian consumers who eschew the consumption of animal products. Smart marketers benefit enormously by investing in halal certification.

The Israeli government is worried about how the promotion of Islamic brands and products may be a hasty decision by international companies since terrorism by "Muslims" is still an issue. Of course, that is an expected opinion since the issue of Palestinians and the Israelis at war still is ongoing. The assumption is marketing or making money from Islamic-labelled products may be helping what Israel labels as terrorism. In most Western nations, in particular the US, many are facing xenophobic and Islamophobic circumstances.

An example of the risks involved in offering Muslim-focused products involves, in the US, an electronic products retailer (Best Buy), which ran an advertisement wishing Muslims "Happy Eid al-Adha", resulting in controversy and negative online responses against the company's offering (Edwards 2009):

> A Best Buy (BBY) ad that wished American Muslims a "Happy Eid al-Adha" has come under fire from conservative Christians, who claim the company stopped saying "Merry Christmas" to its customers in 2006.
>
> Best Buy rep Lisa Svac Hawks, stated:
>
> ... Best Buy's customers and employees around the world represent a variety of faiths and denominations. We respect that diversity and choose to greet our customers and employees in ways that reflect their traditions.

In the United States, the focus on halal products and Muslim consumer demands has resulted in the creation of the American Muslim Consumer Consortium (AMCC),[1] which addresses the needs of American Muslim consumers and encourages companies and entrepreneurs to develop products for this market. In non-Muslim majority nations, the business community recognizes the value of Muslim consumers. Countries such as Russia and China, traditionally intolerant towards their Muslim populations, recognize the potential of halal-based business. Halal-certified products expand the consumer base for both Muslim and non-Muslim majority nations.

In China, "halal only applies to foods of meat, milk, and edible oil. It is forbidden to expand the concept of halal to other fields outside the field of halal food" (Zhou 2022). Meanwhile, China, eager to capture the halal markets observed in Asia and Russia, is working with the Iranian government to establish halal businesses. The efforts of Iran and Russia in pursuing halal trade cooperation demonstrate again the business development toward positioning themselves in a global market that promises valuable economic returns (ibid.)

DETECTING ADULTERATED AND FRAUDULENT HALAL

The confidence of consumers in halal-labelled brands has been the most influential factor in the increased sale of these products. Given the proliferation of food commodities provided by halal-certified companies, the Muslim population, globally, is more eager than at any other time to consume halal food and drinks, and an increasing number of people want to follow the halal lifestyle.

However, according to Hafiz M. Ahmed in *the Halal Times* (2022) the top exporters of halal products are non-Muslim majority nations including Brazil, India, the United States, Russia and Argentina and so, therefore, the issues of *taharah* and *najis* (religious purity and pollution), core concepts for halal, are questionable for many Muslims at large and makes for a conflict between loyalty to a brand and the consumers' trust in halal products originating from a non-Muslim country. In addition, some of the more conservative Muslims question the non-Muslim hands that touch the food. In many instances, orthodox Muslims may even refuse to purchase such products, not only because they are not made in a Muslim nation or because the label on the product is suspicious, but also because they may believe that their first religious obligation is to help and financially support Muslims to excel in their business.

> It must be a wake-up call for Muslims as most of the Halal food they consume is produced and exported by non-Muslim countries. According to recent estimates, almost 85 per cent of Halal food being consumed

by Muslims worldwide is produced in countries where Muslims are in a minority … We do not see any global Halal brands managed by any Muslim-majority countries (Hafiz 2022).

Middle Eastern nations such as Iran have their national regulations for domestic food production. Still, they also import food products, particularly meat, from foreign nations such as Australia and New Zealand. Iran does not accept halal-authority organizations outside Iran that supervise halal slaughterhouses, instead sending their own agents when purchasing meat from non-Muslim majority countries. No reliable global standard halal logo has yet been developed that unifies Muslim halal meat slaughter procedures or other halal products. This absence of standardized procedures is one of the reasons some products are fraudulently labelled.

A widespread movement is now ongoing to enhance halal certification through government or private institutions in Malaysia, Indonesia, Thailand and other countries whose populations include many Muslims (Yun, Lee, and Kim 2020). However, complicated lists of ingredients, including the addition of chemicals and preservatives, make halal assessment difficult for the consumer to ascertain, thus there is still a need to rely on a robust halal certification. Although Indonesia has the largest population of Muslims, it is still ranked tenth in the world for the halal industry market. Malaysia has developed its halal industry on a huge scale and ranks first followed by the United Arab Emirates, Bahrain, Saudi Arabia, Pakistan, Oman, Kuwait, Qatar and Jordan. (Vizano 2020). In 2019, Iran and Russia ranked sixth and seventh in halal tourism. The halal industry is becoming one of the most competitive business sectors in the world as it grows with the rise of the Muslim population, whose growth globally is projected to increase to 2.19 billion by the year 2030 (Business Research Company 2023).

As the Muslim population increases, the production of halal goods increases correspondingly. One of the key points in the growth of the halal industry has been public education regarding the true meaning of the halal logo on products. For example, "in November 2020 Egypt's council of ministers introduced the 'Halal in Egypt' mark [logo] for Egyptian halal exports, while the Philippines' Department of Trade and Industry (DTI) also launched an official national logo" (PR Newswire 2022). Today's technologies are well adapted for tracing halal food chain supplies. Many halal as well as non-halal consumers demand to know what ingredients go into the food. They want to know whether food suppliers follow the ethical rules in handling raw ingredients, and they want to know the details regarding packaging, transportation, and storage to the point of sale. In other words, from the farm to the grocery store, consumers want to be informed.

Food fraud comes in a variety of categories including mislabelling, addition of non-halal additives, and improper feed the animal consumes, such as feeding cows scraps of non-halal meat mixed in the feed. Death before halal slaughter is also forbidden. Food fraud is prevalent with illegal practices common in the meat industry. In these cases, the poultry is no longer halal, even though slaughtered according to halal requirements (Shirazi 2016).

> This type of fraud (i.e., selling dubious meat products as halal) can happen anywhere anytime. However, the unique aspect of this fraud is its direct connection to religion. Muslim consumers select halal food items based almost exclusively on label information. If the label itself is inaccurate, what are the consumer's options? Because halal products can command high prices and generate impressive profits, there is always the danger of fraud (p. 80).

In the United States, the Whole Foods Market company was among the first to provide organically labelled food in response to contemporary trends requiring suppliers to meet standards for the humane treatment of farm animals as well as supporting the fair-trade movement for a more democratic workplace. While the Whole Foods company has done a lot of good, "[M]any of Whole Foods' actions have been controversial and sometimes even illegal, especially where its labour practices are concerned". The Whole Foods company opposes the union organization of its workers and threatens to fire workers who try to organize a union, which action by Whole Foods is illegal (Bluejay n.d.). Whole Foods was also found guilty of false advertising, such as in the sale of Kombucha beverages (fermented tea drinks) marketed to have health benefits.

> [Kombucha drink] contained more than 0.5 per cent alcohol by volume which is over the amount allowed by federal law for a beverage to be labelled as non-alcoholic. Though the labelling error was due to the hard to control nature of kombucha fermentation, Whole Foods became entangled in the lawsuit. The class action lawsuit stated this alcohol content could be harmful to consumers intending to avoid alcohol particularly consumers who are pregnant, breast-feeding, or battling alcohol addiction (Caballero 2019).

Muslim consumers were among the unhappy groups that purchased the Whole Foods Kombucha drink containing more than 0.5 per cent alcohol.

In 2012, reports were made describing how Whole Foods sold unlabelled genetically modified foods in their supermarkets. Many products in Whole Foods were determined to be genetically modified, constituting the false advertising claim of "Nothing Artificial, Ever". Hence, "It is incumbent on policymakers to ensure these standards are upheld and prevent activities that contradict government legislation", (Rejeb et al. 2021) regardless of whether the products are classified halal, kosher or organic.

Adulterated meat, mislabelled halal, is an issue of concern everywhere in Muslim populations. For example, in London, pork DNA was detected in halal chicken sausages served at a primary school in Westminster, central London. The pork DNA report said: "Tests on a sample from Burdett Coutts School revealed the presence of lamb and pork DNA in lean minced beef [used to make the sausages]" (*BBC* 2013). Mixing non-halal meat in the halal food chain is common and happens even in Muslim-majority nations. A cartel in Malaysia was exposed for allegedly selling fake halal meat for forty years. "Products such as kangaroo and horse meat were mixed with [beef] and sold as halal beef". The cartel's operations are believed to begin at slaughterhouses, where government agency officers supervise halal standards. According to the report, the officials would fraudulently certify dubious or low-grade meat products (*South China Morning Post*, 30 December 2020). Whether the foregoing allegations are proven or not, confidence in the halal certification of food is compromised. Midamar Corporation, based in the state of Iowa in the United States, was accused of supplying nearly US$5 million worth of beef to Muslim customers in Malaysia, Kuwait, and the United Arab Emirates. Following investigations, prosecutors "claimed the beef came from a supplier that used bolt stunning to kill cattle and the labels were removed by employees to cover up the real source of the meat" (Arabian Business 2015). Incidents like these create consumer mistrust and loss of confidence in what is supposed to be a highly government-regulated halal industry. Several fraudulent halal products and labels could be eradicated once respected governments get involved in this industry.

Among ASEAN member countries, surprisingly "Singapore, a non-Muslim country, with its halal food industry has gained importance as a globally recognized halal hub due to the country's tourism and business location; stringent food safety laws; and recognized halal standards" (Sugita 2017, p. 1). One of the keys to establishing a trustworthy halal food industry is government involvement and regulation for quality control and accuracy in labelling the ingredients.

In the global halal industry, Malaysia has a good reputation for its halal ecosystem, compliance with global halal standards, and halal certification accreditation. In addition to having excellent credit for its halal matters, "Malaysia aspires to establish a global hub for halal products … [encouraging] participatory approach that involves halal-related research activities from multiple universities" (Rejeb et al. 2021). ASEAN leads in the development of global halal trade due to its use of technology. The top four ASEAN nations—Malaysia, Indonesia, Singapore, and Thailand—are among the top fifteen countries in the Global Islamic Economy Report of 2020/21 for success in halal production (Hidayat and Shiddiq 2022, p. 15). The success is due to engaging technology in many aspects of the halal chain and production, which is a result of cooperation between the scientific support that the universities receive from the government. For example, a consumer with a cellphone, scanning a barcode on the product, can request via an SMS short message service to verify whether the item is government-approved and halal-certified.

Another technique in use to control the halal food chain consists of a blockchain system developed by IBM technologies.[2] A blockchain system records information that is difficult to hack or cheat. "Blockchain technology has been proposed as a viable solution for ensuring halal food authenticity … Numerous use cases illustrate how blockchain networks' trackability and traceability can efficiently contribute to maintaining the halal purity of food products" (Ethis 2022). The system eliminates the need for a third party to "verify transactions and retain records, fostering a trustless [no trusted party required] environment" (ibid.).

Other technologies used to detect adulterated ingredients in halal-labelled food include the use of polymerase chain reaction (PCR), a laboratory technique that rapidly produces millions or billions of copies of a specific DNA segment, which can then be studied in greater detail; enzyme-linked immunosorbent assay (ELISA) that measures antigens, antibodies and glycoproteins in biological samples; and the electronic nose, an electronic sensing device that detects flavours or odours (Farag 2020). In many countries, the sale of fraudulent halal meat issue is a crime punishable by law.

In both Malaysia and Indonesia, despite Muslim-majority populations in both countries, the fraudulent halal issues persist in the meat industry. Dr Aemi Syazwani Abdul Keyon,[3] is an expert in analytical chemistry whose expertise is also used to detect fraudulent and tampered meat products, including *glonggong*. In another study, Muhd Anuar Ramli et al. (2018) noted:

> Clearly, meat fraud activities such as meat adulteration, substitution, stolen livestock, grey market products, smuggling, misrepresentation and mislabelling; are against the *halalan toyibban* principle. Perpetrators, particularly in Malaysian and Indonesian meat industry use harmful and unsafe materials in fraudulent meat products such as *glonggong*, formalin, *tiren*, fake meat, exotic meat, aniline and garbage meat.

Adulterated and mislabelled foods are not a new phenomenon, but global, contemporary consumers now want to learn more about what they eat, what is morally acceptable, and what may be chemically harmful to the consumer or the environment. For these reasons, many Muslims rely on the decisions made by the *ulama* who discuss halal or haram matters in daily lives.

Ulama Disputes Regarding Halal/Haram Status

Devout Muslim consumers follow fatwas (religious decrees) of the *ulama* who issue religious opinions regarding the acceptance or rejection of purchases with the goal of providing halal-informed decisions. Sources for the accuracy of such information are available to any pious Muslim on the Internet, particularly on webpages of the *ulama* who are authorized to impart their opinion. Additionally, new fatwas are generated constantly as new products and services become available to consumers. Muslim consumers submit questions to the ulama whose responses and fatwas constantly flow into the archives of fatwas online. In this section, we examine contradictory fatwas and religious opinions collected from authorities who are invested in issuing fatwas online.

Meanwhile, published academic materials focus on specific concerns of Muslims and how consumer knowledge and religious rulings affect the purchasing perspectives of Muslim youth. A study conducted by Nazlida, Leong, and Mizerski et al. (2016) concluded that fatwas make a difference in the purchasing decisions among younger groups (ibid., pp. 78-94). Another study, cited by Nazlida and Mizerski (2013), states,

> The analyses found that the respondents' motivation in following Islamic teachings had the greatest effects in their deciding to smoke, [to] listen to contentious popular music … but was not relevant for buying the Coca-Cola brand. The results are discussed in terms of the study's theoretical contributions, managerial implications, and future research (Nazlida and Mizerski 2013).

The issue of consuming Coca-Cola and other carbonated drinks containing caffeine appears in one of the questions recorded in this study (in the section regarding fatwas online) and raises the important issue of products containing caffeine.

Since 2010, the government of Saudi Arabia decreed that "only officially approved religious scholars would be allowed to issue fatwas [which] is a step in the continuing efforts of the state to assert its primacy over the country's religious establishment" (Boucek 2010, p. 100). This is the first instance of the Saudi government intruding into the independent *ulama's* fatwas. Consequently, only the *ulama* appointed by the Saudi government are authorized to issue fatwas for the public to follow, and the approved *ulama* must be associated with the Senior Council of Ulama, a governmental entity. This development is the result of the reformation of the clerical power establishment. Limiting the *ulama's* power to issue fatwas began in 2005, but the restrictions were not seriously enforced. The official decree stated that "it is a violation of Islamic law when unqualified individuals issue fatwas, and such actions undermine the official state institutions and cross into 'state jurisdiction'" (ibid.). Some senior Saudi *ulama* were happy about such restrictions, while others rejected the idea of such control. As a result of the decree, fatwas now issued in Saudi Arabia will not be contradictory to the government.

Fatwas are based on the religious knowledge and authority of the *ulama* authorized to issue religious decrees for Muslims. Some fatwas create confusion, such as in "two controversial fatwas—one against Muslims participating in Christmas celebrations ... [and the other] against pluralism, liberalism, and secularism—issued by the Majelis Ulama Indonesia (MUI, Council of Indonesian Ulama)" (Sirry 2013, p. 100). With advancement in Islamic jurisprudence "different religious sects and political factions appeared in the history of Islam" (Jahangir and Shahzadi 2021, p. 1). Some of the contradictions in the fatwas can be understood, as they are issued by different *ulama* in different parts of the world and reflect strong relationships to cultural backgrounds. Among some contentious discussions, we note non-essential commodities such as coffee, *khat* or *paan* debated regarding their status as halal or haram.[4]

For example, the buds and leaves of *khat*, a flowering evergreen shrub (also known as *qat*, *kat*, *chat*, or *qaad*) are chewed as a stimulant and for euphoric effects and are commonly used in Saudi Arabia, Yemen and Eastern Africa such as in Somalia. Health problems are associated with chewing *khat* whose effects include delusions, loss of appetite, breathing difficulties, and increases in blood pressure and heart rate. Heather Douglas and Abdi

Hersi published research on the usage of *khat*, which revealed that among the Somalian people who use the drug regularly, some justified its use as associated with Islam, saying "it has been used generation by generation ... It's been used in the Qur'an; it's been used in religious occasions ..." (Douglas and Hersi 2010, p. 95) which, in fact, is not Islamic and contrary to the Qur'anic verses concerning the use of intoxicants (see Qur'an 4:43 and 5:90-91). Another man in the same study said, "because it is our tradition, it is our way of life, we grow up with it—we enjoy it a lot. It doesn't harm us; it doesn't harm anyone" (Douglas and Hersi 2010, p. 95). Religious opinion on whether *khat* is halal, haram, or *makruh* (discouraged, detested) is varied and not determined.

> Given that the overwhelming majority of khat users in Australia and other common law states are Muslim immigrants, [from the regions that *khat* usage is part of their culture] the uncertain status of *khat* in Islam poses significant challenges to policymakers in immigrant receiving nations. As these communities' cultural norms are largely derived from the Islamic religion, any government response to the use of *khat* should consider these religious and cultural norms (ibid.).

The Islamic legal position on *khat* is ambiguous, and various religious rulings exist that are contradictory in nature. *Khat* is one of the unessential consumer products imbued with many legal and socio-cultural issues, particularly in Western societies in which *khat* is a new drug that holds the possibility of addiction at one end, and the claim of religious and cultural use, among a certain Muslim immigrant base, on the other end. In addition, the controversies and its legal status are the result of ambiguity within Islamic legal rulings (Hersi and Mohamad Abdalla 2013, p. 251). According to Abdi Hersi and Mohamad Abdalla, *khat* should be considered haram, since these two scholars not only look at the definition of intoxicant as defined in the Qur'an, as well as the hadith of the Prophet of Islam declaring haram any substance "that clouds one's mind," but they also take into consideration other factors such as the environmental issues to make their ruling. For example, "the Agricultural Resource Authority of Yemen ... reported that *Khat* is depleting scarce water resources in Yemen" (ibid., p. 251). This is an example of a non-essential product that is declared haram and is a conspicuous waste of water resources.

Paan, another non-essential product, is prepared using *paan* leaves (known as green gold) from the Piper betel vine, which is of Southeast Asian origin. Today, it is found in markets across Asia and Africa. *"Paan* is everywhere in India. The treat—a betel leaf stuffed with a variety of ingredients—can be found in people's homes, at restaurants, shopping centres and markets" (Lal 2020). *Paan* is a disputed product popular in Saudi Arabia and the Gulf countries, and especially popular among guest workers from the subcontinent of India.[5] It is linked with an addictive form of tobacco and associated with "*pan masala* and *gutka* which is a potent mixture of tobacco, crushed betel nut, lime, and clove among other ingredients".[6] Furthermore, "the continuous chewing of *paan* and swallowing of *gutka* trigger[s] progressive fibrosis in submucosal tissue. Human oral epithelium cells experience carcinogenic and genotoxic effects from the slaked lime present in the betel quid, with or without areca nut" (Niaz et al. 2017). In Pakistan and India, oral cancer is the most common type of cancer, due to consumption of *gutka* with its known carcinogenic properties and other hazardous effects, after breast and lung cancer.

As usual, there are differences of opinion about the use of betel nut, which is one of the strongest ingredients used in the preparation of *paan bahar* for chewing. The public can communicate with religious scholars, such as muftis and ayatollahs, via their web pages online. These websites stay updated with new questions and responses generated by religious scholars. The following are examples of several such communications.

Question: Is betel nut haram?
Answer: by Mufti Qamruzzaman, London, UK

Paan is made up of these components (*supari*) Betel nut, *zarda* (smokeless tobacco), tobacco, *chuna* or *soon* (lime), seed, spices. If it is consumed in moderation with the experience of benefit and less harm then it is permissible. One should avoid consuming it beyond necessity. Also, if the tobacco causes intoxication, then it will be Haram to consume. If it is not intoxicating and does not have bad smell then it is permissible, but if it has bad smell then it is *Makruh* [discouraged, detested] to enter the Masjid [mosque] without washing the mouth (Mufti Says 2019).

These kinds of responses are confusing and contradictory.

Question: Is selling or using Betel leaf, Betel nut, or *Paan* haram?
Answer: by Sheikh Assim Al Hakeem.
Islamic Center of Kuwait.

It is haraam to deal with it in any way, whether one inhales it, chews it or deals with it in any of its other forms. It is obligatory upon every

Muslim to give up these things and to hasten to repent to Allaah, and to regret having committed this sin, and to resolve never to go back to it (Assimalhakeem 2020).

Question: ID: 36367Country: India
(1) What is the Islamic ruling about chewing *pan* with tobacco? (2) About *pan* with *supari* or *zarda*? (3) About cigarette smoking (4) About caffeine addictive drinks like tea/coffee/caffeinated cold drinks (Pepsi, Coke)?
Answer: by Ulama of Darul Ifta, Darul Uloom Deoband, India
(Fatwa: 355/143/L=1433) (1) It is unlawful to chew the tobacco or *zarda* (with *pan* or in any other way) which is intoxicating or it is injurious to health. And it is right to chew the tobacco or *zarda* which is not intoxicating and which does not have bad smell and are not injurious to health. But it is *makrooh tanzihi* to chew such tobacco or *zarda* that have bad smell but are not intoxicating or injurious to health. If it is consumed it shall be *makrooh* to enter in the mosque without washing the mouth. (2) Yes, *supari* (betel net) [nut] may be used with *pan* and *zarda*. (3) If smoking is injurious to health, then its use is not lawful. If it is not injurious to health then ... smoking without any need just for entertainment is *makrooh*. It is allowable to drink coffee, tea, Pepsi, Coca Cola etc.
Allah (Subhana Wa Ta'ala) knows Best Darul Ifta,
Darul Uloom Deoband, India (Darul Ifta n.d.).

The last unessential halal-related item to discuss in this section involves the civet cat coffee bean, known as *luwak* in Indonesia and *caphe cut chon* in Vietnam. The coffee beans are collected from the excrement of the Asian palm civet. Various opinions and rulings have been published since *kopi luwak* first became an issue within ASEAN and in the Middle East Muslim-majority nation-states and elsewhere, where a Muslim halal-conscious consumer mentality exists. The Indonesian Ulama Council (Majelis Ulama Indonesia, MUI) stated in 2010 that the coffee beans excreted in the stool of the civet mammal become *mutanajis* (religiously became impure). However, drinking the coffee is permissible if the beans are washed properly, all debris is removed, and only entirely unbroken beans are used, qualifying the drink as halal (Shirazi 2022).

While the Department of Islamic Development in Malaysia (Jabatan Kemajuan Islam Malaysia, JAKIM) also agrees with the MUI's acceptance that civet cat coffee is halal, other religious scholars offer a contradictory opinion about *kopi luwak*. For example, Al Sheikh Ahmad Hujji al Kurdi, a member of the Kuwait National Fatwa Committee, has stated that drinking civet coffee is not permissible. Shi'a ulama have also declared civet coffee haram because it is *najis* (ritually unclean). One can view a clip on Ahlulbayt TV where Shi'a scholar Sayyed-Mohammad-Al Musawi clearly states that *luwak* coffee is haram (Ahlulbayt: General Q&A 2020). In addition, Abdul Halim Abdul Kadir, former president of the Malaysian Ulama Association (Persatuan Ulama Malaysia, PUM), stated in 2010 that drinking civet coffee is prohibited.

Conclusion

While there is great potential in the halal market in the Muslim world, a lack of a standard global halal regulation is a barrier for market development. And because the majority of Muslim nations in the Middle East are dependent upon importation of food from non-Muslim countries, the problem of public confidence comes into play as to whether products are certifiably halal. Until October 2015, "when the United Arab Emirates launched a 'Halal National Mark' to regulate and certify the halal industry, there was no halal standards body in the Middle East and north Africa" (Just Food 2015).

Other Middle Eastern nations such as Iran have their own national regulations for domestic productions, but they also import food products, particularly meat, from foreign nations such as Australia and New Zealand. Iran does not accept halal authority organizations outside the country that oversee and supervise halal slaughterhouses. The Iranian government sends its own agents when purchasing meat from non-Muslim majority countries.

No reliable global halal standards have yet been developed. This lack of standardized procedures makes products vulnerable to fraudulent labelling. Examples abound of Muslim consumers learning that a product they were using, assumed halal, was in fact adulterated and haram. Other nations such as Malaysia, Thailand and Indonesia have implemented a system to standardize and enforce halal certification by providing information through a variety of means. However, the list of ingredients, including chemicals and preservatives, is complicated and often difficult to comprehend by a consumer, thus we must still rely on halal certification (Yun, Lee, and Kim 2020).

Notes
1. The American Muslim Consumer Consortium homepage explains that "The objective of AMCC is to empower Muslim Consumers and entrepreneurs. Since 2009, AMCC has held conferences and Entrepreneur Competition in the US showcasing businesses and entrepreneurs whose products and services come from

socially responsible ideas that benefit consumers as well as comply with Islamic values" (American Muslim Consumer Consortium n.d.).
2. Blockchain is a shared, immutable ledger for recording transactions, tracking assets and building trust.
3. Dr Aemi Syazwani Abdul Keyon is an analytical chemist and an academic at the Department of Chemistry, Faculty of Science, Universiti Teknologi Malaysia, Johor Bahru. Food, pharmaceuticals, environment and forensic-related science are the most frequently researched areas covered by Dr Aemi and her team.
4. The plant *khat* is native to the Horn of Africa and the Arabian Peninsula and has been widely cultivated and consumed for centuries due to its psychostimulant effects (Silva et al. 2022). Botanically, *khat* is known as Catha edulis. "[The] buds and leaves of this plant are chewed for stimulant and euphoric effects, and rationally have been used for medicinal purposes as well as recreationally … khat contains cathinone and cathine, which are the chemicals that produce the stimulant effects" (Alcohol and Drug Foundation 2021). Chronic abuse of *khat* causes physical exhaustion. Its effects are similar to other stimulants, such as cocaine, amphetamine, and methamphetamine.
5. *Paan Bahar* or *Pan Masala* (PM) is a mixture of areca nut with slaked lime, catechu, and other flavouring agents. It is widely available and used by all sections of Indian society. Betel nut is the seed of the fruit of the areca palm. It is also known as areca nut. The common names, preparations and specific ingredients vary by cultural group and individuals who use it. Betel nut is a stimulant drug, which means it speeds up the messages travelling between the brain and the body. Slaked lime, or calcium hydroxide (one of the ingredients in *Paan Bahar*) is known as an inorganic compound with the chemical formula $Ca(OH)_2$. It is used in the preparation of dry mix for painting and whitewashing.
6. *Gutka* is a type of smokeless tobacco that is made in India and is widely used throughout Asia. It is a mixture of tobacco, crushed areca nut (also called betel nut), spices and other ingredients. It is used like chewing tobacco and is placed in the mouth, usually between the gum and cheek. Gutka contains nicotine and many harmful, cancer-causing chemicals. Using it can lead to nicotine addiction and can cause cancers of the lip, mouth, tongue, throat and esophagus. Also called betel quid with tobacco (National Cancer Institute n.d.).

References

Ahlulbayt: General Q&A. 2020. "Is Civet Coffee (Kopi Luwak) Haram?". *YouTube*, 6 January 2020. https://www.youtube.com/watch?v=yXeYYS-MEKc (accessed 25 September 2022).

Alcohol and Drug Foundation. 2021. "Khat". 20 November 2021. https://adf.org.au/drug-facts/khat/ November 20, 2021 (accessed 8 October 2022).

American Muslim Consumer Consortium. n.d. "Home". https://americanmuslimconsumer.com/ (accessed 14 October 2022).

Arabian Business. 2015. "US Firm Extends Invite to Islamic Scholars in Fake Gulf

Halal Food Case". 10 January 2015. https://www.arabianbusiness.com/industries/retail/us-firm-extends-invite-islamic-scholars-in-fake-gulf-halal-food-case-577894 (accessed 26 September 2022).

Assimalhakeem. 2020. "Is Selling or Consuming Betal Nut or Betal Leaf/Paan Haram? — Assim al Hakeem". *YouTube*, 26 June 2020. https://www.youtube.com/watch?v=aAk8BcoJzJw (accessed 25 September 2022).

BBC. 2013. "Supplier of Halal Meat Containing Pork DNA Is Named". 3 February 2013. https://www.bbc.com/news/uk-21312752 (accessed 21 March 2023).

Bluejay, Michael. n.d. "Whole Foods Market: What's Wrong with Whole Foods?" https://michaelbluejay.com/misc/wholefoods.html (accessed 25 September 2022).

Boucek, Christopher. 2010. "Saudi Fatwa Restrictions and the State-Clerical Relationship". *Carnegie Endowment for International Peace*, 27 October 2010. https://carnegieendowment.org/sada/41824 (accessed 21 March 2023).

Business Research Company, The. 2023. "Halal Food Global Market Report 2022". June 2022. https://www.thebusinessresearchcompany.com/report/halal-food-global-market-report (accessed 20 June 2022).

Caballero, Martin. 2019. "Health-Ade, Whole Foods Reach $4M Settlement in Class Action Suit". *Bevnet*, 19 March 2019. https://www.bevnet.com/news/2019/health-ade-whole-foods-reach-4m-settlement-in-class-action-suit/ (accessed 24 September 2022).

China Briefing. 2022. "Halal Certification Procedures in China". 26 August 2022. https://www.china-briefing.com/news/halal-certification-procedures-in-china/ (accessed 7 September 2022).

Darul Ifta. n.d. "Question ID: 36367". https://darulifta-deoband.com/home/en/qa/36367 (accessed 25 September 2022).

Douglas, Heather, and Abdi Hersi. 2010 "Khat and Islamic Legal Perspectives: Issues for Consideration". *Journal of Legal Pluralism and Unofficial Law* 42, no. 62: 95–114.

Edwards, Jim. 2009. "Best Buy Stands by Ad Wishing Muslims 'Happy Eid al-Adha'". CBS News, 30 November 2009. https://www.cbsnews.com/news/best-buy-stands-by-ad-wishing-muslims-happy-eid-al-adha/

Ethis. 2022. "The Rise of the Halal Industry and Tech Innovations in 2022". https://ethis.co/blog/rise-halal-industry-tech-innovations-2022/ (accessed 24 September 2022).

Farag, M. Diaa El-Din. 2020. "Detecting Adulteration in Halal Foods". In *Halal Food Handbook*, edited by Yunes Ramadan Al-Teinaz, Stuart Spear, and Ibrahim H.A. Abd El-Rahim, pp. 283–319. Hoboken, New Jersey: Wiley-Blackwell.

Hafiz M. Ahmed. 2022. "Almost No Muslim Country Among Top 10 Halal Product Exporters". *The Halal Times*, 12 February 2022. https://www.halaltimes.com/muslim-country-among-top-10-halal-products-exporters/ (accessed 25 September 2022).

Hersi, Abdi, and Mohamad Abdalla. 2013. "Sharī'a Law and the Legality of Consumption of Khat (Catha Edulis): Views of Australian Imāms". *International Journal of Humanities and Social Science* 3, no. 21: 1–18.

Hidayat, Sutan Emir, and Shiddiq. 2022. "ASEAN Towards a Global Halal Logistics

through the Digitally Enabled Community". *International Journal of Asian Business and Information Management (IJABIM)* 13, no. 2: 1–15.
Hoesterey, James B. 2012 "Prophetic Cosmopolitanism: Islam, Pop Psychology, and Civic Virtue in Indonesia". *City & Society* 24, no. 1: 38–61.
Jahangir, Humaira, and Pakeeza Shahzadi. 2021. "Evolution of Jurisprudential Principles and the Doctrinal Differences in Historical Perspective". *Journal of Islamic & Religious Studies (JIRS)* 6, no. 1: 1–26.
Just Food. 2015. "Briefing: Middle East: The Halal Food Challenge in the Middle East". https://www.just-food.com/analysis/briefing-middle-east-the-halal-food-challenge-in-the-middle-east/ (accessed 21 March 2023).
Lal, Neeta. 2020. "The History of Paan: An Indian Treat Made with a Betel Leaf That's Recommended in the Kama Sutra and Praised by Ayurveda Practitioners". *South China Morning Post*, 20 November 2020. https://www.scmp.com/lifestyle/food-drink/article/3110313/history-paan-indian-treat-made-betel-leaf-thats-recommended
Mohd Anuar Ramli, Afiqah Salahudin, Mohd Imran Abdul Razak, Muhammad Ammar Harith Idris, and Muhammad Izzul Syahmi Zulkepli. 2018. "Halal Meat Fraud and Safety Issues in Malaysian and Indonesian Markets". *Journal of Halal Industry and Services* 1, no. 1: 1–15.
Muftisays. 2019. "Is Betel Nut Haram?". 15 December 2019. https://www.muftisays.com/qa/miscellaneous/4346-is-betel-nut-haram/ (accessed 1 February 2020).
National Cancer Institute. n.d. "Gutka". https://www.cancer.gov/publications/dictionaries/cancer-terms/def/gutka (accessed 7 September 2022).
Nazlida Muhamad, and Dick Mizerski. 2013. "The Effects of Following Islam in Decisions about Taboo Products". *Psychology and Marketing* 30, no. 4: 357–71.
———, Vai Shiem Leong, and Dick Mizerski. 2016. "Consumer Knowledge and Religious Rulings on Products: Young Muslim Consumer's Perspective". *Journal of Islamic Marketing* 7, no. 1: 74–94.
Niaz, Kamal, Faheem Maqboo, Fazlullah Khan, Haji Bahadar, Fatima Ismail Hassan, and Mohammad Abdollahi. 2017. "Smokeless Tobacco (*Paan* and *Gutkha*) Consumption, Prevalence, and Contribution to Oral Cancer". *Epidemiol Health* 39. https://doi.org/10.4178/epih.e2017009.
PR Newswire. 2022. "Global Halal Food and Beverage Market (2022 to 2030)—Size, Share & Trends Analysis Report". 14 July 2022. https://www.prnewswire.com/news-releases/global-halal-food-and-beverage-market-2022-to-2030---size-share--trends-analysis-report-301586661.html (accessed 7 September 2022).
Rejeb, Abderahman, Karim Rejeb, Suhaiza Zailani, Horst Treiblmaier, and Karen J. Hand. 2021 "Integrating the Internet of Things in the Halal Food Supply Chain: A Systematic Literature Review and Research Agenda". *Internet of Things* 13: 1–18.
Sugita, Ira. 2017. "Halal in Singapore". USDA Foreign Agricultural Service, Global Agricultural Information Network. GAIN Report Number: SN7004.
Shirazi, Faegheh. 2016. *Brand Islam, The Marketing and Commodification of Piety*. Austin: The University of Texas Press.

———. 2022. "Unifying Halal Product Certification: ASEAN's Challenge". *Fulcrum*, 22 September 2022. https://fulcrum.sg/unifying-halal-product-certification-aseans-challenge/

Silva, Barbara, Jorge Soares, Carolina Rocha-Pereira, and Premsyl Mladenka. 2022. "Khat, a Cultural Chewing Drug: A Toxicokinetic and Toxicodynamic Summary". *Toxins* 14, no. 2: 1–12.

Sirry, Mun'im. 2013. "Fatwas and their Controversy: The Case of the Council of Indonesian Ulama (MUI)". *Journal of Southeast Asian Studies* 44, no. 1: 100–17.

South China Morning Post. 2020. "Malaysian Cartel Allegedly Sold Fake Halal Meat to Muslims for 40 Years". 30 December 2020. https://www.scmp.com/news/asia/southeast-asia/article/3115837/malaysian-cartel-allegedly-sold-fake-halal-meat-muslims-40 (accessed 21 March 2023).

USDA Foreign Agricultural Service. 2017. "Halal in Singapore". 28 March 2017. http://efaidnbmnnnibpcajpcglclefindmkaj/https://apps.fas.usda.gov/newgainapi/api/report/downloadreportbyfilename?filename=Halal%20in%20Singapore%20_Singapore_Singapore_3-28-2017.pdf (accessed 21 March 2023).

Vizano, Nico Alexander, Anis Fittria, Mohamad Nuryansah, Muhammad Rikza Muqtada, Gufron, M. Farhan, and A. Purwanto. 2020. "Halal Medicine Purchase Intention among Southeast Asian Consumers". *European Journal of Molecular & Clinical Medicine* 7, no. 7.

Yun, Eun Kyeong, Hee-yul Lee, and Dong-Hwan Kim. 2020. "Is Halal Certification Necessary for Exporting to Islamic Countries? Focus on OIC Countries". *Cultura: International Journal of Philosophy of Culture and Axiology* 17, no. 1: 173–92.

Zhou, Qian. 2022. "Halal Certification Procedures in China". China Briefing, 26 August 2022. https://www.china-briefing.com/news/halal-certification-procedures-in-china/

3

EVOLUTION OF THE HALAL INDUSTRY AND LIFESTYLE

Mohammad Hashim Kamali

Introduction

This chapter is presented in two parts. Part one is on the emergence of a halal lifestyle in Southeast Asia and beyond, whereas part two addresses halal-related developments in Malaysia. Halal as a concept and value category is an integral part of shariah and is not new. However, its more recent manifestations and growth into an industry are linked with the development of a certain lifestyle and culture among Muslims. Halal as a concept began with a focus on food and drinks but further developed to include clothes, cosmetics, recreation, housing, tourism, banking and finance, halal pharmaceuticals and medicine and even halal dating and matchmaking. However, not all aspects of the halal industry are expounded in the shariah textbooks. Questions, therefore, arose from time to time over doubtful matters and the role of ʿurf (social custom) and fatwa in determining such issues. Similar questions arose over the qualification of halal slaughterers, whether non-Muslims and women were qualified to carry out the halal slaughter, and whether machine slaughter, slaughtered meat imported from non-Muslim countries, electric stunning and so on, were shariah-compliant.

The twentieth-century reassertion of Muslim identity projected Islam as a comprehensive way of life and placed a fresh emphasis on the Islamic lifestyle and culture. Even Muslims who are not so pious in other respects still tend to observe certain aspects of this lifestyle, especially halal food, partly because dietary laws are usually observed from early childhood as part of the religious and family traditions. Halal, like the hijab, tends to be entrenched in the custom and culture of Muslim societies, hence is a part of their identity and lifestyle (Alatas 2022, pp. 39–40; Suzanna 2007, pp. 40–41; Kamali 2021, pp. 6–7).

An anti-halal movement also gained traction in the West as a negative response to these developments. Thus, in Europe, North America and Australia, campaigns against the Muslim presence revolved around visible signifiers such as women wearing the hijab, *burqa* or *niqab*, the building of mosques and minarets, halal certification and restaurants. The Italian cities of Genoa and Bergamo imposed bans on kebab shops in the name of safeguarding hygiene and culinary traditions. A scare campaign against halal food certification in Australia threatened various food suppliers with consumer boycotts saying that the fees they paid for halal certification were funding terrorism and campaigns to introduce shariah law in Australia. Other companies took the opportunity to cite their lack of halal certification as evidence of their national loyalty and preservation of Western values (Shakira 2015, pp. 85–86; Ruiz-Bejarano 2017, pp. 132–38).

Halal in Southeast Asia

Halal in Southeast Asia has been expanding as part of the emerging modern religious-cum-moral economies. Southeast Asia, most notably Indonesia, Malaysia, Brunei and Singapore, took initiatives to develop and regulate their halal standards and certification regimes, primarily in response to internal demands but also larger enhanced participation in international markets (Lever and Fischer 2018, p. 3).

Majelis Ulama Indonesia (Indonesian Ulama Council, MUI) has been fostering a halal lifestyle through halal certification for many years. MUI was initially requested by President Suharto to promulgate a state policy on halal and establish an institution to monitor the lawfulness of halal production. Established in 1989, the Assessment Institute for Foods, Drugs and Cosmetics of Indonesian Ulama Council (Lembaga Pengkajian Pangan, Obatan-obatan dan Kosmetika Majelis Ulama Indonesia, LPPOM MUI) has for long been the sole halal certifier in Indonesia. MUI's role in creating a halal lifestyle was strengthened during the presidency of Susilo Bambang Yudhoyono (2004–14), who endorsed MUI on many issues, including the halal project (Syafiq 2022, pp. 76–77).

Halal lifestyle is popular among the Muslim youth, who currently make up a significant segment of the population. The Muslim world is experiencing a "youth bulge", with 60 per cent of the population of Muslim-majority countries under 30 years old, while 43 per cent are under 25, amounting to 780 million, or more than 11 per cent of the world population (Africa Islamic Economic Foundation 2020, pp. 2–4). This generation of young Muslims are agents of change for the halal industry as they embrace an Islamic lifestyle, are proud of their religious identity and are becoming more knowledgeable about preserving halal as a part of their daily lives. They also have high purchasing power and consumption patterns (Janmohamed 2016, pp. 48–50; Dinar Standard 2022, pp. 96–97). Aspects of the halal lifestyle primarily associated with the youth are halal fashion, halal cosmetics, halal dating and matchmaking, as elaborated below.

Halal Fashion, Cosmetics, Dating and Matchmaking

The growth of fashion as an Islamic lifestyle encourages Muslims to be both covered and fashionable, modest and beautiful. Muslims, especially the youth, spent more than US$368 billion on halal/modest fashion in 2021. Globally, this Muslim market for fashion ranks third, just behind the United States and China. High-end labels in the fashion industry, such as Dolce & Gabanna, Gucci and Nike, started paying special attention to Muslim fashion by releasing special collections of headscarves and *abayas* (Waninger 2015, pp. 9–10; Gonzalez-Rodriguez 2018). In Southeast Asia, competition among halal fashion brands is fierce due to the emergence of new local designers and the entry of renowned international brand names into the market following easy access to cheaper raw materials from China and Vietnam. Another catalyst for the rapid growth of this industry is that, unlike halal food and halal pharmaceuticals, halal fashion need not go through halal certification procedures and can be practised without prior preparation (Muhammad, Faridah, and Abdul Kadir 2020, pp. 1278; Susilawati, Yarmunida, and Elwardah 2021, p. 42).

The huge demand for halal cosmetics and beauty products is driven by rapid growth in the demographics of young and religiously conscious professional Muslims (Suhana, Suhaiza, and Zainorfarah 2016, pp. 55–56; Hew 2019, p. 322). It has also gained traction among modern eco-ethically conscious consumers willing to pay a premium for organic, natural and earthy cosmetic products to suit their lifestyle. Muslims' spending on cosmetics was estimated at US$64 billion in 2018 and is expected to reach US$95 billion by 2024 (Dinar Standard 2019, p. 127). Southeast Asia is the largest producer of halal cosmetics, at around 40 per cent of the total production. The market is currently estimated at US$1,037.7 million, thus showing a growth rate of 10.2 per cent from 2015 to 2020 (Mohamed

Azmi et al. 2015, p. 2). The halal market in Southeast Asia has developed rapidly due to a well-established halal regulatory environment in cosmetics, particularly in Malaysia and Indonesia. For instance, in Malaysia, halal cosmetics contribute 10–20 per cent of the total local cosmetics market. Following the implementation of Halal Product Assurance Law No. 13/2014 in Indonesia, halal certification was made mandatory in 2019. Currently, around 80 per cent of the country's market share of cosmetics have halal certification, and its US$5.5 billion pharmaceuticals market is due to become fully halal-certified by 2024 (Africa Islamic Economic Foundation 2020, p. 6; Dinar Standard 2019, pp. 116–18).

In recent years, the number of Muslim web-based dating sites and mobile dating applications has been growing to promote online halal dating and online-cum-offline halal matchmaking. This happens in tandem with the growing popularity of *hijrah* movements that call for replacing dating with *ta'aruf* (getting to know each other) before marriage. Websites and mobile applications such as Singlemuslim (United Kingdom), Muzmatch (Bangladesh), Salaam Swipe (Canada) and Minder (United States of America) have gained popularity, with thousands of users signing to their platforms. In Southeast Asia, platforms such as Marriage Conference (Malaysia), Indonesia Tanpa Pacaran (Indonesia without Dating) and Mat & Minah (Singapore) are rapidly growing (Eva 2021, pp. 233–34). The BaitulJannah app and website currently have more than 1 million youth users from all over Malaysia, Singapore and Brunei (Baituljannah n.d.).

According to Kuwait Finance House research, the value of the global halal economy was expected to be US$6.4 trillion in 2018. Of this total, Islamic finance and halal food sectors were to contribute US$3.9 trillion and US$1.6 trillion respectively. Additionally, according to the Global Islamic Economic Indicator (GIEI), Malaysia and the United Arab Emirates (UAE) are two among the fifty-seven member countries of the Organization of Islamic Cooperation (OIC) and sixteen non-OIC countries with the best halal ecosystems. Halal ecosystem signifies a dynamic system consisting not of an isolated development but a complex network of businesses, institutions, government agencies and NGOs. It is equipped with the means to detect instances of non-compliance according to an established set of criteria.

The halal industry expanded further over time not only in Muslim-majority countries such as Turkey, Indonesia, Pakistan and Egypt but also in China, Japan, South Korea and elsewhere. Interest was also shown regarding new halal products such as the halal vaccines, genetically modified organisms, and the environmental impact of halal, especially regarding meat eating.

Halal in Malaysia

The evolution of the halal industry began with the conceptual development of halal through a set of halal standards published by the Department of Islamic Development Malaysia (JAKIM) between 2008 and 2017. Sixteen halal standards were published in separate booklets relating to animal slaughter, food, pharmaceuticals, halal additives, cosmetics, halal tourism, halal certificates, halal parks, preparation and processing of halal products, and halal management matters.

Malaysia holds a special position in the global halal market, partly because of the general perceptions and demand of the Muslims of Malaysia (also Indonesia) and prevailing consumer behaviour among them that shows a keen interest in halal consumption and lifestyle. Muslims today demand an all-encompassing halal environment and seem to be strongly motivated even to boycott brands that violate Islamic teachings (Tieman 2019, p. 14).

When Malaysia launched its first Malaysia International Halal Show Case (MIHAS) in Kuala Lumpur, then Prime Minister Abdullah Ahmad Badawi declared in 2004 that establishing Malaysia as a "global halal hub" was a major priority of the government. Malaysia also became the only country in the world where the halal industry is backed by the government, which allows a synergy between the private and public sectors. The private sector players focus on production, manufacturing and services, while the government agencies, like the Halal Industry Development Corporation (HDC) and JAKIM, provide halal certification and training. In most other countries, private players dominate the halal industry (Laili 2017, p. 12). HDC was established with the purpose of developing the halal industry internationally.

Two events are held annually in Malaysia; MIHAS, as already mentioned, and the World Halal Forum (WHF), both tasked with spearheading the networking and internationalization of the halal industry. MIHAS is organized by Malaysia's External Trade Development Corporation (MALTRADE) under the Ministry of International Trade and Industry, and it provides a value-adding platform that promotes cross-border investments and business partnerships. Malaysia's global halal hub concept aims to create opportunities for small and medium industries (SMEs) to penetrate halal markets in the Middle East, OIC countries, and elsewhere.

The halal industry in Malaysia has developed in the following four areas: halal standards, halal certificates, halal parks, and halal pharmaceuticals, as explained below.

Halal Standards

Halal food under the halal standards currently in force in Malaysia refers to food and drink that are permitted under shariah law and clear of any ingredients of non-halal animals or animal products not slaughtered according to the shariah. The food must also be clear of impurities, filth, poisonous, and intoxicating contents that are hazardous to health. It is required, furthermore, that no contaminated equipment or parts are used in the preparation of halal food, its processing, packaging, storage, or transportation, and that it does not contain any human parts or its derivatives not permitted under shariah law (Department of Standards Malaysia 2009, clause 2).

The first national halal standard was released in 2004, effectively making Malaysia the first country to have a systematic halal assurance system, eventually transforming the halal industry from a traditional cottage industry to a vibrant sector of the economy.

The Department of Standards Malaysia (DOSM), the issuing authority of halal standards in the country, is a department under the Ministry of Science, Technology and Innovation. DOSM was established to develop uniform halal standards for industry practices in Malaysia. It is the issuance, in other words, of halal standards that also promote standardization and accreditation as a means of advancing the national economy, public health and safety, and domestic and international trade.[1] Malaysia's Halal Standards (MS) are developed through consensus by committees that comprise a balanced representation of producers, users, consumers and other interested parties. To the extent possible, MS are consistent with international standards. Approval of a standard as an MS is governed by the Standards of Malaysia Act 1996 (Act 549).

MS are reviewed periodically. The use of MS is voluntary except when made mandatory by the regulatory authorities, local by-laws and regulations. An interesting feature of the MS is that they incorporate both Islamic and scientific components that give the country a competitive edge in terms of good manufacturing practices that include hazard analysis of critical control points. A technical committee on Halal Food and Islamic Consumer Products has been set up that provides seminars and courses to educate the public on MS and certification procedures.

Prior to 2004, the country had no national standards for its halal products and only referred to informal documents and procedures introduced by JAKIM. MS 1500–2004 was the first documented standard on halal food established by the government of Malaysia to produce coordinated halal guidelines for the country. This was aimed at boosting Malaysia's exports and capturing the global halal food market. The basic purpose was to ensure a set basis for regulating trade with other countries and the halal production activities and businesses within Malaysia (Raja Nerine 2013, p. 26). Standards Malaysia has been mandated to develop local halal standards. The first of these was formally launched in August 2004 by then-Prime Minister Abdullah Ahmad Badawi. However, in 2009, this standard was replaced by *MS 1500-2009: Halal Food—Production, Preparation, Handling and Storage—General Guidelines*. MS 1500-2009 covers the basic shariah requirements in terms of providing practical guidelines for the food industry operation and handling of halal food, including nutrient supplements. It also provides basic requirements for halal food products and trade in Malaysia.

It is not mandatory to adhere to MS 1500-2009, and it only serves as a guide for firms related to food processing and handling. It also does not cover all the halal certification requirements and procedures. MS 1500-2009 has also been supplemented by additional standards, in particular, MS 1480 on Food Safety According to Hazard Analysis and Critical Control Points and MS 1514-2001 on general principles of food hygiene, which highlight key hygiene controls at every level of the food production chain—all of these four standards are interconnected and used together. Notwithstanding the optional nature of these standards, many firms in Malaysia are keen, however, to adopt them for customer appeal and global market access (ibid. 2013, p. 27). The sixteen halal standards currently in force certify not only food items but also food premises, cosmetics, packaging, pharmaceuticals, *Halalan Toyyiban*, usage of animal bone, skin and hair, Muslim hospitality services, personal care, shariah-compliant management and services.

Many of these standards have been revised from time to time and replaced. As mentioned, MS 1500-2009 on Halal Food is the revised version of its original introduced in 2004. At the outset, this standard provides practical and basic guidelines for halal food products and food businesses in Malaysia (Department of Standards Malaysia 2009, p. 1).[2] Basic guidelines evidently imply that juridical details, scholastic differences, and *fiqh* (jurisprudential) information from which the standards were taken are not included. MS 1500-2009 consists of eleven pages of text, two appendices and a bibliography of the relevant statutes—all in seventeen pages; its style is concise and confined to statute-like declarations that establish positions of validity or otherwise under the shariah, Malaysian laws, and operational procedures.

The DOSM Standards clearly show that halal products and services have acquired a degree of specialization in sector-by-sector-based developments. Whereas the general principles of halal are observed in all sectors, there are sectoral variations, logistics and implementation details. Both the general and sector-based developments are governed by regulations, standards, and circulars that are somewhat piecemeal and call for consolidation.

Establishing unified standards internationally is also desirable for the future growth of the halal industry. There are numerous certification bodies around the world applying standards that are modified to suit their local custom and culture. These country standards also differ in accordance with their interpretation of the Islamic principles and the *madhhab* (school of thought) of Islamic law they may be following. Currently, there is a certain lack of synchrony among Muslim countries and their procedures for the issuance of halal certificates. This also translates into disparities in the numerous halal stamps or logos issued across regions and globally, affecting, in turn, consumer confidence as to what they may see to be more authentic.

As of 2022, JAKIM recognizes eighty-four halal certification bodies from forty-six countries, meaning that their certified products can be exported to Malaysia, just as Malaysia can also export to those countries. Efforts are made in Malaysia and elsewhere to unify the numerous standards currently obtained in the Muslim world. Malaysia's awareness of its own leading role is manifested in a June 2017 announcement on the setting up of an International Halal Authority Board (IHAB) as part of the Malaysian Halal Council's (MHC) agenda for 2018–20. It was also announced that MHC would establish a halal international research academy to be the first of its kind in the region.

MS 1500–2009, as already mentioned, articulates most of the basic positions on halal, haram, and *najis* (filthy, impure) in foodstuffs, and the shariah-compliant animal slaughter. A great deal of the rulings provided in this standard tend to also feature in almost all of the other over a dozen or so halal standards. MS 1500–2009 begins with a one-page Foreword that specifies the main changes it has made to its first edition. The standard then features on its first page its requirements for the production, preparation, handling, and storage of halal food.

Halal food, accordingly, means food and drink and their ingredients that are permitted under shariah law and fulfil the following conditions:

1. The food or its ingredients do not contain any component or product of animals that are non-halal under shariah law, or products of animals which are not slaughtered according to shariah.

2. The food does not contain any ingredient that is considered *najis* by the shariah.
3. The food is safe for consumption, non-poisonous, non-intoxicating and non-hazardous to health.
4. The food or its ingredients are not prepared, processed or manufactured using equipment contaminated with *najis* according to the shariah.
5. The food does not contain any human parts or their derivatives that are not permitted by shariah law.
6. During its preparation, processing, packing, storage, or transportation, the food is physically separated from any other food that does not meet the requirements stated in (1), (2), (3), (4) or (5) or anything that is decreed as *najis* by shariah law.

It is stated that these standards are developed to safeguard the life and well-being of consumers and the general public, and promote domestic and international trade. It is also a means to promote international cooperation in food safety and health. When all these standards are duly observed, the authorized agency issues a halal certificate that establishes the shariah permissibility and halal status of the food concerned.

Halal Certificates

Halal certificates were first introduced in 1974 when the Research Center for the Islamic Affairs Division in the Prime Minister's Office started to issue halal certification letters for products that met the halal criteria at that time. Halal certification has since played a focal role in the overall development of the halal industry in Malaysia, especially with regard to meeting international market demands for higher standards in the production and management of halal products. This also led to the creation of a new section, the Halal Hub, under the expanded JAKIM, responsible for monitoring the halal industry, including halal certification. Suitable amendments in the Trade Description Act of Malaysia 2011 gave JAKIM a stronger mandate to regulate the halal industry. Only companies and businesses that complete the halal certification procedures may use JAKIM's halal logo on their products and premises. Halal certification in Malaysia thus requires the following:

1. Every producer or manufacturer with halal certification must produce only halal products.
2. Every company that applies for the halal certificate must ensure that the source of the ingredients they use is halal. Their suppliers and subcontractors supply halal goods and have halal certificates.

3. A company that is listed under the Multinational as well as Small and Medium Industry category is required to establish an Internal Halal Audit Committee and appoint an Islamic Affairs Executive to oversee and ensure compliance with halal certification procedures.
4. It is also required to have a minimum of two permanent Muslim workers of Malaysian nationality in the kitchen/handling/food processing section.
5. Equipment and appliances used on the premises must be clean and free of contamination by impurities based on Islamic law and not detrimental to health.
6. Transportation used must be for halal product delivery only.
7. Religious worship paraphernalia is prohibited on the premises/food processing area (Department of Standards Malaysia 2014; Raja Nerine 2013, pp. 29–30).

Many of these requirements correspond with the rules of Islamic jurisprudence (*fiqh*) that anything which comes into contact with pig and porcine products, non-halal carcasses, and blood is also contaminated and, therefore, non-halal. This is the main reason manufacturers are required to produce only halal products at their factories. Requirement (4) envisages Muslim employees as witnesses to the process of food production. This can also be said regarding requirement (7), as worship of objects is unacceptable in Islam.

JAKIM, which supervises halal certification procedures, also monitors halal downstream activities such as handling and packaging. Imported products are certified by certain organizations accredited by JAKIM and government agencies such as the Department of Veterinary Services and the Food Safety and Quality Division of the Ministry of Health that issues clearance on suspected hazardous food substances. Malaysia's halal hub concept, moreover, aims to establish benchmarks for the eventual development of Global Halal Standards not only for food production and processing but also for pharmaceuticals, cosmetics, and preservatives (Sabariyah 2006, pp. 20–21). Once a halal certificate is issued to a company, it may print and display JAKIM's halal logo on its products, advertisements, premises and outlets.

Moreover, Malaysia's halal hub concept aims to establish benchmarks for the development of Global Halal Standards not only for food production and processing but also for pharmaceuticals, cosmetics and preservatives (ibid., pp. 20–21). Known as the Malaysia International Halal Authorities and Bodies System (MYIHAB), the system features a centralized database under

JAKIM's Halal Ecosystem Solutions, aimed at setting up an International Halal Accreditation Board. JAKIM's office monitors the applications for International Halal Certification, while recognized halal certification bodies in Malaysia act as JAKIM's monitoring agents abroad to assist the government in the process (Sabariyah 2006).

Halal Parks

As part of its Global Halal Hub policy, the government of Malaysia has taken measures in both its Second Industrial Master Plan and the National Agricultural Policy to support the halal industry by creating several halal parks located in strategic places in the country. Several smaller halal parks operate in Selangor, Kedah, Melaka, Negeri Sembilan, Perak, and Pahang. In contrast, the bigger ones are the Pulau Indah Industrial Park in Selangor, the Free Trade Zone in Johor, and the largest in Sarawak (ibid. 2006; Halal Development Corporation Berhad n.d.). The halal park is a means of clustering a big part of a halal value chain in one place. Next to clustering advantages (like shortening of the supply chain, better access, cost reductions, and innovations), it can create a base for halal food products with common halal standards in a controlled location. Different halal parks offer different infrastructure facilities and benefits, but overall, they all encourage green designs and accessibility of raw materials and ingredients, energy efficiency, and intercompany linkages. It is noted, however, that Malaysia faces a certain shortage of raw materials for halal products. Shortages are noted of livestock, especially cows, goats and poultry, which means that many halal ingredients, including meat, need to be imported for the industry to continue on its growth path (Raja Nerine 2013, pp. 34–35).

Iskandar Halal Park (IHP) in Johor started in November 2015 as a joint venture collaboration between United Malayan Land Berhad (UM Land) and Johor State via Johor Biotechnology & Biodiversity Corporation (J-Biotech) to create a 350-acre international halal park under the Johor State investment company chaired by the Chief Minister of Johor.

IHP is an integrated industrial park comprising an industrial, commercial, and corporate headquarters, scientific laboratories, data centre, foreign worker enclaves, integrated packaging and warehousing facilities as part of a regional marketing and clearing house, youth park, one-stop recreation centre and business facilities. These were all developed in three phases, eventually making IHP the first premium bio-halal industrial park in Malaysia (United Malayan Land Berhad n.d.).

Another development was the launching in 2018 of the world's first halal laboratory in Seremban, known as the Malaysia Halal Analysis Centre (MyHAC). The laboratory helps to boost the halal industry internationally. Halal-certified products in Malaysia are thus buttressed by scientific laboratory analysis to confirm the halal status of a product's ingredients (Nur Aqidah 2018).

Halal Pharmaceuticals

Halal Pharmaceuticals (HP) are a natural extension of the traditional manufacture of pharmaceuticals. This extension can even push the boundaries of manufacturing outwards generally. Muslims in Malaysia and elsewhere are becoming increasingly more aware of the medicine and supplements they take, hence the exponential growth of the halal pharmaceutical industry. In 2016, the sector was valued at US$83 billion, a 6 per cent growth over the previous year. It is expected to grow 8 per cent year-on-year to reach US$132 billion by 2022. As of 2021, the market value for halal pharmaceuticals stood at US$100 billion. Malaysia has been increasing its exports of pharmaceuticals which, according to MATRADE, were valued at RM1.31 billion (US$317 million) in 2015, an increase of 15.8 per cent over 2014 (Dinar Standard 2022, pp. 135–36).

Malaysia has fairly well-developed supporting industries, such as halal logistics, halal parks, warehousing and transportation, which augur well for the further development of HP (Laili 2017, p. 13). Malaysia has produced HP since 2014 and implemented a seven-point development scheme under the halal certification programme, including food, logistics, manufacturing, cosmetics, slaughterhouses, consumer goods (such as toiletries), and pharmaceuticals. Each scheme has a special team overseeing the certification process, and they normally collaborate with the private sector industries. For cosmetic products, for instance, the team collaborates with the Cosmetics, Toiletries and Fragrance Association, while for manufacturing, the team collaborates with the Federation of Malaysian Manufacturers. When there are issues with pharmaceutical products, for instance, there will be collaboration to solve them. Both sides try to facilitate each other's work, especially relating to the production of new halal pharmaceuticals. Furthermore, the Halal Hub Committee comprises experts and researchers who look into all issues the industry faces to fulfil the requirements of MS (ibid.).

Malaysian pharmaceutical companies like Pharmaniaga and AJ Pharma are spearheading innovation in the halal pharmaceutical sector, investing substantial amounts into the development of halal vaccines. The construction of the world's first halal insulin and vaccine plant in Puchong, Selangor, valued at RM300 million, began in 2020 and is expected to be completed by 2023. This would enable Malaysia to also export these products to other countries (Bernama 2022).

According to the State of the Global Islamic Economy Report 2017/18, the UAE has the best-developed Islamic economy for HP and cosmetics, followed by Singapore and Malaysia. This is based on four criteria: trade, governance, awareness and social (MIHAS 2018).

Within the HP sector, halal nutraceuticals have been identified as a major growth segment that can experience rapid growth if supported by strategic investment. Developing new products based on primary research is critical for HP to become a viable business model to market its products to a broader range of consumers.

JAKIM's Halal Hub Division has been active in publishing the world's first HP Standard—the MS2424: 2012 Halal Pharmaceuticals General Guideline—in collaboration with the National Pharmaceutical Regulatory Agency (NPRA) and subject matter experts from shariah and science disciplines. Before this development, pharmaceutical manufacturers referred to the halal food standard MS1900 as a stand-in guide. This was not ideal, as it was not tailored to the peculiarities of the pharmaceutical industry. Upon publication of the MS2424, JAKIM's Halal Hub Division has successfully developed a certification system that can be used not only by pharmaceutical companies in Malaysia but also by halal certifying bodies around the world.

In 2016–17, Malaysia's HP industry saw several key developments, including the world's first halal licence for prescription medicine given by Malaysia's religious authority, JAKIM, to the Chemical Company of Malaysia (CCM) in 2017. Meanwhile, Indonesia was gearing up for mandatory halal certification of its products in 2019, and the UAE required all its halal imports to be certified as halal.

Indonesia's Halal Product Assurance Law came into force in October 2019, and its range of products due to be halal-certified is scheduled to take five years (until 2026). The first stage of implementation began in October 2019, covering food, beverage, and animal slaughter. The halal certification mandate for drugs, cosmetics, chemicals, and biological products came into force in the second stage of the new halal quality regime in October 2021 (Luthviati and Jenvitchuwong 2021, pp. 162–64; *Jakarta Globe*, 17 October 2021).

The CCM was the first to get involved in halal certification for pharmaceutical products around 2000. This development milestone marked the transition in the sector from vitamins and health supplements to over-the-counter medicines such as painkillers, analgesics, eye drops, cough mixtures, ointments, and creams.

Among the challenges halal pharmaceuticals must address is the general public's low level of knowledge and awareness. Although Malaysia has a large Muslim population, HP are not well known. For the HP market to expand, it needs to be seen as part of the religious requirements for Muslims to be better informed of HP, including not only medicines but also vitamins and health supplements. Another challenge facing HP is a general shortfall of raw materials for the industry. This shortage occurs despite Malaysia's biodiversity, which HP could tap into to develop resource-based biogeneric drugs. More investment should be encouraged in Active Pharmaceutical Ingredients (APIs) for this to happen.

Experts have also identified another major challenge: the limited focus on halal. There is a critical life-saving role for HP, which is not well recognized. This lack of recognition is why growing numbers of people, especially children, are not being inoculated against diseases due to suspicion about vaccine ingredients, such as porcine gelatine and other non-halal ingredients. The conventional sector has not addressed this challenge either. It may be noted in this connection that AJ Pharma is working on the world's first non-animal origin vaccine.

The number of halal pharmaceutical players, excluding traditional medicines and cosmetics manufacturers, has significantly increased in recent years. The CCM chair, Normala binti Abdul Samad, commented that according to Islam, non-halal medicines are allowed to be consumed only if there is no other alternative, as one of the main tenets of *Maqasid Shariah* (higher objectives of the shariah) is the preservation of life and health. Muslims worldwide are becoming better informed and often demand pharmaceutical products that contain only halal ingredients (Salama 2017).

"When we got halal certification in 2013, we were the first, and we now see 20 to 30 companies out of around 70 pharma manufacturers in the country, so the sector has grown quite well", Leonard Ariff, Group Managing Director of CCM, told Salaam Gateway.[3] Ariff estimated the overall pharmaceutical sector to grow by 10 to 12 per cent a year, while CCM's exports are growing at close to 15 per cent. Demand is driven at the domestic level by the country's 31.7 million people, around 60 per cent of whom are Muslim, although uptake of HP is still low overall.

"What sells the most in the halal segment, at 35 per cent of the market, is food and beverage, while ingredients and pharmaceuticals are about ten per cent. Acceptance is still low at the moment", said Dr Tabassum Khan, Managing Director of AJ Pharma Holding and Chairman of Saudi Arabia's AJ Biologics of Aljomaih Group, which has facilities in Malaysia (ibid.).

The following four suggestions were made to push HP into a new growth trajectory: (1) The government and the pharmaceutical industry should carry out a "communication blitz" to raise public awareness about HP; (2) Greater investment both locally and abroad. Local pharmaceutical companies should venture into partnerships with foreign companies for large-scale manufacturing to meet the huge potential demand; (3) Expanded research and development collaboration between manufacturers and universities; and (4) To penetrate and conquer the global HP market, the government should foster global collaboration to develop an internationally recognized certification scheme (Xavier 2017, p. 16).

From Halal Industry to Halal Economy

Market surveys show that non-Muslims are increasingly embracing halal, driven by heightened health and ethical consciousness, social responsibility, and an alignment with the values underlying halal.

Malaysia has prepared its Halal Industry Master Plan 2030 (HIMP 2030), intending to promote the internationalization of the local halal industry by leveraging the country's globally recognized halal certification.

The internationalization of the halal industry in Malaysia has also entailed the creation of an online e-marketplace to market and sell its halal products and services internationally. This led Malaysia's ninth prime minister, Ismail Sabri Yaakob, to speak of a halal economy for Malaysia. In his "Tun Abdullah Badawi's Lecture on Halal Economy" on 30 May 2022, Ismail Sabri noted that the current regulatory proposals were limited to the Islamic Financial sector via Bank Negara Malaysia and the Securities Commission. He added that a more comprehensive halal sector could be realized through the establishment of a shariah-compliant Commission. He identified six sectors of the halal economy being developed: halal food, tourism, fashion, cosmetics and pharmaceuticals, media, and recreation. He further added that the rapid growth of Islamic finance can now look toward expanding the halal into all six sectors (Teh Athira 2022).

Conclusion

The all-around enthusiasm for the growth of halal not only as a viable sector of the economy but for the whole economy to become halal, as Ismail Sabri spoke about, necessitates steady growth in all sectors of the economy. The Muslim population of Malaysia, and even their fellow non-Muslims, are endorsing the halal and its growth path in the country. All the various segments of the halal industry reviewed above have shown unprecedented growth. This promise of a vibrant future for halal as an important aspect of Islam may also bring new challenges along the way. Yet, the existence of a sound infrastructure in Malaysia, as shown by its lead role internationally, bodes well for realizing the anticipated transition to a halal economy. It is well to note that halal is not a destination, so to speak, but a journey towards further refinement and growth at every level of the economy, and it is to this more qualitative phase of achievement that Malaysia may be moving. From food and drink to tourism and pharmaceuticals, there will be a greater focus on better quality, diversity, and attractive packaging and presentation to mark a successful transition to a halal economy.

One may further recommend a number of strategies to facilitate this transition. Firstly, increase publicity and advertising to enhance the understanding and visibility of halal. The increased awareness will also indirectly address Islamophobic misconceptions that often perceive halal as a tool for Islamization. Secondly, there is a need to diversify halal products and services. This diversification can be achieved through improved networking within the OIC countries, with certain regions, including the Middle East and Southeast Asia, potentially being more cost-effective producers of specific goods and services. Such efficiencies could be formalized through inter-region agreements. Thirdly, improving alignment and standardization among the various Muslim *madhhabs* and cultural zones is essential, as it would further internationalize halal products and services. This standardization effort can form part of the aforementioned proposal to increase publicity efforts, making halal a means of promoting better networking in the marketplace. Finally, we should encourage mutual understanding and appreciation among Muslim countries by leveraging the potential of halal. This strategy can also serve as an aspect of halal tourism, aiming to introduce Muslim countries, their attractions, and products to the broader world and promote exchanges between Muslim countries.

Notes
1. This statement appears as a Foreword to MS 1500–2009.

2. The 13-item bibliography on p. 16 only refers to Malaysian laws and other existing standards, but no reference is made to the *fiqh* sources.
3. CCM is a public listed company on Bursa Malaysia. Established in 1963, it plays a key role in the development of the pharmaceutical and chemical industries whilst actively developing halal initiatives in the country.

References

Africa Islamic Economic Foundation. 2020. *The Global Halal Industry: An Overview*. Tamale: Africa Islamic Economic Foundation.

Alatas, Syed Imad. 2022. "Women and Islamisation in Malaysia: Contestations on the Practice of Islam". In *The Politics of Muslim Identities in Asia*, edited by Iulia Lumina, pp. 33–47. Edinburgh: Edinburgh University Press.

Baituljannah. n.d. "Baituljannah Official Website". https://baituljannah.com/ (accessed 9 September 2022)

Bernama. 2022. "Pharmaniaga Setting up RM300 Mil Plant to Produce Halal Insulin, Vaccines". *New Straits Times*, 16 May 2022. https://www.nst.com.my/business/2022/05/796562/pharmaniaga-setting-rm300-mil-plant-produce-halal-insulinvaccines (accessed 9 September 2022).

Department of Standards Malaysia. 2009. "Malaysian Standards MS 1500-2009: Halal Food—Production, Preparation, Handling and Storage—General Guidelines (Second Revision)". *Kuala Lumpur: Department of Standards Malaysia*. https://law.resource.org/pub/my/ibr/ms.1500.2009.pdf (accessed 10 September 2022).

———. 2014. "Malaysian Standards MS 1900-2014: Shariah-Based Quality Management Systems—Requirements with Guidance (First Revision)". *Kuala Lumpur: Department of Standards Malaysia*. https://www.iium.edu.my/media/59852/MS%201900%202014SHARIAH%20BASED%20QMS.pdf (accessed 9 September 2022).

Dinar Standard. 2019. "State of the Global Islamic Economy Report 2019/20". https://cdn.salaamgateway.com/special-coverage/sgie19-20/full-report.pdf (accessed 9 September 2022).

———. 2022. "State of the Global Islamic Economy Report 2022: Unlocking Opportunity". *DinarStandard*. https://cdn.salaamgateway.com/reports/pdf/State+of+the+Global+Islamic+Economy+Report+2022_V2_Updated.pdf (accessed 9 September 2022).

Eva F. Nisa 2021. "Online Halal Dating, Ta'aruf, and the Shariatisation of Matchmaking among Malaysian and Indonesian Muslims". *Cyber Orient* 15, no. 1: 231–58.

Gonzalez-Rodriguez, Angela. 2018. "Macy's Eyes 230 Billion Dollars Muslim Fashionistas' Opportunity with Dedicated Fashion Range". *FashionUnited*, 11 February 2018. https://fashionunited.uk/news/business/macy-s-eyes-230-billion-dollars-muslim-fashionistas-opportunity-with-dedicated-fashion-range/2018021028099 (accessed 10 September 2022).

Halal Development Corporation Berhad. n.d. "HDC Halal Parks (2012)". http://www.hdcglobal.com/publisher/halal_park_location_operation (accessed 3 October 2017).

Hew, Wai Weng. 2019. "Religious Gentrification: Islam and the Remaking of Urban Place in Jakarta". In *Ideas of the City in Asian Settings*, edited by Henco Bekkering, Adèle Esposito, and Charles Goldblum, pp. 307–30. Amsterdam: Amsterdam University Press.

Jakarta Globe, The. 2021. "Indonesia Begins Mandatory Halal Certification on Drugs, Cosmetics". 17 October 2021. https://jakartaglobe.id/business/indonesia-begins-mandatory-halal-certification-on-drugs-cosmetics (accessed 10 September 2023).

Janmohamed, Shelina. 2016. *Generation M: Young Muslims Changing the World*. London: I.B. Tauris.

Kamali, Mohammad Hashim. 2021. *Shariah and the Halal Industry*. New York: Oxford University Press.

Laili Ismail. 2017. "Halal Is Not Just about Food—HDC". *New Straits Times*, 19 November 2017. https://www.nst.com.my/news/nation/2017/11/304887/halal-not-just-about-food-hdc (accessed 21 November 2017).

Lever, John, and Johan Fischer. 2018. *Religion, Regulation, Consumption: Globalising Kosher and Halal Markets*. Manchester: Manchester University Press.

Luthviati, Resti Dian, and Suviwat Jenvitchuwong. 2021. "Implementation of Halal Product Assurance in the Pharmaceutical Sector in Indonesia". *Journal of Human Rights, Culture and Legal System* 3, no. 3: 160–75.

Malaysia International Halal Showcase. 2018. "Halal Pharmaceuticals a New Frontier". 7 February 2018. https://mihas.com.my/halal-pharmaceuticals-a-new-frontier/ (accessed 8 February 2018).

Mohamed Azmi Hassali, S.K. Al-Tamimi, Omar Thanoon Dawood, Ashutosh Kumar Verma, and Fahad Saleem. 2015. "Malaysian Cosmetic Market: Current and Future Prospects". *Pharmaceutical Regulatory Affairs* 4, no. 4: 1–3.

Muhamad Izzuddin Zainudin, Faridah Haji Hasan, and Abdul Kadir Othman. 2020. "Halal Brand Personality and Brand Loyalty among Millennial Modest Fashion Consumers in Malaysia". *Journal of Islamic Marketing* 11, no. 6: 1277–93.

Nur Aqidah Azizi. 2018. "Deputy Prime Minister Launches World's First Halal Laboratory in Seremban". *New Straits Times*, 28 March 2018. https://www.nst.com.my/news/nation/2018/03/350678/dpm-launches-worlds-first-halal-laboratory-seremban (accessed 10 September 2022).

Raja Nerine, Raja Yusof. 2013. *Halal Foods in the Global Retail Industry*. Serdang: Universiti Putra Malaysia Press.

Ruiz-Bejarano, Barbara. 2017. "Islamophobia as a Deterrent to Halal Global Trade". *Islamophobia Studies Journal* 4, no. 1: 129–45.

Sabariyah Din. 2006. *Trading Halal Commodities: Opportunities and Challenges for the Muslim World*. Johor Bahru: Penerbit Universiti Teknologi Malaysia.

Salama. 2017. "Malaysia: World's First Halal Certification for Prescriptive Medicine Issued to CCM". *Halal Focus*, 2 February 2017. http://halalfocus.net/malaysia-worlds-first-halal-certification-for-prescriptive-medicine-issued-to-ccm/ (accessed 3 October 2017).

Shakira Hussein. 2015. "Not Eating the Muslim Other: Halal Certification, Scaremongering, and the Racialisation of Muslim Identity". *International Journal for Crime, Justice and Social Democracy* 4, no. 3: 85–96.

Suhana Mohezar, Suhaiza Zailani, and Zainorfarah Zainuddin. 2016. "Halal Cosmetics Adoption among Young Muslim Consumers in Malaysia: Religiosity Concern". *Global Journal Al-Thaqafah (GJAT)* 6, no. 1: 47–59.

Susilawati, Nilda, Miti Yarmunida, and Khairiah Elwardah. 2021. "The Halal Fashion Trends for Hijabi Community: Ideology and Consumption". *DINAR: Jurnal Ekonomi Dan Kewangan Islam* 8, no. 2: 35–46.

Suzanna Eddyono. 2007. "Halal Food and Identity". *Jurnal Harmoni Sosial* 2, no. 1: 39–52.

Syafiq Hasyim. 2022. "Islamic Populism and Identity Politics of MUI: Islamic Leadership, Halal Project and the Threat to Religious Freedom in Indonesia". In *The Politics of Muslim Identities in Asia*, edited by Iulia Lumina, pp. 66–80. Edinburgh: Edinburgh University Press.

Teh Athira Yusof. 2022. "PM: Shariah Compliance Panel Needed to Regulate Halal Industry". *New Straits Times*, 30 May 2022. https://www.nst.com.my/news/nation/2022/05/800674/pm-shariah-compliance-panel-needed-regulate-halal-industry (accessed 11 September 2022).

Tieman, Marco. 2019. "Safeguarding Halal Reputation". *New Straits Times*, 22 February 2019. https://www.nst.com.my/opinion/columnists/2019/02/462817/safeguarding-halal-reputation (accessed 11 September 2023).

United Malayan Land Berhad. n.d. "Iskandar Halal Park". www.umland.com.my/Project/39/Iskandar-Halal-Park (accessed 29 March 2018).

Waninger, Kelsey. 2015. "The Veiled Identity: Hijabistas, Instagram and Branding in the Online Islamic Fashion Industry". Master's thesis, Georgia State University.

Xavier, John Anthony. 2017. "New Halal Frontier Products". *New Straits Times*, 8 August 2017. https://www.nst.com.my/opinion/columnists/2017/08/265299/new-halal-frontier-products (accessed 3 October 2017).

DRIVERS OF SHARIAH-COMPLIANT LIFESTYLE IN INDONESIA
Majelis Ulama Indonesia

Syafiq Hasyim

Introduction

In Indonesia, some Islamic groups continue to struggle for the revival of the Jakarta Charter of 1945, "that sought to implement shariah laws" (Endang Saifuddin 1979; Ahmad Syafii 2001). In 2002, some Muslim political parties lobbied to amend Article 29 of the Indonesian Constitution to include the Jakarta Charter provisions (Nadirsyah 2007). Although the formalization of shariah through political and constitutional means has not materialized, some factions in Indonesia continue to have this aspiration through other means. The failure of the Islamist push in 2002 means that Indonesia is unlikely to become an Islamic state in its traditional and legalist form. However, this does not nullify the shariahtization (the inclusion of shariah into state laws) agenda of those who argue that shariah can be implanted and embedded in the Pancasila doctrine. Islamist groups such as the former members of the Hizbut Tahrir Indonesia (HTI) and Islamic Defender Front (Front Pembela Islam, FPI) were not the only organizations championing this course; Islamic organizations such as Indonesian Council of Ulama (Majelis Ulama Indonesia, MUI), Muhammadiyah, and Nahdlatul Ulama (NU)—considered moderate and apolitical movements—are also on the same page. Muhammadiyah and NU members often proclaim their openness and inclusivity, but the two organizations never outrightly reject the implementation of shariah in the public sphere. They only express clear opposition to shariahtization in the realm of politics and law—such as in the case of establishing a shariah state and the legislation of *hudud* law—but refrain from commenting on the so-called shariah lifestyles that have garnered the interest of many Indonesian Muslims.

This chapter argues that shariahtization in Indonesia implemented through Islamic political conduits is garnering less followership when compared to it being championed through *fatwa*-making, especially on matters dealing with the Islamic way of life (i.e., lifestyle). Groups aspiring for political Islam are decreasing in numbers and influence, while those who champion a shariah-compliant lifestyle are gaining traction (Burhanuddin, Hui, and Negara 2023). Indonesian Muslims generally approve halal food and beverage regulations, shariah-compliant lifestyles, and Islamic economic practices. By contrast, most Indonesians do not support forming an Islamic state. This project, which I term "shariahtization through lifestyle", centres on the role of MUI as the primary driver of shariahtization (Syafiq 2022).

In discussing shariahtization in Indonesia, this chapter will first examine the history of MUI, tracing its evolution from its challenging origins to becoming Indonesia's main driver of a shariah-compliant lifestyle. It then discusses MUI's shariah initiatives since its establishment in 1975, and analyses how MUI's *fatwas*—which provide legal opinions—endorse the enforcement of shariah banking, financial regulations, and halal certification.

MUI and the Shariah Initiative

MUI was established in 1975 with strong endorsement from President Suharto's New Order regime (Moch 2005; Muhammad Atho 1993; Wahiduddin 2012; Syafiq 2020, 2023). During the Suharto administration from 1966 to 1998 (Vatikiotis 1998), Suharto reached an agreement with a number of prominent Indonesian *ulama* (religious scholars) to establish MUI. According to this agreement, MUI's role was to serve as a dialogue partner with the Suharto government, and to issue *fatwas* which could provide guidance or *tawṣiyya* (recommendations) in response to inquiries from government officials or the Muslim community (Syafiq 2023). MUI could issue *tawṣiyya* voluntarily, even without any specific request. Given its history, Suharto stipulated that MUI's organizational structure should differ from existing Islamic organizations such as NU, Muhammadiyah, and Persatuan Islam (Persis). For instance, MUI was not allowed to manage programmes or recruit members directly from the grassroots level because they were already affiliated with NU, Muhammadiyah, Persis and other Muslim organizations. MUI's primary role was *fatwa*-making, a role agreed upon between Suharto and several prominent Indonesian *ulama*.

Notably, it is through this role that MUI later emerged as a prominent driver of shariahtization; its *fatwas* provide the grounds that facilitate the implementation of shariah in a non-Islamic state such as Indonesia.

During the initial phases of its establishment, MUI issued *fatwas* covering four main categories: *ibadah* (worship), *aqidah* (belief), social and cultural issues, and food, drugs, and cosmetics (MUI 2003). It also issues fatwas on Islamic finance, banking, insurance, which we can collectively term as part of shariah economy. It is important to note that not every *fatwa* related to the shariah economy was included in MUI's *fatwa* compilation. *Fatwas*, specifically those addressing the shariah economy, fall under the purview of the National Shariah Board (Dewan Syariah Nasional, DSN), and are compiled in Himpunan Perbankan Syari'ah (Anwar et al. 2019). Later, MUI's *fatwas* concerning halal food, drugs, and cosmetics were handled by Lembaga Pengkajian Pangan, Obat-obatan, dan Kosmetika-Majelis Ulama Indonesia (LPPOM-MUI), the institution set up by MUI to provide halal certification. These *fatwas* were thus separated from the organization's main legal compilation (Himpunan Fatwa Halal Majelis Ulama Indonesia 2008). This means that *fatwa*-making within the institution is a complex process that has its champions and stakeholders.

During Suharto's presidency, MUI pursued shariahtization discreetly, despite the state granting it some freedom to be the *ummah*'s (Muslim community) spokesperson. While MUI issued *fatwas* and *tawsiyya*, they did not use these Islamic legal instruments to dictate shariah legislation and the processes associated with it. Notably, the earlier generations of MUI leaders never had any shariahtization agenda. If they did, they never expressed it publicly. Authoritarian rule under the New Order regime instilled fear among most Islamic organizations, and MUI was not immune to such fear. Consequently, all *fatwas* and recommendations typically aligned with Suharto's agenda, and Pancasila doctrine.

Suharto's resignation in 1998 provided an opportunity for MUI to reorient its mission and distance itself from the ruling regime. This reform culminated in MUI embarking on overt shariahtization efforts. In the past, MUI refrained from publicly expressing its objectives and primarily focused on promoting individual piety. It held the position that shariah was a private matter. However, after 1998, this discourse saw a noticeable shift when MUI began championing the strengthening of shariah in both the private and public spheres. Leveraging its authority to issue *fatwas* and *tawsiyya*, MUI emphasized that shariah should not only be confined to the private realm but extended to the public domain. As a result, shariahtization became MUI's foremost agenda.

MUI asserts that as the world's most populous Muslim country, Indonesia should align with shariah norms. It therefore advocated for the shariahtization of the nation. Sahal Mahfudh, the former general chairman of MUI (2002-14), supported the gradual implementation of shariah in the country. Mahfudh acknowledged that Indonesia is not a shariah state but believed that shariah could still be integrated into the political system. He proposed including shariah principles in national legislation, emphasizing that such legislation would be tolerable as long as it does not intend to replace the existing political structure. In other words, including shariah in Indonesian law should only be a concern if the intention is to establish an Islamic state.

Ma'ruf Amin succeeded Mafhudh as the MUI general chairman in 2015 and later became a prominent advocate of shariah legislation in Indonesia. Amin argued that although Indonesia is not an Islamic state, the implementation of shariah by-laws is not prohibited. Referring to the first principle of Pancasila, the philosophical foundation of Indonesia, Amin firmly believes that shariah should be incorporated into the legal system without contradicting Pancasila or existing Indonesian laws. Under Amin's leadership from 2015 to 2020, MUI directed its efforts towards strengthening the presence of shariah in every aspect of Indonesian society, thereby lending unequivocal support to all shariah-based legislation in the country. As part of these efforts, MUI played a crucial role in advocating the implementation of shariah banking and financial systems in Indonesia. Amin approached the central bank of Indonesia, negotiating for the accommodation of an Islamic finance and banking system into the national financial system. Amin also established the DSN (National Shariah Board) as an umbrella institution for shariah-compliant banks and finance institutions. DSN persuaded conventional national banks and financial institutions in sectors such as insurance and leasing to offer shariah-based products.

MUI's shariah legislation model can be characterized in three forms. Firstly, MUI directly focuses on shariah legislation and regulation, aiming to address the demands of the Muslim community seeking a shariah-based system. To achieve this objective, MUI approaches them to consolidate their support for its legislative agenda. They raise awareness among the Muslim grassroots, underscoring the importance of implementing shariah-based legislation and policymaking in the country. One example of this approach was MUI's push to enact the State Law on Pornography legislation in 2008. MUI utilized persuasion and discourse on the importance of pornographic law to mobilize conservative Muslims, organizing mass demonstrations demanding the legislation of the pornography law. Through this protest,

MUI sought to exert pressure on Indonesian lawmakers to support their cause. Recognizing the deeply polarized nature of Indonesian society on the issue, MUI sought to swing public opinion to align with their standpoint. As a result, State Law No. 44/2008 on Pornography was passed, partially fulfilling MUI's objectives. Another example of MUI's first type of approach is their involvement in the Joint Decree from the Minister of Religious Affairs, General Attorney and Minister of Home Affairs in 2008. By reaffirming their 1981 *fatwa* regarding the heterodoxy of Ahmadiyah, MUI successfully persuaded Susilo Bambang Yudhoyono's (SBY) government in 2008 to restrict the public activities of the Ahmadiyah community.

The second shariah legislation strategy does not involve direct participation from MUI but operates through initiatives proposed by lawmakers. These proposals can be put forth by either the executive or legislative bodies. MUI's role in this process is to encourage the lawmakers of Indonesia to introduce shariah into the legislative agenda. The legislative process involves two key bodies: the executive body, which includes government departments and ministries, and the legislative body (Dewan Perwakilan Rakyat, DPR). When MUI proposes a particular legislation agenda, it engages in lobbying efforts targeting either the executive or legislative bodies. Usually, MUI prepares the legal drafts or conceptualization of the proposed law before presenting the agenda to the legislators. MUI's success in achieving its mission is facilitated by its strong connection with Indonesian lawmakers. Since the Suharto era, personnel within MUI have developed personal skills to effectively approach and persuade the people in government and members of parliament. It is worth noting that in the post-reform era of Indonesia, some government officials and DPR members also hold positions as board members of MUI.

The third strategy involves endorsement and public expressions of support. Indonesia's executive and legislative bodies typically propose shariah legislation and policy regulation initiatives. In this context, MUI's role is to provide moral and theological grounds to support the significance of such legal and policy-making initiatives. One example is State Law No. 33/2014 on Halal Product Assurance, initially proposed by Indonesia's legislative body through *hak inisiatif* (legislative initiative), a constitutional power granted to the DPR. MUI's general stance was to support the legislation of the law by providing shariah justification for this process. This pattern also emerged in the legislation of the State Law on Pornography in 2008. MUI provided moral and theological justification highlighting this law's importance in safeguarding Indonesian society's public morality.

Shariah Economy

MUI has long promoted an economy based on Islam or shariah. One significant collaboration it had was with Ikatan Cendekiawan Muslim Indonesia (ICMI), an organization for Muslim intellectuals sponsored by the New Order regime. Through their collaboration, they established the first Islamic bank in the 1990s, known as Bank Islam Muamalat (BMI) (Hefner 2000). As this initiative began during the Suharto era, the push for shariahtization was not so apparent. For instance, MUI and ICMI did not actively lobby against the issue of *riba* (usury). The establishment of the Islamic bank aimed to provide Muslims with an alternative avenue to safely keep their savings and facilitate credit borrowing. While BMI introduced a non-*ribawi* (non-usury-based) system to account holders, it struggled to gain widespread adoption. Limited public campaigns were conducted to highlight the importance of BMI. Unfortunately, BMI, which operated as a non-*ribawi* bank, faced poor performance and needed an injection of new investments. It eventually went bankrupt as a result of its failure to attract new investments. It is worth noting that BMI was not the only ICMI project that failed to gain traction; the Baitul Mal wa Tamwil (BMT), which are small banks providing microfinance services, also experienced similar outcomes.

The underperformance of BMI, shariah banks and other shariah-related financial institutions did not completely halt the shariah economy project. Although ICMI's influence diminished after its sponsor, Suharto, fell from power, the project continued under MUI's leadership. In 1999, MUI established the DSN and was tasked to supervise the adherence to shariah principles in shariah banks and financial institutions in accordance with the Qur'an and Hadith (Anwar et al. 2019, p. 4). The DSN appoints members of the Shariah Supervisory Council (Dewan Pengawas Syariah, DPS), who serve as MUI representatives in Islamic banks and institutions issuing *fatwas*. The DPS is mandated to supervise the products and systems of Islamic banks and financial institutions and address any issues or cases concerning the shariah economy and finance through the issuance of *fatwas*. DSN also endorses the implementation of a shariah-compliant financial system in national insurance and financial institutions (Moch 2013, p. 74).

The DSN plays a crucial role in promoting a shariah-compliant lifestyle, particularly in the economic sphere. Its mission revolves around applying shariah teaching in the management system of shariah banks and financial institutions and monitoring and enforcing shariah compliance.

Consequently, the DSN also has the right to impose sanctions, determined by its guidelines, on shariah banks and financial institutions that do not comply with shariah principles (Anwar et al. 2019, p. 4). The establishment of DSN was based on a Memorandum of Understanding (MOU) between MUI and Bank Indonesia, the central bank and highest authority in Indonesia's banking sector. The MOU designates the DSN as the *pembina* (builder) and *pengawas* (observer) of shariah-compliant banking.

From establishing the DSN in 2000 until the beginning of President Joko Widodo's (Jokowi) term in 2014, the development of Islamic banks and financial institutions remained stagnant. Compared to conventional banks, the market share of Islamic banks remained under 6 per cent, with conventional banks holding the majority share of 94 per cent. Although the SBY government supported MUI's shariah economy project, it did not create an enabling environment conducive to implementing a shariah economy. While SBY's administration enacted the legislation on State Law No. 21/2008 on shariah banking, it did not provide further measures to facilitate the concrete implementation of the shariah economy.

Ironically, despite the initial strained relations between MUI and Jokowi during his first term (2014-19), his administration helped advance the institutionalization of Islamic banking and finance more concretely and comprehensively. Jokowi successfully positioned the shariah economy as an important national agenda. As part of this effort, the government agreed to establish Bank Syariah Indonesia (BSI), which differs from the earlier BMI. The bank's name reflects Jokowi's willingness to accommodate MUI's vision for shariah banking and finance, as including the word "shariah" aligns with MUI's project objectives. This move is particularly understandable given that Jokowi's vice-president is Ma'ruf Amin, a senior figure within MUI who has long championed Islamic banking and finance. In his role within the government, Ma'ruf Amin oversees the advancement of the country's shariah banking and finance sector.

During his second term, Jokowi further endorsed his ministries to create an enabling environment to promote the advancement of shariah banking and finance. Ministers such as Sri Mulyani, Erick Thohir, and others in his cabinet were deployed to support the success of shariah banking and finance in their respective capacities. For instance, Minister of Finance Sri Mulyani was appointed the general chairman of the Association of Islamic Economic Experts (IAEI). At the same time, Erick Thohir assumed the role of the general chairman of the Shariah Economic Society (Masyarakat Ekonomi Syariah, MES). Additionally, the Governor of Bank Indonesia is the primary adviser to MES. Significantly, Vice-President Ma'ruf Amin was appointed the general chairman of the National Committees of Shariah Economy and Finance (Komite Nasional Ekonomi dan Keuangan Syariah, KNKS). These appointments thus demonstrate state actors' active promotion of shariahtization in the economic and finance sectors during Jokowi's administration.

With the state actively promoting shariah banking and finance, the effects of shariahtization have become more apparent, leading to the expansion of BSI. BSI's assets approximately amount to IDR214.6 trillion (US$14 million), with an initial capital of IDR20.4 trillion (US$1.3 million). Patrons of shariah banking and finance welcomed this growth which signals the stability of the shariah financial system. Furthermore, this growth is expected to have positive spillover effects on other sectors such as tourism (including haj and umrah, and shariah-compliant tourism), investments, and trade.

Halal Industry

Prior to MUI's growing concerns with the halal status of consumable products and the eventual establishment of LPPOM in 1989, Indonesian Muslims generally understood the issue of a product's halal status to be a private matter. While their understanding may not extend to the technicalities of the method of slaughtering or the chemical properties of consumables, most understood the prohibition against pork and alcohol, and that meat had to be slaughtered according to Islamic rites. However, they still had the personal freedom to consume any goods they wished, whether halal or haram (prohibited). Well-established Muslim organizations such as NU and Muhammadiyah did not see the need to control their members' consumption patterns, although they did issue *fatwas* on issues concerning halal and haram. Even then, not all *fatwas* are adhered to by the Indonesian public in their daily lives. This approach aligned with their general understanding that the legal enforcement of shariah was not their primary organizational goal.

However, the situation started to change when MUI established LPPOM under the direction of Suharto. This was prompted by an incident involving Dancow's milk product which was suspected of being contaminated with pork. The issue had serious repercussions, adversely affecting dairy farmers in East Java in the 1990s. Research conducted by Tri Susanto from the University of Brawijaya revealed that all products suspected of containing pork experienced a 40-75 per cent drop in sales. Considering East Java was a vital milk-producing region in Indonesia, the threat to national milk supply greatly concerned Suharto. He therefore sought MUI's assistance in addressing the issue and ensuring its prevention in the future. Hassan Basri, then general chairman of MUI, thus established LPPOM (Syafiq 2023).

Since then, the LPPOM has assumed the role of a halal certification institution, assessing and certifying national and international companies seeking halal certification for their products. Initially, the scope of halal certification focused on food, drugs and cosmetics. Although LPPOM-MUI was established in response to the government's request, obtaining halal certification remained voluntary. However, MUI, as the primary organization to which the LPPOM belongs, actively approaches and persuades restaurant owners, companies, and producers to obtain halal certification for their products. In addition to employing shariah-based arguments, MUI asserts that halal certification not only indicates that food and beverages meet religious requirements, but that these products also embody the concept of *tayyib*, which promotes general goodness or healthiness. Hence, in emphasizing the importance of halal certification, MUI also assures consumers that the products are healthy and of high quality.

Despite its initial slow progress, MUI has consistently developed and improved the halal certification system, emphasizing its significance to stakeholders. MUI also routinely campaigned for the recognition of halal certification as an added value for businesses in Indonesia. After Suharto's resignation in 1998, the popularity of MUI's halal certification became more noticeable. During this period of political change, MUI adapted and reoriented its organizational alliance away from the Suharto regime towards its rivals. Under President Abdurrahman Wahid, MUI's position as an *ulama* organization faced ideological challenges and was undermined due to Wahid's status as an *ulama* himself. Unlike previous presidents, Wahid did not rely on MUI for advice on Islamic issues as he had religious legitimacy and credentials from NU, which was founded by his grandfather. This lack of theological reliance meant that, unlike their relationship with Suharto, MUI could not dictate Wahid's perspectives. Despite their less-than-harmonious relationship, Wahid supported an endowment fund to support MUI, envisioning it as an independent organization separate from state influence, similar to NU and Muhammadiyah. Wahid believed that if MUI remained financially dependent on the state, it could be instrumentalized by the state to legitimize the government's interests. He also surmised that MUI could present its shariahtization agenda within the state's apparatus if it remained closely aligned with the ruling elite. However, even with

Wahid's endowment fund, MUI's dependency on the state did not change significantly.

Following that, MUI experienced a resurgence in strength and significance during SBY's presidency. SBY relied on MUI to establish his Islamic legitimacy in the face of potential challenges from many Indonesian Muslim organizations. MUI thus became a crucial ally for the SBY government in shaping the regime's image and public communications. They even defended SBY against challenges raised by NU and Muhammadiyah. SBY developed close ties with Ma'ruf Amin, making him a member of the Presidential Advisory Council (Wantimpres) for almost two terms from 2007 to 2009 and 2009 to 2014. This further elevated MUI's prominence during SBY's presidency, which elevated several of MUI's key programmes, including halal certification. However, tensions arose between SBY and MUI when SBY's Minister of Religious Affairs, Suryadharma Ali, proposed State Law No. 33/2014 just days before the end of SBY's presidential term. The bill sought to transfer MUI's monopoly on halal certification to the state. While MUI generally supported the legislation of halal certification in the state law, they disagreed with the notion of the state taking control of the halal certification process. However, despite their disagreement, they did not publicly confront the minister regarding the issue.

State Endorsed Shariah-Compliant Lifestyle

The enactment of State Law No. 33/2014 resulted in a significant shift in the regulation of shariah-compliant lifestyles, transferring the responsibility from a non-state domain to the state, thus marking the state's direct involvement in the matter (Syafiq 2022). With the passing of this law, the Indonesian government came to oversee halal issues, leading to the establishment of the State Agency of Halal Product Assurance (Badan Penyelenggara Jaminan Produk Halal, BPJPH). The transfer of responsibility from LPPOM-MUI to BPJPH thus reflected the evolving role of the state in shariahtization.

However, the enactment of the law posed a challenge to religious diversity in Indonesia and the country's status as a Pancasila state. With the passing of the law, every Indonesian business producing and selling goods, regardless of religion or belief, had to comply with the requirements of the shariah. In other words, non-Muslims would be forced to obtain halal certification for their products and adhere to the theological lawfulness or unlawfulness of a given product. While non-Muslims recognize that certain goods are considered haram from a shariah perspective, they may not view them as prohibited based on their beliefs. For example, a product contaminated with pork may be considered unlawful from Muslims' theological and legal standpoints. Still, it may be viewed as lawful theologically and unlawful legally for non-Muslims. Further complications will arise when halal certification becomes mandatory in October 2023. All producers, regardless of religion and belief, will have to comply with halal regulations. Furthermore, all restaurants without halal certification will automatically be categorized as non-halal restaurants.

Overall, such a law has an impact on a Muslim's personal consumption choices. While an individual previously had the freedom to consume products without halal certification, the encompassing nature of the law means that there is greater policing of their choices. While they still have the freedom to consume non-halal products, they are prohibited from dining at restaurants without halal certification. Moral and social sanctions for dining at non-halal restaurants have become significant concerns, despite the absence of halal certification not implying that non-halal foods and drinks are being served. Consequently, many Indonesian Muslims have questioned the need for the state to regulate eating and drinking through legislation.

State Law No. 33/2014 can be regarded as the first state legislation that attempts to shape a shariah-compliant lifestyle not only for Indonesian Muslims but non-Muslims too. A survey conducted by the ISEAS – Yusof Ishak Institute found a significant growth in the demand for shariah-compliant products (survey period: 21–28 July 2022). Approximately 90 per cent of Indonesian Muslims expressed a preference for halal products. The Indonesian government is supportive of this trend as they can leverage it to stimulate the economy through channels catering to shariah-compliant practices. When a product gains popularity and virality, Indonesian Muslim consumers endeavour to find out if it is halal. For example, Mixue, a popular ice cream franchise from China, faced controversy regarding its halal status and eventually had to apply for halal certification from BPJPH. MUI also issued a *fatwa* confirming that all ingredients used in Mixue's products have been certified halal since 15 February 2023. Another notable incident involved Hollywings, a restaurant that promoted its products by offering free alcoholic drinks to individuals with the names Muhammad and Maria. In response, MUI reiterated its *fatwa* stating that any food or beverage containing alcohol is not halal. The restaurant was thus deemed as non-halal, and its business permit was eventually revoked. An individual by the name of Feriyawanansyah even sued six of the restaurant's staff for alleged blasphemy. Another example was the case of Lina Mukherjee, an online content creator and artist who faced legal action due to her content featuring pork consumption while reciting the *basmalah*. This was a violation of blasphemy laws as it was regarded as the propagation of hatred towards Islam.

MUI IN THE POST-BPJPH ERA

MUI's role in the halal agenda reached a turning point with the takeover of the halal certification process by BPJPH as mandated by State Law No. 33/2014. However, this assumption is incorrect. While LPPOM-MUI no longer has the full authority to issue halal certificates, MUI still plays an important role in the process overseen by BPJPH. According to the state law on Halal Product Assurance and the Government Regulation on Job Creation, MUI's role in issuing halal *fatwas* remains intact. Clients seeking halal certification now need to approach BPJPH to initiate the certification process for their products. BPJPH collaborates with the Halal Auditor Institute (Lembaga Pemeriksa Halal, LPH), which includes LPPOM. After undergoing auditing and product investigation, BPJPH consults MUI for *fatwas*. According to the state law on Halal Product Assurance, MUI is responsible for issuing *fatwas* on halal matters, a core component of the halal certification process. Without a MUI-issued *fatwa*, BPJPH cannot issue a halal label. However, MUI's role in the post-implementation of State Law No. 33/2014 is somewhat diminished compared to the period between 1989 and 2019, as MUI no longer leads the entire halal certification process. Efforts to reduce MUI's authority in publishing halal *fatwa* were made during serial public hearings in preparation for the State Law on Job Creation.

However, MUI's role in the halal project differs from its role in the shariah economy. Currently, through the DSN, MUI continues to play a role in driving the development of the shariah economy in collaboration with the Monetary Authority (Otoritas Jasa Keuangan, OJK) and the central bank. All shariah-based economic and financial products and services must obtain MUI's approval through the DPS, demonstrating MUI's monopoly in this field (Lindsey 2012). Additionally, MUI holds the authority to recruit and deploy DPS members. Islamic banks, financial institutions and companies must make a request to MUI for the deployment of DPS members. It is important to note that these DPS members represent the *ulama* institution rather than the finance institutions and banks, thereby maintaining their loyalty to MUI.

By examining the cases associated with halal food and the shariah economy, it is evident that MUI plays a significant role in shaping shariah-compliant lifestyles in Indonesia. The adoption of shariahtized practices in various aspects such as food, drink, fashion and others, has proven to be an effective way to implement the principles of the shariah.

Shariah as a Key Reason for MUI's Survival

MUI is a prominent Muslim organization in Indonesia known for its institutional endurance. It has faced numerous challenges since its establishment in 1975 but has consistently overcome them. It has even proven adept at turning challenges into opportunities for growth. Despite initial assumptions that MUI would decline following Suharto's resignation, the organization not only preserved but also expanded its portfolio.

Shariahtization has played a pivotal role in maintaining MUI's influence and relevance among Indonesian Muslims. Unlike other Muslim organizations, and learning from its failures when dealing with the Suharto regime, MUI recognizes the need to embrace shariah as a means for survival and has achieved relative success. It stands out as the only Islamic organization in Indonesia that explicitly advocates for the formalization of shariah, doing so without calling for the establishment of an Islamic state. It firmly upholds the importance of a Pancasila state, considering it non-negotiable. MUI asserts that Indonesians must embrace the Pancasila state, regarding it as a consensus (*ijma'*) among Indonesians. Ma'ruf Amin often refers to Indonesia as *dar al-mithaq wa al-shahada*, or "a house of agreement and testimony" (NU Online 2019). The concept of *dar al-mithaq* highlights the collective agreement among Indonesians to have Indonesia as a Pancasila state. In contrast, *dar al-shahada* emphasizes their role as witnesses in loving and contributing to the development of the country.

However, MUI's loyalty to the principles of the Pancasila state and its simultaneous support for the implementation of shariah at the state level poses certain practical challenges. Indonesian Muslims, most of whom are Sunnis, adhere to the principle of consensus. Yet, MUI is not a monolithic *ulama* organization. Its board members come from diverse Islamic organizational backgrounds, each with their own understanding of the Pancasila state and shariah. The board members affiliated with modernist Islamic organizations like Muhammadiyah, the Indonesian Islamic Propagation Council (Dewan Da'wah Islamiyah Indonesia, DDII), and Persis differ from those affiliated with traditionalist organizations such as NU, especially in how they aim to position shariah in the Pancasila state. Modernist Islamic organizations tend to prioritize shariah principles over the Pancasila state. This can be seen from the supporters who advocate for a redefinition of the Jakarta Charter; including shariah as an obligation for Indonesian Muslims to apply, they primarily come from a modernist background. While both groups agree on implementing shariah, they differ in their views on how extensively it should be incorporated into the state system, and who should lead its implementation. For example, NU believes the responsibility for implementing shariah should lie with the Muslim community rather than the state. On the other hand, Persis advocates for the formalization of shariah by the state.

Conclusion

Despite various political and economic challenges, MUI remains Indonesia's main driver of shariah-compliance. MUI's role in issuing *fatwas* at the national and regional level sets it apart from other Islamic organizations. Additionally, MUI's new role as *sadiq al-hukumah*, or a "trusted advisor to the government" in the second term of the Jokowi-Ma'ruf administration has facilitated smoother cooperation with government offices, aiding in the push for the formalization of shariah initiatives, as seen with shariah economy and halal project.

Despite the diverse Islamic backgrounds of MUI's board members, there is a noticeable tendency for them to share a similar understanding regarding the formalization of shariah within Indonesia's legal framework. Notable figures such as the late Kyai Sahal Mahfudh, Ma'ruf Amin, the late Ichan Sam, Slamet Effendy Yusuf, and many others with a NU background have shown acceptance of the formalization of shariah. As an organization, MUI can explain why NU ulama should support MUI's agenda of formalizing Sharia.

The continued significance of MUI in promoting a shariah-compliant lifestyle is partly attributed to the relatively limited interest of other Muslim organizations like NU and Muhammadiyah in outwardly advocating for it. While MUI's role in halal certification may have faced some obstacles, it does not imply a complete absence of shariahtization efforts. As the sole authority for issuing halal *fatwas*, MUI remains a key driver of shariah-compliance in various aspects of the Indonesian Muslim lifestyle, including entertainment, tourism, and many others. The endearing influence of MUI as a promoter of shariah-compliance stems from its historical role in spearheading the shariahtization process in Indonesia. No other Muslim organization in Indonesia is as dedicated to advancing the implementation of shariah as MUI. The continued existence of MUI is closely intertwined with its ongoing pursuit of implementing shariah in the country.

References

Ahmad Syafii Maarif. 2001. *Syariat Islam Yes, Syariat Islam No: Dilema Piagam Jakarta Dalam Amandemen UUD 1945* [Islamic Shariah Yes, Islamic Shariah No: The Jakarta Charter Dilemma in the 1945 Constitutional Amendment]. Jakarta: Paramadina.

Anwar Abbas, Asrarun Niam Sholeh, Ichwan Sam, Hasanudin, Cecep Mashanul Hakim, and Endy Muhammad Astiwara. 2019. *Himpunan Fatwa Perbankan Syariah, Dewan Syariah Nasional MUI* [Compilation of Fatwas on Shariah Banking, MUI National Shariah Board]. Jakarta: Emir Cakrawala Islam.

Burhanuddin Muhtadi, Hui Yew-Foong, and Siwage Dharma Negara. 2023. *The Indonesia National Survey Project 2022: Engaging with Developments in the Political, Economic and Social Sphere*. Trends in Southeast Asia, no. 3/2023. Singapore: ISEAS – Yusof Ishak Institute.

Endang Saifuddin Anshari. 1979. *Piagam Jakarta 22 Juni 1945* [Jakarta Charter: 22 June 1945]. Bandung: Pustaka Perpustakaan Salman ITB.

Hefner, Robert.W. 2000. *Civil Islam: Muslims and Democratization in Indonesia*. Princeton: Princeton University Press.

Himpunan Fatwa Halal Majelis Ulama Indonesia. 2008. Jakarta: Direktorat Jenderal Bimbingan Masyarakat Islam Departemen Agama RI.

Lindsey, Tim. 2012. "Monopolising Islam? The Indonesian Ulama Council and State Regulation of the 'Islamic Economy'". *Bulletin of Indonesian Economic Studies* 48, no. 2: 253–74.

Majelis Ulama Indonesia. 2003. *Himpunan Fatwa Majelis Ulama Indonesia*. Jakarta: Departemen Agama.

Moch Nur Ichwan. 2005. "'Ulamā', State and Politics: Majelis Ulama Indonesia after Suharto". *Islamic Law and Society* 12, no. 1: 45–72.

———. 2013. "Towards a Puritanical Moderate Islam: The Majelis Ulama Indonesia and the Politics of Orthodoxy". In *Contemporary Developments in Indonesian Islam: Explaining the "Conservative Turn"*, edited by Martin van Bruinessen, pp. 60–104. Singapore: ISEAS – Yusof Ishak Institute.

Muhammad Atho Mudzhar. 1993. *Fatwa of the Council of Indonesian Ulama: A Study of Islamic Legal Thought in Indonesia 1975–1988*. Jakarta: INIS.

Nadirsyah Hosen. 2007. *Shari'a and Constitutional Reform in Indonesia*. Singapore: Institute of Southeast Asian Studies.

NU Online. 2019. "KH Ma'ruf Amin Sebut Indonesia adalah Darul Mitsaq" [Kyai Haji Ma'ruf Amin Says Indonesia is Abode of National Consensus]. 25 June 2019. https://www.nu.or.id/nasional/kh-maruf-amin-sebut-indonesia-adalah-darul-mitsaq-yS512 (accessed 29 May 2023).

Syafiq Hasyim. 2020. "Fatwas and Democracy: Majelis Ulama Indonesia (MUI,

Indonesian Ulema Council) and Rising Conservatism in Indonesian Islam". *TRaNS: Trans-Regional and -National Studies of Southeast Asia* 8, no. 1: 21–35.

———. 2022. *The Halal Project in Indonesia: Shariatization, Minority Rights and Commodification*. Trends in Southeast Asia, no. 12/2022. Singapore: ISEAS – Yusof Ishak Institute.

———. 2023. *The Shariatisation of Indonesia: The Politics of the Council of Indonesian Ulama (Majelis Ulama Indonesia, MUI)*. Studies in Islamic Law and Society. Leiden: Brill.

Vatikiotis, Michael. 1998. *Indonesian Politics Under Suharto: The Rise and Fall of the New Order*. Politics in Asia Series. London and New York: Routledge.

Wahiduddin Adams. 2012. "Fatwa MUI dalam Perspektif Hukum dan Perundang-Undangan". In *Fatwa Majelis Ulama dalam Perspektif Hukum dan Perundang-Undangan* [MUI Fatwas from the Perspective of Law and Legislation], edited by Nahar Nahrawi, Nuhrison M. Nuh, Asrorun Ni'am Sholeh, and Abidin Zainal, pp. 3–17. Jakarta: Puslitbang Kehidupan Keagamaan Badan Litbang dan Diklat Kementerian Agama RI.

THE EMERGENCE OF ISLAMIC FINANCE AND ITS IMPACT ON THE LIVES OF MUSLIMS IN THAILAND

Tawat Noipom

INTRODUCTION

Islamic finance in Thailand has been expanding since the establishment of the first Islamic Financial Institution (IFI), Pattani Islamic Saving Cooperative Limited, in 1987. This led to the establishment of an Islamic bank, Islamic sections in commercial banks, more than thirty Islamic cooperatives, Islamic asset management firms, Islamic insurance (*takaful*) companies, and informal social financial institutions. The literature on Islamic finance in Thailand has duly discussed the basic features of Islamic finance such as shariah-compliant contracts, service quality, acceptance of IFIs, and the use of Islamic finance among Muslim clients. Only recently have issues related to the performance and impact of Islamic finance on clients' households been discussed.

Until now, scholars are at odds as to whether Islamic finance improves the lives of the Thai population (Muslims and non-Muslims) and adapts to a new set of banking rules and regulations. This chapter examines the impact of Islamic finance on a multicultural society such as Thailand. More specifically, it aims at identifying the forces behind the emergence of the Islamic finance industry, evaluating the current state of the industry, and scrutinizing Islamic finance's impact on society. How does Islamic finance operate in a non-Muslim country? Has there been a complete development plan that ensures that the Islamic finance industry benefits clients of different religious groups? It argues that the Thai government can address the gap of financial exclusion and at the same time ensure better coexistence of various religious groups in the country.

Muslims in Thailand and Their Socio-economic Status

Thailand is a predominantly Buddhist country where religion shapes the country's political culture and people's worldview (Yusuf 2009). Muslims represent the largest religious minority group and can be found nationwide. The majority of Muslims live in the four southernmost provinces of Pattani, Yala, Narathiwat and Satun, and in general, they are found to be poor, undereducated and unemployed (Tawat 2013). The current southern conflict, which began in 2004, has worsened their socio-economic conditions; they rely on agriculture and unskilled low-paying jobs.

Scholars have proposed various theories about Islam's introduction to Thailand. One fact is that in 128 A.D.—several centuries before the founding of the Kingdom of Sukhothai—Arab and Persian Muslims were found active in the ports of the Tenasserim and the Isthmus of Kra, the first truly Thai kingdom (Forbes 1982). Today, Muslims in Thailand consist of Haw Chinese Muslims in the north, Indian or Pathan living across the country, Sulawesi Muslims who migrated from Macassar in Indonesia, and the Malay Muslims, the largest group, residing in the Deep South (Kersten 2004). In these provinces, Muslims form a majority of the total population and have close social and cultural relationships and historical experiences with the Malays in Malaysia, especially in Kelantan, Perlis and Kedah (Kersten 2004; Nisakorn 2009). The ethnic Malay inhabitants converted to Islam during the fourteenth and fifteenth centuries through Arab traders. Pattani, which was independent at the time, was fully incorporated into Thailand after the Anglo-Siamese Treaty in 1909 (Syed 1998). Thereafter, attempts have been made to assimilate ethnic Malays into the Buddhist-dominant state. In Thailand's modern history, Muslims living in the south, who are ethnically different from the majority of Thais, have been trying to separate from Thailand and have caused continuous rebellion and conflicts in the area (Thanet 2008; Forbes 1982).

The number of Muslims residing in Thailand is debatable. The Survey on Conditions of Society, Culture and Mental Health 2018 conducted by the National Statistical Office indicated that the total population of Thailand is 63.3 million, of which 3.6 million or 5.4 per cent were reported to be Muslims. In the National Census 2010, the reported Muslim population was 2.9 million or 4.6 per cent. The real size of the Muslim population is probably higher than that reflected in official data. Some other reports, for example, show that the number of Muslims is around 6 million or approximately 10 per cent of the total population (Isra 2005), while a recent report suggests that the number of Muslims is 7.4 million (MuslimThaiPost n.d.). According to the Division of Islamic Organization and Haj Affairs Promotion, Department of Provincial Administration, Ministry of Interior, the number of mosques in Thailand reached 4,028 in December 2021. Most of the mosques are located in the southern region (14 provinces) and the central regions (25 provinces), with 3,416 mosques and 342 mosques respectively. There are also 51 mosques and 33 mosques in the north (17 provinces) and the northeast (20 provinces) respectively. Interestingly, 186 mosques are found in Bangkok—the capital city—alone. Out of 77 provinces, 40 provincial Islamic councils have been formed.

Even though Thailand's Human Development Index (HDI) 2019 value was 0.777 and was ranked 79 out of 189 countries within the high human development category, the country's economy is characterized by regional disparity and inequality. Statistics on Thailand's socio-economic conditions often indicate that the four southernmost provinces are experiencing high poverty, low education levels, and high unemployment rates (Tawat 2013). According to the National Statistical Office's reports, these provinces constantly record the lowest per capita income. These provinces also report negative economic growth. As such, the poverty incidence of these provinces has been among the highest in Thailand, with just over 23 per cent of the total population living below the poverty line. According to the 2022 statistics on poverty and income distribution issued by the Office of National Economic and Social Development Council, the headcount ratios of these provinces, which indicate poverty incidence, are 43.96 per cent, 17.49 per cent, 24.65 per cent, and 7.08 per cent, respectively, which are far higher than the country's average of 6.84 per cent and the southern region average of 11.63 per cent. This severely affects the poorest segment, living in rural areas (Tawat 2013; Isra 2005).

In terms of educational attainment, the four southernmost provinces have not performed as well compared to the country's standards. Based on the statistics issued by the Office of the National Economics and Social Development in August 2021, the average mean years of schooling of those aged 15 and older in these provinces is 8.4 years compared to 8.9 years of the country's average. The statistical figures of Pattani and Narathiwat were significantly lower than the national average, recording modest figures of 8.2 years and 7.8 years respectively. The average ordinary national educational test (O-net), including subjects such as the Social Sciences,

Thai Language, English, Mathematics and Science, for students in Grade 6 in these provinces has consistently been below Thailand's mean scores. For example, in 2015, the mean scores for these provinces were 32.00, 34.10, 31.37, and 32.24 respectively. These scores are significantly lower than the average 34.81. The scores of Pattani, Narathiwat and Yala have been consistently lowest in the south and in the whole country (Tawat 2013). Most young Muslims attend Islamic private schools for secondary education and informal traditional Islamic schools or *pondok,* and some of these students reach higher education. This affects the career opportunities and choices of the young people in these provinces.

The unemployment rates of the four southernmost provinces have been consistently higher than the national average, and the economy is dominated by agriculture. The National Statistical Office reported that the average unemployment rate of the four provinces in 2021 was 3.7 per cent, compared to the average rate of the southern region (3.0 per cent) and the country average (1.9 per cent). Narathiwat recorded the highest unemployment rate (8.7 per cent), while Yala registered the lowest rate (0.8 per cent). The rates for Pattani and Satun were 2.7 per cent and 2.4 per cent respectively. The manufacturing sector dominates the other regions in Thailand. In the four southernmost provinces, the economy relies on agriculture such as fisheries, crops, livestock, agricultural services, and simple agricultural processing (Tawat 2013). The main crops of these provinces are rubber, durian, rambutan and palm oil, and the prices of these crops have fluctuated but are low most of the time. Slow industrialization indicates the failure of attempts to eradicate poverty. The recent southern unrest since 2004 and the government's low expenditure allocation have worsened this situation (Isra 2005; Jitpiromsri and Sobhonvasu 2006).

THE EMERGENCE OF ISLAMIC FINANCE IN THAILAND

Muslim leaders, Islamic scholars and Muslim activists have had long discussions on how best to resolve the plight of Thai Muslims, particularly those living in the Deep South. Having the above socio-economic positions, an IFI to serve the Muslim communities excluded Thailand's mainstream financial system. The first official IFI was established in Pattani province only in the early 1980s. Since then, various forms of IFIs have been created in the country, ranging from Islamic cooperatives, Islamic windows in conventional banks, a full-fledged Islamic bank, Islamic asset management companies, and *takaful* companies. According to Surin (1988), the *chularajamuntri* or the official head of Thai Muslims, introduced the idea of having a separate charitable fund to assist the poorer sections of the Muslim community. For certain political and socio-economic reasons, a fully-fledged Islamic bank could not be formed. Thus, local Muslim leaders opted for an Islamic cooperative (Tawat 2013).

The establishment of the first Islamic cooperative required cooperation from various stakeholders and was not without obstacles. The Muslim political leaders, religious leaders, and academics in the Muslim-populated region were the main drivers of this endeavour. They initiated the idea of Islamic banking, mobilized dedicated Muslim groups and individuals, and actively negotiated with government officials. Den Tomina, a Muslim politician and the son of the renowned Pattani Muslim scholar and reformer Haji Sulong, led the steering team which was instrumental in negotiating with the related government authorities from the start. Muslim religious leaders at the Pattani Provincial Islamic Council and academics at Prince of Songkla University, Pattani Campus, also played an important role in this process, providing necessary support to the steering team. The management team from neighbouring Bank Islam Malaysia Berhad (Malaysia's first Islamic bank) was also invited to give talks on the principles and operations of an IFI at Prince of Songkla University, Pattani Campus.

After knowing that no Islamic bank could be created, the steering team decided to establish a cooperative. Two government authorities were directly involved: the Cooperative Promotion Department (CPD) and the Cooperative Auditing Department (CAD), both under the Ministry of Agriculture and Cooperatives (MOAC). The officials from both departments had no idea how a cooperative could operate without interest, especially a saving cooperative applied for by the Muslim leaders. After long discussions and negotiations, the first Islamic cooperative, the Pattani Islamic Savings Cooperative Limited, was officially registered on 28 October 1987. The establishment of an IFI not only demonstrated the negotiating power of Muslim politicians but also fulfilled the Thai government's intention to allow Islamic teachings and support the coexistence between Muslims and non-Muslims in Thai multicultural society. The success of this cooperative encouraged the formation of similar shariah-compliant financial institutions in South Thailand, paving the way for a full-fledged Islamic bank in the country (Sudin and Yamaruding 2003).

Many conventional banks then saw the potential of Islamic financial products and ventured into this untapped market. Sri Nakhon Bank was the first bank to offer shariah-compliant products in 1997, but the bank was closed during the 1997 Asian Financial Crisis. The Government Savings

Bank (GSB) initiated an Islamic window in several branches in Muslim areas in 1998, mainly to attract savings from Muslim communities. In 1999, the Bank for Agriculture and Agricultural Cooperatives (BAAC) followed suit and opened an Islamic window for the first time. A state-owned commercial bank, Krung Thai Bank, then entered the market by creating full-fledged Islamic branches in 2002 called Krung Thai Shariah. This was a major development for Islamic finance in Thailand. At about the same time, the Thai parliament approved the Islamic Bank of Thailand Act 2002 based on an agreement signed under the Indonesia-Malaysia-Thailand Triangle (IMT-GT) in which the establishment of an Islamic bank was critical to allow the Muslims to participate in the country's financial system, possibly improve their well-being, and potentially attract funds from Islamic countries (Sudin and Yamaruding 2003). The full-fledged Islamic bank, Islamic Bank of Thailand (Ibank), started its operations in June 2003 (Islamic Bank of Thailand 2022), offering shariah-compliant products and services based on a special act, the Islamic Bank Act B.E. 2545 and the Islamic Bank Act (No. 2) B.E. 2561.

CURRENT STATUS OF ISLAMIC FINANCE IN THAILAND

Islamic finance in Thailand now faces the following characterizations, progress and challenges: different institutional forms, standardized products, commercialization of Islamic financial products, the lack of shariah governance practices, and the lack of qualified personnel. These will be tackled in greater detail in the following paragraphs.

IFIs have now been in various forms such as Ibanks, Islamic cooperatives, Islamic asset management firms, *takaful* companies and informal social finance institutions. These not only allow Muslims from all walks of life to actively participate in the country's financial system but also fulfil their financial needs while conforming to what they consider to be Islamic principles. However, these IFIs face problems in different forms from time to time. They should improve several aspects to effectively serve the needs of their diverse customer segments.

Ibank was established under the Islamic Bank of Thailand Act B.E. 2545 and started offering services in June 2003. The bank is a special commercial bank under the supervision of the Ministry of Finance. In 2018, some amendments were made to the original Islamic Bank of Thailand Act B.E. 2545 and the Islamic Bank of Thailand Act (No. 2) B.E. 2561 was introduced. In November 2005, another bank, the Krung Thai Bank, transferred eighteen branches offering shariah-compliant finance to Ibank, following the instruction from the Ministry of Finance. With almost twenty years of operation, Ibank's performance has not met expectations. Even though the bank has fulfilled the needs for shariah-compliant finance, it has consistently incurred losses. Non-performing loans (NPLs) have been very high, especially from non-Muslim borrowers. The bank has only reported profit in the past few years after the government injected more capital into the Ibank system (ManagerOnline 2017). Another bank, BAAC, operated its Islamic banking services via the Islamic window mainly for agricultural projects of Muslim clients. Hardly any specific financial records on the shariah-compliant unit have been reported.

Likewise, Islamic cooperatives fall under the supervision of the MOAC (more specifically the CPD and the CAD). Even though the Islamic cooperative has not been recognized as one of the official cooperatives, it is allowed to operate effectively in Muslim-populated areas across the country. Most Islamic cooperatives have been operating in Pattani, Yala, Narathiwat and Satun and are registered under either saving cooperatives or service cooperatives. Until recently, the CPD allowed all Islamic cooperatives to include the words "Islamic Cooperative" in their official names. In 2021, the number of cooperatives operating on Islamic principles, listed by the Islamic Cooperatives Network, reached thirty cooperatives with 278,803 members and total assets of approximately THB12,230 million (US$327 million).[1] Many more Islamic cooperatives have not registered with the Islamic Cooperative Network, and their exact numbers are not known.

As for Islamic asset management firms or brokers, at least two companies have offered shariah-compliant services to Muslim clients. These companies are MFC Asset Management Company Limited and DAOL (Thailand) PCL (previously known as KTBST Holding PCL). The former manages an Islamic fund called "MFC Islamic Fund" which has been offering the service since 22 September 2004 (www.mfcfund.com), while the latter started offering Islamic wealth management services called "KTBST-Islamic" (now DAOL-Islamic) in 2017. The services offered by this company include Islamic Equity Account, Islamic Smart Algo, Islamic Private Fund, Sukuk, and LTF-RMF (ManagerOnline 2017). Shariah supervisory committees have been appointed by both companies to ensure the halalness of their products and services, and clients of these companies may choose to use foreign-based shariah screening criteria because no such criteria have been formulated in Thailand. These services have become popular, especially among younger Muslim professionals.

Another form of IFI is *takaful* companies. The first *takaful* company to operate in Thailand was Finansa Life Assurance PCL (now Phillipe Life Assurance PCL) in 2006 (Abbas and Tawat 2022). At present, three insurance companies offer life insurance, while several companies provide other types of *takaful*. These insurance companies present both conventional insurance and *takaful* products, which are termed "One Company, Two Systems". The performance of these companies has been encouraging as more middle-class Muslims are looking for shariah-compliant insurance services to suit their financial needs. More educational and promotional activities are needed to ensure a wider acceptance of *takaful* products.

In the past few years, many Muslim individuals and organizations in Thailand have been trying to establish Islamic social financial institutions such as *zakat* (tithe or Islamic tax) institution, *sadaqah* house (charitable house), and *waqf* institution (endowment). This initiative has impacted the lives of Thai people, Muslims and non-Muslims alike. Unfortunately, no Islamic social financial institution has been officially registered. Islamic foundations, mosques, and provincial Islamic councils continue to oversee the *zakat*, *sadaqah* and *waqf* activities although the social financial activities form a small part of their operations. Most Islamic financial products offered by IFIs, especially Ibank and Islamic cooperatives, are standardized and traditional. There has been a lack of product innovation in the Islamic financial sector. Ibank and Islamic cooperatives have provided banking financial products and services based on traditional shariah contracts such as *murabahah, mudarabah* and *wadi'ah*. On the assets side, *murabahah*-based loan/financing remains the most popular product among IFIs. It forms at least 70 per cent of its loan/financing portfolio. Ibank largely provides loans on the same basis, except that it provides additional products and services for international trade and personal loans based on *bai-inah*. Investment-related products and services are based on the Islamic contracts of *mudarabah* and *musharakah*. These products often comprise a small part of Ibank and cooperative loans/financing. This may not be desirable as Asutay (2012) argues that IFIs may best fulfil the value-loaded objectives of the Islamic moral economy by using the participative products of *mudarabah* and *musharakah*. These products better allow the parties to the contract to share risks and improve real economic activities in the economy. On the liability side, Ibank and Islamic cooperatives attract funds through *wadi'ah* savings accounts and *mudarabah* investment accounts. *Ar-rahnu* service is now available in many Islamic cooperatives to fulfil any urgent financial needs for the working capital of businesses and short-term financial needs such as income shocks, healthcare expenses, consumption needs, and educational expenses. In addition, some Islamic cooperatives provide microinsurance and funeral welfare services to their members. The *takaful* products and services are based on the *qabalah* and *mudarabah* models, which are used in Malaysia. This practice is not a surprise because IFIs in Thailand, in general, have duplicated the Islamic products and services from their neighbours in Malaysia.

Islamic finance is now commercialized, and this is motivated by other factors beyond religious interest as perceived at the beginning of its formation. In Thailand, apart from being interest-free, quality services, returns, confidence in the cooperatives, and social responsibility have become significant factors for patronizing Islamic finance in Thailand. Non-Muslims have also been active clients of both Ibank and Islamic cooperatives, particularly on the *mudarabah* investment account (Natchanan, Tanayu, and Longprasert 2017). In 2019, non-Muslims comprised 69.61 per cent of the total Ibank clients, while Muslims comprised only 31.39 per cent (Thaipost.net 2019). Moreover, Islamic cooperatives can offer higher returns than conventional financial institutions and have been reported to be well-received by non-Muslim clients who want to invest their money in the cooperatives' investment account of *mudarabah*. Thus, participation in the Islamic finance segment is motivated by business or commercial purposes. Most clients have recorded their satisfaction with their services, responsiveness, empathy, Islamic compliance, assurance, and tangibles, which are all conventional aspects of service quality (Parichard, Anlaya, and Useng 2020).

This development is not all well-received, especially when in 2021 Ibank needed a capital injection. Some Buddhist activists were against the idea of the government injecting fresh capital to improve Ibank's financial situation. They exclaimed that Ibank is for a minority group, so public money (through taxes) must not be used. Some interest groups even proposed that the government create a Buddhist-specialized bank so that the Buddhists, who are the majority, can benefit from it. This is part of proposals to ensure that the majority religious group deserves special treatment, in response to several specific policies of the government in promoting Muslims' participation in the socio-economic sphere of the country. In many cases, the issue is due to misconceptions about Islamic finance and the government's policies targeting the Muslim community in the past.

As for shariah governance, IFIs have not adopted effective shariah governance frameworks and practices. This somewhat leads to criticisms and heated debates on social media that IFIs in Thailand promote "Islamic capitalist ideology", focusing on profit maximization as opposed to shariah governance and social objectives, termed by some Thai Muslim academics as the "souls of Islamic finance". Even though most IFIs have appointed shariah supervisory committees, their role is limited. In fact, Ibank has not adopted any internationally recognized governance framework. The bank has followed certain shariah guidelines it duplicates from other Islamic banks and resolutions from its in-house shariah supervisory committee, and these can be problematic. Ismaae and Maroning (2019) state that five major aspects of shariah governance issues in Ibank consist of the lack of clear policy and legislation, taxes and fees burden, lack of operational standards, lack of shariah experts, and lack of government support. Islamic cooperatives also experienced the same problems. However, these might not be damaging since IFIs rely on traditional Islamic products and contracts.

Another issue is the lack of qualified personnel to oversee these Islamic institutions, and this requires immediate attention. Since the beginning of its introduction in Thailand, Islamic finance experts and practitioners were not available; and until today there have been no specific plans to tackle this. As stated by Hama (2016), the staff of IFIs do not have the required knowledge and skills such as Islamic law, financial management skills, and project management skills to effectively perform their jobs. Most Islamic cooperatives established during the first decade of the Islamic finance industry, for instance, recruited Islamic religious teachers as staff. This may have been acceptable at the beginning considering the modest funding and small group of clients. However, as the cooperatives expand, they need staff who understand both dimensions of Islamic finance, and they are hard to find. Ibank faced the same issue, and their priority has been to recruit staff, many of whom are non-Muslims, who have experience in the conventional banking system. They are then trained in various aspects of Islamic finance. Since they might not be well versed in Islamic law, this affects the image of the bank, resulting in lower acceptance among Muslim clients.

Impact of Islamic Finance on the Lives of Muslims

The performance of Islamic finance in Thailand in the first three decades has shown mixed results. Most literature on the performance of Islamic finance has focused on evaluating financial inclusion, proposing performance indicators, examining Islamic contracts, and assessing the quality of services. Ibank has offered Islamic finance products and services for financial inclusion. Financial performance in the past few years has not been promising, incurring losses and accumulating NPLs. Few scholarly writings offer insights into the impact of Islamic cooperatives, and this chapter highlights some of them. Tawat (2013) examined the impact of Islamic cooperatives on the lives of Muslim households and introduced several impact factors, including productive assets, self-employment, housing, income, children's education consumption, healthcare, and religious practices. In general, the findings of this study indicate that Islamic finance has improved income, the ability to acquire productive assets, housing and self-employment. The impact can be either direct or indirect. Islamic financial products offered by IFIs, especially Islamic loans/financing, often have a direct impact on the ability to purchase productive asset-holding, housing and self-employment. However, the client's household income is indirectly improved because of the utilization of Islamic financial products and services.

The clients of Islamic cooperatives purchase productive assets and use them to engage in mainly small and medium economic activities such as petty trade, minimarts, and rubber tapping. These assets provide the necessary components for motorcycles, vehicles, and office computer production, and a range of other tools and equipment. The level of improvement depends on the initial number of productive assets owned by the clients and the awareness of financial products offered by IFIs. Clients with a higher number of productive assets can correctly find productive assets that better suit their economic activity and acquire those assets using Islamic financial products and services. In addition, clients who are professionals can obtain accurate information about Islamic financial products and services on offer. Therefore, they can identify suitable assets for their business or other economic activities. Information on Islamic financial products and services is now available on the IFIs' websites and social media platforms.

Another significant impact is the cooperatives' ability to improve housing conditions in the Deep South. It was found that Islamic loans/financing can improve clients' opportunities to build new houses, expand existing ones, and repair them. Most IFIs offer *murabahah* loan/financing for housing-related purposes. Clients can request IFIs to purchase houses or hardware for them in the first instance, and they can repay the institution by instalment. Cooperative members with longer membership would be familiar with information relating to the rules and regulations of the cooperatives, and they would benefit more from housing-related products and services. Moreover, older groups of clients tend to use Islamic loans or financing for housing building and repairs.

Moreover, Islamic loans and financing increase production opportunities and generate income for Muslim households directly or indirectly. In some cases, the loans/financing enhance business opportunities from working capital injection, purchase of productive assets, and house expansion, all from financial services. To illustrate, prayer hat makers borrow from IFIs to purchase raw materials to continue producing hats that will be exported to Saudi Arabia during the haj season. In another example, motorcycles bought using *murabahah* financing are used for mobile food stalls in Thailand. Some clients expanded their houses and later used these spaces for homemade products and minimart. These Islamic finance services have been used effectively by small and medium-sized entrepreneurs. Clients utilize Islamic loans to purchase productive assets and acquire business capital or liquidity injections. Therefore, they can improve their economic activities, resulting in an increase in income. The level of impact tends to depend on the initial income level of the clients and awareness of the products and services.

The IFIs can also indirectly increase food and non-food consumption, enhance children's education, improve household access to healthcare, and upgrade Islamic activities and practices of Muslim clients, among others. These resulted from improved income-generating activities in the clients' households through loans/financing. Consequently, as household income increases, they use this income on better-quality food and non-food items. As for the impact of Islamic finance on educational opportunities for children living in these households, the impact can be either direct or indirect. In some Islamic cooperatives, members can opt for emergency loans or Islamic pawnbroking (*ar-rahnu*) and then directly pay tuition fees or purchase the educational equipment needed for their children. In some cases, they buy motorcycles for their children so that they may ride them to school. In addition, Islamic finance can also increase access to healthcare by households, especially medication for serious illness, which is not covered under the country's healthcare system.

However, this impact is an indirect one, meaning that Islamic loans/financing improve economic activities and increase the income of households that can be used for healthcare expenses. Participating in Islamic finance also encourages regular Islamic practices such as congregation prayers, paying *zakat*, *waqf*, and *sadaqah*, avoiding interest, and going to haj. In cooperatives, in particular, the members are usually grouped in various Islamic talks and other activities to ensure that the members can improve their Islamic knowledge and practices. Tawat (2013) illustrated the impacts of Islamic cooperatives in Thai households in Figure 5.1.

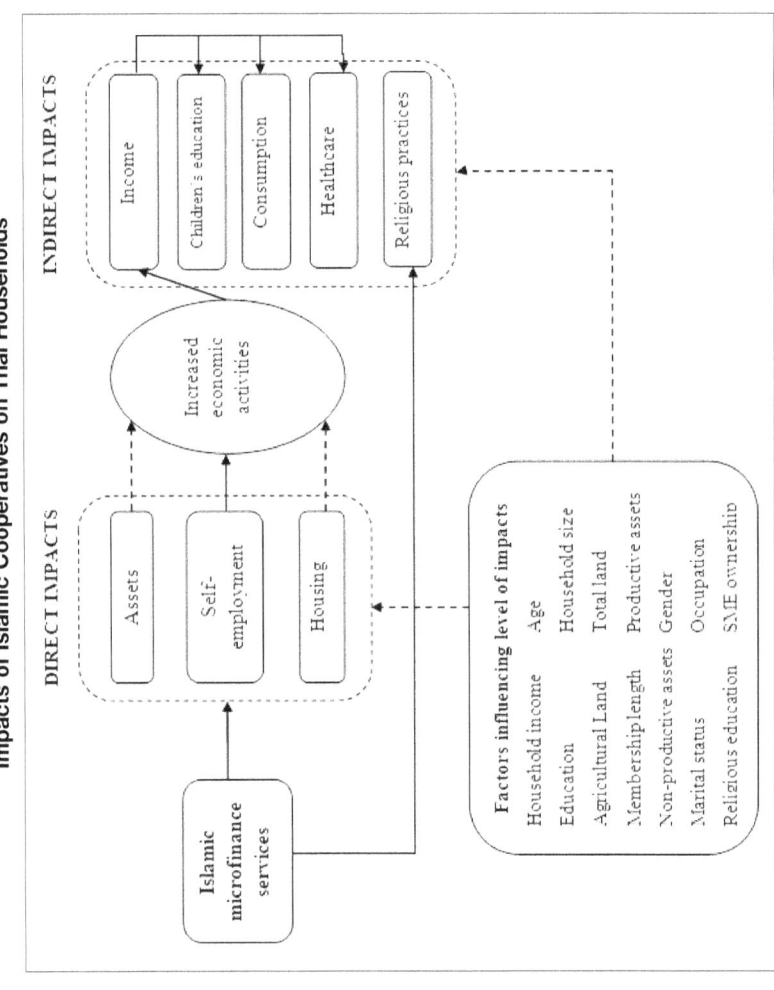

FIGURE 5.1
Impacts of Islamic Cooperatives on Thai Households

Source: Tawat (2013).

In terms of outreach to a considerable number of clients, Islamic finance in Thailand can reach many Muslim and non-Muslim clients. The number of clients served by financial institutions is termed as "breadth of outreach". Ibank, for example, which started operations in 2003, operated 130 branches across Thailand in 2021 in Muslim and non-Muslim areas. The bank has provided its products and services to and targeted both Muslim and non-Muslim clients. According to the Islamic Cooperatives Network, the number of Islamic cooperatives and Islamic funds registered as active members reached thirty members, and at the end of 2021 reported a total asset of THB12,230 (approximately US$327 million). The clients or members of the cooperatives and Islamic funds hit 278,803 in the same year.

In terms of the depth of outreach, IFIs can reach low-income and financially excluded groups. As mentioned in the previous paragraph, the IFIs have served several Muslims who were initially excluded from the Thai financial system because of their beliefs. The question is whether they can effectively help the Muslim poor, specifically Muslims in the four southern border provinces, one of the poorest regions of the country. In general, there is no specific data available to prove that IFIs can reach the poorest of Muslims. Ibank, understandably, targets the public and its participation in recent Islamic microfinance programmes failed and resulted in large NPLs. Since then, the bank has focused on clients with similar characteristics to those patronizing conventional financial institutions and has adopted strict policies on loans, and more specifically, collateral requirements. This does not strongly support the claim that Ibank can reach poorer Muslim clients. As for Islamic cooperatives, their members should in principle target low-income groups of the Muslim community, adapting the principles of Islamic moral economy and helping the poorest. In practice, this might be contradictory when looking at the profile of the members who are mostly middle-class professionals, not the farmers who form much of the population in the provinces. The cooperatives may have fulfilled the objective of financial inclusion of Muslims but not the Muslim poorest who are required to prove creditworthiness like conventional financial institutions. In fact, many of them do not have the required collaterals and are turned away by the cooperatives. In short, the poorest Muslim groups in Thailand may not benefit significantly from Islamic finance.

Conclusion

Muslims constitute the largest minority group in Thailand, and most of them live in the southern provinces of Pattani, Yala, Narathiwat and Satun. This region is known for extreme poverty, low education, high unemployment and violence. The introduction of Islamic finance was considered to be a panacea to improve the abovementioned socio-economic conditions of the Muslims and to implement a key Islamic principle in daily life. However, Islamic finance in Thailand has not been established simply as a political solution, although there is a genuine belief that Muslims will be more proactively integrated into the economy and the measures can alleviate poverty. Muslim political leaders, religious leaders, academics and government agencies were all involved in this establishment until the Pattani Islamic Saving Cooperative Limited was created in 1987. A Muslim politician, Den Tomina, was active in the negotiation process between the steering group, consisting of members from different Islamic ideologies, and related government agencies such as the CPD and the CAD under the MOAC. Pattani religious leaders and academics, mainly from the then College of Islamic Studies (now Faculty of Islamic Sciences), Prince of Songkla University, Pattani Campus, played supporting roles in the process. More importantly, the establishment of IFI was not possible without the central government's policy on Muslims' inclusion and coexistence in Thai society. Unlike the earlier phases, each Islamic cooperative is likely to belong to the members upholding the same Islamic ideology. The cooperatives, however, cooperate with each other through the Islamic Cooperative Network.

The emergence of Islamic finance in Thailand initially suggests that it is a religious requirement for the Muslim community to have access to financial products and services in line with Islamic teachings. After three decades since its inception, Islamic finance, with promising financial performance, has become more commercialized. Unlike the earlier stage of its establishment where religious requirements were predominant, service quality, return and other conventional banking indicators have become relevant. From time to time, politics is important in driving Islamic finance forward, especially when Ibank needs special treatment such as capital injection and restructuring. At first, Muslims in the southernmost provinces accepted the idea of Islamic finance and participated in Islamic cooperatives. This is not the case for Ibank, where non-Muslims formed the main clients. A considerable portion of the southern Muslim communities, especially the conservative groups, were reluctant to use the bank's products and services, citing the fact that the bank belonged to a non-Islamic government and might be completely non-Islamic. This perception changed over time. As for non-Muslim communities, most do not voice any grievances except for some small Buddhist activist groups who have expressed their concerns about the government's policy towards Islamic finance on social media. There has been some misunderstanding and the Central Islamic Council of Thailand, the main Islamic organization, often duly responds to their queries.

Impact studies have confirmed that Islamic finance in Thailand has improved the socio-economic conditions of Muslim clients, i.e., income, accumulation of productive assets, consumption, housing, healthcare, children's education, and Islamic practices. These impacts can be either direct or indirect, and very much depend on certain characteristics of the clients, especially their awareness of Islamic finance products and the length of their participation. IFIs perform well on financing outreach in general and the breadth of outreach in particular. It is also argued that IFIs in Thailand need to focus more on participative modes of financing such as *mudarabah* and *musharakah* so that more people can benefit from their products and services.

In Thailand, Islamic religious consumerism and commoditization have taken place in Muslim society for a few decades. These have formed an effort to preserve their identity and to bring Islamic principles into practice. Halal products and finance, apart from other religious practices, have become relevant for the country's economic development. Unlike their Buddhist counterparts, their religious consumerism and commoditization are limited to their communities, and in fact, very much confined to their religious practices. It might be sensible to suggest that as a minority group, Muslims in Thailand have engaged in religious consumerism and commoditization because they need to preserve their Islamic identity and religion.

Note
1. The calculation is based on the exchange rate US$1 = THB37.5592.

References
Abbas Labduang, and Tawat Noipom. 2022. "Model and Operations of Islamic Insurance (Takaful) in Thailand". *Journal of Humanities and Social Sciences* 18, no. 1: 184–208.
Asutay, Mehmet. 2012. "Conceptualising and Locating the Social Failure of Islamic Finance: Aspirations of Islamic Moral Economy vs the Realities of Islamic Finance". *Asian and African Area Studies* 11, no. 2: 93–113.
Forbes, Andrew D.W. 1982. "Thailand's Muslim Minorities: Assimilation, Secession, or Coexistence?". *Asian Survey* 22, no. 11: 1056–73.
Hama, Z. 2016. "Islamic Bank of Thailand: Realities and Challenges". *Al-Nur* 21, no. 2: 23.
Islamic Bank of Thailand. 2022. "History". https://www.ibank.co.th/th/about/history (accessed 21 July 2022).
Ismaee Sani, and Maroning Salaeming. 2019. "Conditions and Problems of Shari'ah

Supervision in Islamic Bank of Thailand". *Journal of Yala Rajabhat University* 14, no. 2: 288–98.

Isra Sarntisart. 2005. "Socio-Economic Silence in the Three Southern Provinces of Thailand". *Journal of Public and Private Management* 12, no. 2: 67–88.

Jitpiromsri Srisompob and Sobhonvasu Panyasak. 2006. "Unpacking Thailand's Southern Conflict: The Poverty of Structural Explanations". *Critical Asian Studies* 38, no. 1: 95–117.

Kersten, Carool. 2004. "The Predicament of Thailand's Southern Muslims". *American Journal of Islam and Society* 21, no. 4: 1–29.

ManagerOnline. 2017. "iBank Executives Have Informed the NCTC That More Than 100 Bankers Have Been Damaged". 26 June 2017. https://mgronline.com/stockmarket/detail/9600000064793 (accessed 21 July 2022).

MuslimThaiPost. n.d. "How Many Muslims in Thailand?". https://news.muslimthaipost.com/news/33076 (accessed 21 July 2022).

Natchanan, N., Tanayu Puwittayathorn, and S. Longprasert. 2017. "Islamic Bank of Thailand Imagine, Upper Southern Region Towards the Customer's Perceived". *Journal of Management Sciences Suratthani Rajabhat University* 4, no. 1: 179–202.

Nisakorn Klanarong. 2009. "Border Crossing of Muslim Women in Southern-Border Provinces of Thailand". *Asia Pacific Viewpoint* 50, no. 1: 74–87.

Parichard Benrit, Anlaya Smuseneto, and Useng N. 2020. "A Causal Relationship Model of the Service Quality Influences on Customer Satisfaction of Islamic Bank in Three Southern Border Provinces". *Journal of Public Administration and Politics* 9, no. 2: 148–70.

Sudin Haron, and KuMajdi Yamaruding. 2003. "Islamic Banking in Thailand: Prospects and Challenges". *International Journal of Islamic Financial Services*, 5, no. 2: 1–11.

Surin Pitsuwan. 1988. "The Islamic Banking Option in Thailand". In *Islamic Banking in Southeast Asia*, edited by Muhammad Ariff, pp. 164–71. Singapore: Institute of Southeast Asian Studies.

Syed Sirajul Islam. 1998. "The Islamic Independence Movements in Patani of Thailand and Mindanao of the Philippines". *Asian Survey* 38, no. 5: 441–56.

Tawat Noipom. 2013. *Assessing the Performance and Scope of Islamic Microfinance in Thailand: Developments and Prospects.* Durham: Durham University.

Thaipost.net. 2019. "Stop Mocking 'Buddhist' against 'Islam': The Office of Chularatchamontri Issued a Clarifying Statement After the Ill-Wishers Disseminated the Message from the Truth". 20 December 2019. https://www.thaipost.net/main/detail/52903 (accessed 21 Julu 2022).

Thanet Aphornsuvan. 2008. "Origins of Malay Muslim "Separatism" in Southern Thailand". In *Thai South and Malay North: Ethnic Interactions on a Plural Peninsula*, edited by Michael Montesano and Patrick Jory, pp. 91–123. Singapore: National University of Singapore Press.

Yusuf, Imtiyaz. 2009. "The Thai Muslims and Participation in the Democratic Process: The Case of 2007 Elections". *Journal of Muslim Minority Affairs* 29, no. 3: 325–36.

Part II
SOCIALIZATION OF LIFESTYLE AND NEOLIBERAL CAPITALISM

6
SHARIAH COMPLIANCE AND ITS IMPACT ON READING CULTURE IN MALAYSIA

Azhar Ibrahim

> Islamization has not succeeded in imprinting upon the Muslim consciousness the crucial importance of eliminating poverty, exploitation, corruption and greed. Neither has it strengthened the Muslim commitment to inter-ethnic harmony or public accountability or social justice.
> *Chandra Muzaffar*

INTRODUCTION

Since the emergence of Islamic revivalism in the Malay-Indonesian world in the 1970s, the region has witnessed various forms and intensities of Islamic politics and group interests. It is marked by the greater assertion of Islamic observances, practices and ideas, especially in the public sphere. In recent decades, the call for Islamic revivalism or Islamization has been noticeable in Malaysia and neighbouring Indonesia. The religious elite (*ulama*) in Brunei, Singapore, and Southern Thailand have also participated in such assertions to some extent.

In a nutshell, Islamization has evolved in two directions. The first involves a social process whereby Islamic values and practices have been gradually entrenched in Muslim societies, as a result of numerous factors at work. As a social process, it has shaped Muslim societies over an extended period, introducing new values and traditions, and affirming existing ones. On the other hand, the second direction is a conscious effort to Islamize the community, resulting in exclusivist orientations and anti-pluralist modes of thinking which are motivated by several factors. Both directions have resulted in greater compliance with the shariah. This would refer to adherence to general Islamic principles, or to specific observances which are stipulated by Muslim governing authorities.

Overall, the period of intense Islamization witnessed the persistent claim that "Islam is the panacea to all human predicaments", that "Muslims need no other systems", and that "all other systems are corrupt and unIslamic". As these assertions became popular and were eventually normalized, those who critically scrutinized such claims were relegated to the background and dismissed as "liberal". However, such assertions and trends warrant sociological and historical scrutiny, as they may have (un)intended consequences on a society characterized by religious, cultural and ethnic pluralism. These consequences may be cultural, religious or linguistic, and may affect inter-religious and inter-ethnic relations.

While many have focused on the rise of political Islam in the context of revivalist ideologies and orientations, few studies have scrutinized and assessed the impact of cultural and intellectual Islamism that has been articulated and growing within the Muslim community over the last five decades. Thus, this chapter will discuss the second direction of Islamization—which can also be referred to as socio-cultural Islamism—and how it has had an impact on reading culture in Malaysia. More specifically, the chapter will explore the following questions: (1) What are the reasons for the emergence of shariah compliance in reading culture, and how has it manifested; (2) What is the impact of shariah compliance on culture and knowledge production; and (3) What lies ahead? While the chapter will focus on Malaysia as the subject of investigation, references and comparisons will be made to neighbouring Indonesia, since the nature of interaction between the two countries—specifically between the literary and religious elite—has changed significantly over the years.

Islamic Revivalism: From the Calling for Shariah to Shariah Compliance

In the Malay world, the 1970s witnessed a crucial turning point that would shape society's Islamic orientation or style of thinking. Arguably, this era continues to impact contemporary religious life until today. Much has been said about this period, which scholars often refer to as Islamic resurgence (Chandra 1987), Islamic revivalism (Azhar 2014), the *dakwah* movement (Zainah 1987), the reflowering of Islam (Nagata 1987), or Islamism (Ahmad Fauzi 2008). Preferring the term "resurgence" to "revivalism", Chandra describes the period as follows:

Islamic resurgence is a description of the endeavour to re-establish Islamic values, Islamic practices, Islamic institutions, Islamic laws, indeed Islam in its entirety, in the lives of Muslims everywhere. It is an attempt to re-create an Islamic ethos, an Islamic social order, at the vortex of which is the Islamic human being, guided by the Quran and the Sunnah (Chandra 1987, p. 2)

Clearly, the religious elites championed the incorporation of the Islamic worldview—in line with the principle that Islam is *ad-deen*, or a way of life—in all aspects of social, economic and political life. The strength of the movement, which originated from the urban centres of Malaysia, Indonesia and Singapore, led the Malaysian government under Mahathir Mohamad (1981–2003) and later the Indonesian government under Suharto (1966–98) to embark on state-led Islamization policies. As will be discussed shortly, Mahathir adopted the co-optation strategy to include Islamic revivalist activists into the government machinery and the ruling party United Malays National Organization (UMNO), while Suharto adopted a savvier pluralist method to divide the traditionalist and modernist camps, as he began to offer carrots, rather than sticks, to Muslim activists since the 1990s (Norshahril 2018).

A number of global and local factors combined to trigger this movement. Among others, the feeling of dispossession of global Muslims after the fall of the Ottoman caliphate in the 1920s, the defeat of Arab nations at the hands of Israel in the Arab-Israeli conflict in the 1960s, the loss of Palestinian lands to the hands of Israel who were backed by the US, and the Soviet Union's attempts to capture Afghanistan in 1979. Basically, the Muslim world felt it was at the beck and call of the superpowers after the Second World War and during the Cold War. On the flip side, the Iranian Revolution of 1979 which witnessed the rise of 77-year-old cleric Ayatollah Khomeini leading a revolution to topple the Western-allied Shah of Iran, inspired Muslims across the world, including those in Southeast Asia, that Islam and the *ulama* could be the agents of social change. Many Southeast Asian students and activists travelled to Iran to witness the revolution. This was despite the fact that most of them were Sunni, while Iranian Islam is Shi'a. Iran's geopolitical rival, Saudi Arabia, had to counter the interest in Iranian Shi'ism's revolutionary spirit. With its edge in funding capabilities via petro-dollars, they have embarked on exporting Salafi-Wahhabism to many parts of the Islamic world, including Southeast Asia.

Malaysia also experienced demographic and socio-economic changes because of Mahathir's and his predecessors' developmental policies. Access to university education increased for males and females, and the country experienced rapid urbanization and migration from rural villages to the capital, Kuala Lumpur. By the 1980s, the country was thriving, recovering from the bloody 1969 racial riots. The Malay middle class was slowly emerging, and with them came new demands and lifestyles suited to their socio-economic status. For instance, they patronized eating outlets, entertainment and fashion that distinguished them from the underclass, lived in high-end apartments, and drove fancy cars. But with this appetite to uplift their lifestyles, they negotiated their tastes with the parallel revivalist discourse supported by the politicians and religious elites. The political domain also witnessed significant changes. The Malay nationalist UMNO also facilitated Islamization from within the party by co-opting *ulama* and activists into the party. The well-known figure who joined UMNO was youth activist Anwar Ibrahim. There were also significant changes to the education domain, from the strengthening of the shariah courts to the formation of Islamic universities such as the International Islamic University of Malaysia (IIUM). There were also other Islamization policies that were introduced and strengthened during this period, and this has been well documented (Azhar 2014; Norshahril 2018). The state-backed calls for greater integration of shariah—which is defined in a legalistic fashion—into policies. Some of these include the growth of the halal certification process and the Islamic banking and finance industry (which will be discussed in other chapters in this volume).

By the 1990s, Islamic revivalism was already at its peak. In the 1990 general election, the Islamic Party of Malaysia (PAS) made significant inroads into the political domain by capturing the state of Kelantan. PAS ruled Kelantan from the 1950s up to the 1970s. It reinvented itself from a Malay nationalist-Islamic party to an Islamist party and regained control of the east coast state after being out of power for over a decade. The state was led by cleric Nik Aziz Nik Mat and aimed to introduce a shariah criminal code which was blocked by the federal government. The 1990s also saw the strengthening of the Department of Islamic Development of Malaysia (Jabatan Kemajuan Islam Malaysia, JAKIM), the federal-level religious department. There were also several institutions that were made more prominent, one of them being the Malaysian Institute of Islamic Understanding (Institut Kefahaman Islam Malaysia, IKIM).

Revivalism was not only experienced at the state and political level but also the societal level. Activist groups had their own interpretation of how to bring the call for shariah into their organizational struggle. One such organization was the Islamic Youth Movement of Malaysia (Angkatan

Belia Islam Malaysia, ABIM), whose leader Anwar Ibrahim joined the government, and later rose to become UMNO's deputy president and the country's deputy prime minister. Another group that was active at the grassroots and took pride in its followers which numbered in the thousands, was Al-Arqam led by the charismatic Ustaz Ashaari Mohammad. In 1994, the movement was banned by Mahathir's government for spreading "deviant" teachings.

While much has been discussed about the impact of Islamic revivalism on the political and civil society domain, less attention has been dedicated to the impact on socio-cultural aspects, especially reading culture. On the one hand, there is greater scrutiny on publications and circulation of reading materials that are not in line with Malaysia's Sunni (Ahlus Sunnah wal Jamaah) school of thought. Shi'ism is totally banned, and Shi'as cannot practise their faith in the country, especially in the open (Mohd Faizal and Tan 2018). However, the impact of revivalism can also be felt through the creeping Islamization discourse in the literary scene. The following sections will analyse this aspect further.

Shariah Compliance and the Constriction of the Discursive Terrain

Shariah compliance can be viewed as a subset of socio-cultural Islamism. Those who call for it mainly seek the observance of practices that are in line with the principles of the shariah. However, calls to comply with the shariah are often made in general and even vague terms, without in-depth clarification and elaboration. Yet, despite its ambiguity, shariah compliance has become the standard measure as to whether one accepts Islam in its totality, which would therefore earn him or her the title of a "good Muslim", as opposed to one who may just be a "nominal Muslim" or worse still, a "liberal Muslim" who works with the enemies of Islam.

Thus, while socio-cultural Islamism may be a vague concept, it connotes the sacrality and authenticity of standard Islamic practices and contributes to the euphoria surrounding greater Islamization, ranging from public policies to cultural claims and assertions. Between the 1970s and 1990s, the Malaysian state machinery directed its resources towards facilitating Islamization and shariah compliance. However, it was not just a top-down process. There were also several ground-up initiatives originating from civil society organizations (CSOs) within the Malay/Muslim community.

The calls for greater Islamization in all aspects of Malay/Muslim life shaped the discursive terrain of the country—especially those expressed in Malay. The changes in the discursive terrain were largely due to the Islamization of knowledge phenomenon which emerged in the 1970s, and which is part of the enthusiasm for greater shariah compliance. For those who actively partake in facilitating this phenomenon, it is believed that the knowledge systems which people build can only be valid and relevant if they are first "Islamized". This would mean removing any secular or Western elements within a given body of knowledge. They argued that Muslims must not accept ideas and knowledge if they do not align with Islamic ethos, traditions, and values. In contrast, proponents of the Islamization of knowledge claimed that "Revealed Knowledge", or the knowledge which originates from a divine source, is foundational and complete or sufficient for Muslims and even the whole of humankind.

As this attitude towards knowledge gradually became entrenched in the minds of the educated Malay elite, their reception towards other forms and traditions of knowledge became increasingly limited and even hostile. It is not uncommon for them to regard these other forms of knowledge as "secular" or "worldly" in contrast to "religious" or "revealed" knowledge. The most apparent manifestation of this dichotomy and hostility is the rejection of knowledge and ideas from the West, whereby they are dismissed as "*kafir*" or a danger to Islam and Muslims.

However, it is not just Western knowledge which is the victim of such an attitude. The continuous emphasis on the importance of the Islamization of knowledge has also resulted in reduced reception towards other knowledge systems, including those from Indonesia. This exclusivist attitude towards scholarship and other intellectual paradigms has serious ramifications not only on reading culture but also on the development of Malay academic and cultural discourse.

Exclusivism Underlying Socio-cultural Islamism and Sastera Islam

In the cultural domain, the call for *Sastera Islam* (Islamic Literature) has gained traction among those who think that the cultural and artistic paradigms have failed to encapsulate or project an Islamic worldview. These calls gained momentum between the 1980s and 1990s and led to further calls to inculcate an Islamic way of reading and producing literature. Such efforts questioned the literary orientation that had been established and accepted among the Malay literati. This included the norms of *sastera untuk masyarakat* (literature for society), any elements of marhaenism, or the affirmation of *kemanusiaan* (humanism).[1] The ideals of *sastera untuk masyarakat* and humanism were deemed to be unaligned with the perceived Islamic conception of literature, for all endeavours must be directed solely towards God (Kuntum 1991). Moreover, humanism, literature and philosophy are Western and Christian imports which Muslims should shun. For proponents of *Sastera Islam*, human acts which are aimed at improving society's well-being are regarded as this-worldly or secular. Such acts are therefore deemed un-Islamic, as they claim that Islam is the very antithesis of secularism.

It is no surprise that anti-secularism has become common in Malay intellectual, cultural and religious discourse. In fact, almost all problems in society are linked to secularism. This has been the case since the publication of *Islam and Secularism* by Syed Muhammad Naquib Al-Attas, a world-renowned Malaysian intellectual figure. While other countries in the Global South have busied themselves with reformist and post-colonial debates which focus on the demerits of neoliberalism, globalization, and the hegemonic forces of Western knowledge production, Malay discourses—except for a minority of academic circles—have been preoccupied with the issues of secularism, Westernizing trends, and even the perceived threat of Christian evangelism.

Additionally, other "-isms" are also subject to scrutiny. When groups within progressive circles call for the affirmation of pluralism, human rights, civil liberties, democratization, and multiculturalism, certain conservative groups—including the Islamists within the establishment—view such values as a real threat and danger towards Islam and Muslims. For example, in Indonesia, such sentiments were evident from the reactions against Indonesian reformist intellectuals like Gus Dur, Nurcholish Madjid (Cak Nur), and Buya Syafii, whose calls for such values were deemed aberrant or liberal, if not simply anti-Islam. The conservative voices against such values had become so strong to the extent that in 2006, the Indonesian Ulama Council (Majelis Ulama Indonesia, MUI) issued a fatwa that outlawed secularism, pluralism and liberalism (Syafiq Hasyim 2015). "Sipilis", a derogatory portmanteau of the word, was even coined.

Similarly, in Malaysia, the National Fatwa Council declared in 2006 that "liberalism is a heretical teaching and deviates from the shariah" (Muzakarah Jawantakuasa Fatwa Majlis Kebangsaan 2006).[2] In 2014, the Selangor State Fatwa Committee declared Sisters in Islam (SIS)—a vocal CSO active in championing women's rights—as having transgressed the true teachings of Islam (Lim 2023). It even urged the Malaysian Communication and Multimedia Commission to censor the organization if it were found to produce and disseminate the ideas of liberalism and religious pluralism.

In this vein, any criticism levelled against the religious establishment of bureaucracy in the form of the Department of Islamic Development Malaysia (Jabatan Kemajuan Islam Malaysia, JAKIM) is simply dismissed as going against Islam. Those who voice such criticisms are known as the "liberal group" or *pelonggar agama* (those who are lax in religious observances). A senior government official who was formerly part of JAKIM even likened these "obstructors" to Western Orientalists such as "Ignaz Goldziher, Joseph Schacht and NJ Culson who for a long time propagated the idea that Islamic teachings are a legacy that resulted from past jurists' creation" (Abdullah Muhammad Zin 2018).

At the height of the *dakwah* movement in Malaysia, the criticisms against secularism were made alongside condemnation of humanism for its this-worldliness. By the 1990s, the condemnation extended to feminism. More specifically, they targeted feminism among Muslim women as it was perceived as part of the Western agenda to undermine Islam. However, while feminist discourse was almost completely deplored in Malay discourse, it was only in studies of literature that it was tolerated to a certain extent. In contrast, in Indonesia, Muslim women's feminism made great inroads into intellectual circles, and this is evident from the variety of translated and original works on the subject which still can be found today.

Similarly, proponents of *Sastera Islam* were also against concepts like pluralism and multiculturalism. In Malaysia and Indonesia, conservative groups deemed the advocacy for pluralism and multiculturalism as attempts to weaken the Muslim *ummah* and undermine their faith by diluting their *tauhidic* (monotheistic) worldview. Again, those who championed such values were regarded as following "Islam Liberal", a label which assumes a pejorative connotation. In the case of Indonesia, intellectual figures such as Gus Dur, Nurcholish Madjid and Buya Syafii were seen as proponents of Islam Liberal and therefore obstructors of shariah compliance and Islamization in the country.

In an article published on the website of the Malaysian Institute of Islamic Development (Institut Kefahaman Islam Malaysia, IKIM), there is a clear rejection of multiculturalism which the author argues undermines Islam in Malaysia. In fact, multiculturalism is conflated with secularism. It is perceived as an alien ideology that originates from the Western liberal tradition and is both anti-religious and secular in origin. Overall, multiculturalism robs Malaysia of its Malay-Muslim identity. The author claims that

Multiculturalism, as understood and propagated by its proponents in this country is not based on diversity, but rather it strives to debunk Islam as a socio-political order. The ideological components of Malaysian multiculturalism can be summarized as a cultural relativism which finds the prominence of Islam in this country intolerable. It rests on the attitude that religion should not be allowed to "interfere" in our social and political life. Hence, it is important that every Malaysian, especially the Muslims, be made to accept "the fact" that Malaysia is a "secular country". The Malaysian multiculturalism's hostility towards Islam and its repudiation of an identifiable Malaysian culture (based upon Islam) is augmented by a radically new definition of community, one that deviates from the traditional/religious emphasis on family, neighbourhood, house of worship and school, towards an emphasis on race, gender, occupation, and sexual preference (Md. Asham Ahmad 2006).

The view that other groups are at work to undermine Islam and Muslims is not uncommon, and the rejection of multiculturalism at this level can mean a few things. Most crucially, while religious and ethnic minorities can be tolerated, their culture and intellectual tradition are not to be accepted as they are perceived to be against the teachings of Islam. When such ideas are normalized, one can expect a shrinking of interest in knowing and understanding the culture of non-Muslims and non-Malays. As such, it is no surprise that religious authorities have sanctioned Muslims against wishing their Christian friends "Merry Christmas" as it is tantamount to affirming the divinity of Jesus Christ as the Son of God, a doctrinal position that Muslims cannot accept. The translated paragraph below exemplifies this view.

> Christmas Day is a celebration in conjunction with two things: Jesus as the son of God and second: the sacrifice of Jesus by God himself to eliminate the sins of humans ... Muslims are not only required to avoid such beliefs but are also prohibited from helping or supporting it ... Included in the general command "... do not be supportive in committing sins ..." is that we should not help and support the beliefs of Christians. Among others, do not say "Merry Christmas" because with this greeting or anything similar to it, we uphold their beliefs and congratulate them on their beliefs. This is prohibited and very much contrary to what is demanded of us (Hafiz Firdaus Abdullah 2007).[3]

Apart from celebratory greetings, there is a long list of don'ts that Malaysian Muslims should follow. For example, expressing "Rest in Peace" (RIP) is unacceptable (*The Vibes* 2022). Furthermore, the nomenclature of products labelled as "hot dog" or alcoholic products labelled "Timah" are deemed as insulting or demeaning to Muslims (*Straits Times*, 18 October 2016; Nambiar 2021). In addition, attending a Japanese cultural festival, Bon Odori, was considered unIslamic by conservative circles (*New Straits Times*, 6 June 2022).

While Muslim religious scholars and preachers in Indonesia are at the forefront of the discourse which promotes multiculturalism, pluralism, and democratic citizenship, Malaysian religious scholars—even the more progressive ones—have not ventured creatively and critically into those areas.[4] Instead of engaging in progressive discourse, the Malay religious and cultural discourse is flooded with criticisms against pluralism, as part of the growing denunciation of Islam Liberals which is prevalent throughout the region (Kamaruzzaman 2011).

It is therefore unsurprising that Indonesian works which are critical of Islam Liberal and the other above-mentioned values can easily be found in the Malaysian reading market (H. Hartono 2001; Husaini 2005). This is partly due to the bureaucratic monitoring by Malaysian religious authorities in censoring books for import into Malaysia from Indonesia. The selection process demonstrates the orientation of the establishment. Indonesian writers such as Adian Husaini and H. Hartono Ahmad Jaiz who actively chastise Islam Liberal circles have become the intellectual heroes among conservative groups in Malaysia because they denounced secularism and pluralism, including scathing criticisms against those who promote such ideas. On the other hand, the works of internationally renowned scholars such as Fazlur Rahman, Bassam Tibi, Mohamed Arkoun, Hasan Hanafi, and Abdullahi an Naim, which are easily available in Indonesia and are commonly discussed, are not discussed in Malaysian intellectual circles.

Thus, while knowledge production busied itself with calls towards Islamization, the Malay publishing industry also witnessed a robust demand for books which had Islam as their central theme, often covering topics on religious foundation, legal matters in *fiqh* (jurisprudence), or devotional tracts to affirm religious duties and rituals. Even the Institute of Language and Literature (Dewan Bahasa dan Pustaka, DBP), which used to publish books on commendable topics in literary and language studies, has become subject to this trend of publishing works with Islamic themes, including those with a more conservative bend.[5] There are even publishers such as PTS Litera who have stated that their foremost mission and policy is to produce and publish works which "comply with the shariah" (Masliza Nawi 2012). The company's website states,

PTS Litera is open to themes based on writers' creativity as long as it complies with the shariah, maintains the quality of linguistic style and expression, uses High Malay, and upholds the principle of enlightening people (ibid.)

An example of an author who meets the standard of shariah-compliant literature is Abdul Latip Talib, who is marketed as Malaysia's best writer of historical novels. Some of his titles include *Mustafa Kamal Ataturk: Penegak Agenda Yahudi* and *Runtuhnya Islam Andalusia: Pelengkap Kemasyhuran Ratu Isabella*. Other titles include Hamka's *Tenggelamnya Kapal Van Der Wijck*, and Taufiq Rahman Al-Azizy's *Syahadat Cinta*. There are also books which were written specifically about *Sastera Islam*. These include *Teori dan Pemikiran Sastera Islam di Malaysia* by Nurazmi Kuntum, *Polemik Sastera Islam* by Kassim Ahmad, and Shahnon Ahmad and *Sastera Melayu Islam: Konsep, Teori dan Aplikasi* by Samsina Abd. Rahman.

Turning Away from Regional and Global Intellectualism

Before intense Islamization and calls for greater shariah compliance, Malay discourse saw a healthy influence of works from both Eastern and Western intellectual traditions. There was a steady engagement with Indonesian works, as well as translations of other texts from around the world. The Malay literary and intellectual scene benefited from such diverse bibliographic sources. Some of such titles include Kuntowijoyo's *Maklumat Sastra Profetik*, Abdul Hadi W.M.'s *Kembali ke Akar, Kembali ke Sumber: Jejak-Jejak Pengumulan Kesusastraan Islam di Nusantara*, Emha Ainun Nadjib's *Sastra yang Membebaskan: Sikap Terhadap Struktur dan Anutan Seni Moderen Indonesia*, and Y.B. Mangunwijaya's *Sastra dan Religiositas*. However, as explained above, when Islamization was at its height, literature from the West was shunned as it was deemed as anti-Islam.

However, the shunning away from exogenous bibliographic sources was most apparent in the attitudes towards Indonesian publications. From the early 1900s to the 1960s, Malay cultural and intellectual circles received a steady inflow of Indonesian texts, ranging from literary, linguistic, cultural, historical and even religious themes. These publications were important references for the development of Malay cultural and intellectual discourse. However, as a result of Islamization, many of these works were viewed as theologically aberrant, too modern, or too dangerous for Muslims to be exposed to. Over time, Malay discourse in Malaysia was effectively divorced from reformist and progressive Islamic thought to the point that an entire generation of Malay readership was cut off from the Indonesian intellectual and religious scene since the latter was invariably labelled as too liberal and wayward.

Moreover, with this zeal to pursue an Islamic intellectual project, Malaysian discourse has not been able to actively partake or has simply neglected other discursive projects that have been developing in the Global South. This includes discourses on ecological justice, feminist rights, liberation theology and subaltern history. The dominant academic and intellectual circles either show little interest or outrightly reject publications on such themes as their epistemic sources are deemed unIslamic. Exogenous ideas are therefore seen with great suspicion and are always thought to undermine Islam and Muslims. Such thinking accentuates in-group exclusivism, whereby prejudice and the feeling of superiority are normalized. In a socio-cultural realm where there is constant suspicion or rejection of "Other" traditions, one cannot expect any kind of cultural and intellectual progression.

However, such an attitude is also directed towards endogenous reformist voices. Indeed, throughout the period of active Islamization, reformist ideas were dismissed or relegated to the margins. Some were even subjected to censure and pressure. This was also the case with regard to alternative voices within academic discourse which did not necessarily have anything to do with religion. For example, the late Syed Hussein Alatas' calls for autonomous knowledge production in Southeast Asian social sciences received hardly any attention from the Malaysian academic scene. This contrasts with calls for the Islamization of knowledge which has been well received and promoted by various Malaysian intellectuals and institutions.

Conclusion

The turn towards shariah compliance in Malaysian reading culture was cemented during the period of Islamic revivalism in the 1970s and 1980s. With the search for authenticity, the increasing involvement of the religious bureaucracy in the daily lives of Muslims, the greater desire for "Islamic products", and the lack of space for groups who are critical of exclusivist tendencies, the literary terrain in Malaysia has evolved from one that was open to diversity, to one that has become narrow in its scope and interests. As a result of such constriction, attitudes such as critical thinking and creativity have been stifled in a bid to ensure conformity to expected standards. As a result, the quality of the literature produced is affected, and so is the quality of discussions within literary circles.

Furthermore, the preoccupation with *Sastera Islam* or shariah-compliant literature means that other forms of literature are not given attention. These include those which are about philosophical rational discourse, socio-historical discourse, and literary narratives and poetics. This is in contrast to the past when religious figures such as Syed Sheikh Al-Hadi and Hamka also had a strong interest in literature. Their works were even translated and actively transmitted across the Malay world.

While the challenges of nurturing harmony and moderation in contemporary Malaysia are many, the task of bringing about public enlightenment must be part of the intellectual endeavours of the progressive and reformist groups. To mitigate the effects of the phenomenon of socio-cultural Islamization, there are three steps which can be taken. Firstly, there is a need to rethink the centrality of identity politics. Instead of emphasizing identity, it is crucial that attention is given to the politics or discourse of redistribution to balance or mitigate the euphoria surrounding Islamization and shariah compliance. Secondly, there is a need to provide and nurture more spaces for critical programmes and cultural discourses which can serve as a counterweight against cultural and religious conservatism. Finally, greater effort should be made at using culture, the arts and education in the public sphere to serve as a ballast against the turn towards conservatism. This way, the literary elite may be able to promote a "cultural movement" (*gerakan kultural*) just as leading Indonesian intellectuals, religious leaders, writers, artists and student activists did.

Notes

1. Marhaenism or Marhaenisme is an ideology that was developed by Sukarno. He conceptualized it based on Marxist ideas, and referred to members of the proletariat as "Marhaens".
2. The Deliberation of the National Fatwa Committee of the 74th Islamic Religious Affairs Council, which convened from 25 to 27 July 2006, decided that liberal ideas on Islam are deviant and against Islamic law.
3. Interestingly, a question about greeting Christians "Merry Christmas" was posed by a Muslim audience member when a leading Indonesian scholar, Prof M. Quraish Shihab, gave a talk in Singapore in 2002. See Shihab (2003).
4. Read, for instance, Mohd Asri Zainul Abidin, *Islam in Malaysia: Perceptions and Facts* (Petaling Jaya: Matahari Books, 2010).
5. For an example of DBP's publication, see Khalif Muammar A. Harris, *Islam dan Pluralisme Agama: Memperkukuh Tauhid pada Zaman Kekeliruan* [Islam and Religious Pluralism: Strengthening Tawhid in an Age of Confusion] (Kuala Lumpur: Dewan Bahasa dan Pustaka, 2015).

References

Abdullah Muhammad Zin. 2018. "Pluralisme, Liberal Ancam Institusi Islam" [Pluralism and Liberalism Threaten Islamic Institutions]. *Berita Harian*, 10 March 2018. https://www.bharian.com.my/rencana/muka10/2018/03/397782/pluralisme-liberal-ancam-institusi-islam (accessed 14 August 2023).

Ahmad Fauzi Abdul Hamid. 2008. "Islamist Realignments and the Rebranding of the Muslim Youth Movement of Malaysia". *Contemporary Southeast Asia* 30, no. 2: 215–40.

Azhar Ibrahim. 2014. *Contemporary Islamic Discourse in the Malay-Indonesian World: Critical Perspectives*. Malaysia: Strategic Information and Research Development Centre (SIRD).

Chandra Muzaffar. 1987. *Islamic Resurgence in Malaysia*. Petaling Jaya: Fajar Bakti.

H. Hartono Ahmad Jaiz. 2001. *Tasawuf, Pluralisme, dan Pemurtadan* [Sufism, Pluralism, and Apostasy]. Jakarta: Pustaka Al-Kautsar.

Hafiz Firdaus Abdullah. 2007. "Jawapan kepada Astora Jabat Berkenaan Hukum Mengucapkan Merry Christmas" [Response to Astora Jabat Regarding the Ruling on Saying Merry Christmas]. In *Membongkar Aliran Islam Liberal* [Unveiling the Liberal Islamic Movement], pp. 187–99. Johor Bahru: Perniagaan Jahabersa.

Husaini, Adian. 2005. *Islam Liberal, Pluralisme Agama dan Diabolisme Intelektual* [Liberal Islam, Religious Pluralism, and Intellectual Diabolism]. Surabaya: Alternatif Buku Baik.

Kamaruzzaman Bustamam-Ahmad. 2011. "Contemporary Islamic Thought in Indonesia and Malay World: Islam Liberal, Islam Hadhari, and Islam Progresif". *Journal of Indonesian Islam* 5, no. 1: 91–129.

Khalif Muammar A. Harris. 2015. *Islam dan Pluralisme Agama: Memperkukuh Tauhid pada Zaman Kekeliruan* [Islam and Religious Pluralism: Strengthening Tawhid in an Age of Confusion]. Kuala Lumpur: Dewan Bahasa dan Pustaka.

Kuntum, Nurazmi. 1991. *Teori dan Pemikiran Sastera Islam di Malaysia* [Theory and Thought in Islamic Literature in Malaysia]. Kuala Lumpur: Dewan Bahasa dan Pustaka.

Lim, Ida. "In 2-1 Ruling, Court Rejects Sisters in Islam's Bid to Challenge Selangor Fatwa Declaring it as Deviant". *Malay Mail*, 14 March 2023. https://www.malaymail.com/news/malaysia/2023/03/14/in-2-1-ruling-court-rejects-sisters-in-islams-bid-to-challenge-selangor-fatwa-declaring-it-as-deviant/59496 (accessed 14 August 2023).

Masliza Nawi. 2012. "Mematuhi Syariah—Prinsip Utama Penerbitan Buku PTS [Adhering to the Shariah—The Main Principle of PTS Book Publishing]". *PTS*, 12 March 2012. https://pts.com.my/berita/mematuhi-syariah-prinsip-utama-penerbitan-buku-pts (accessed 14 August 2023).

Md. Asham Ahmad. 2006. "Debunking Multiculturalism". *Institute of Islamic Understanding Malaysia*, 22 August 2006. https://www.ikim.gov.my/v5/print.php?grp=2&key=1096 (accessed 14 August 2023).

Mohd Asri Zainul Abidin. 2010. *Islam in Malaysia: Perceptions and Facts*. Petaling Jaya: Matahari Books.

Mohd Faizal Musa, and Tan Beng Hui. 2018. "State-backed Discrimination against Shia Muslims in Malaysia". *Critical Asian Studies* 49, no. 3: 308–29.

Muzakarah Jawantakuasa Fatwa Majlis Kebangsaan. 2006. "Aliran Pemikiran Liberal: Hukum dan Implikasinya kepada Islam di Malaysia [Liberal School of Thought: Its Laws and Implications for Islam in Malaysia]". *E-Sumber Maklumat Fatwa*. http://e-smaf.islam.gov.my/e-smaf/fatwa/fatwa/find/pr/16319 (accessed 14 August 2023).

Nagata, Judith. 1984. *The Reflowering of Malaysian Islam: Modern Religious Radicals and Their Roots*. Vancouver: University of British Columbia Press.

Nambiar, Pradeep. 2021. "Why Timah, Why Not 'Captain Speedy', Asks Mufti". *Free Malaysia Today*, 18 October 2021. https://www.freemalaysiatoday.com/category/nation/2021/10/18/why-timah-why-not-captain-speedy-asks-mufti/ (accessed 14 August 2023).

New Straits Times. 2022. "Muslims Advised Not to Participate in Bon Odori Festival—Idris". 6 June 2022. https://www.nst.com.my/news/nation/2022/06/802827/muslims-advised-not-participate-bon-odori-festival-idris (accessed 14 August 2023).

Norshahril Saat. 2018. *The State, Ulama and Islam in Malaysia and Indonesia*. Singapore: ISEAS – Yusof Ishak Institute.

Shihab, M. Quraish. 2003. *Pergaulan Masyarakat dalam Islam* [Social Interaction in Islam]. Singapore: Jabatan Belia Masjid Ba'alwi.

Straits Times. 2016. "Rename 'Pretzel Dog' to 'Pretzel Sausage', Malaysia's Islamic Body Tells Auntie Anne's". 18 October 2016. https://www.straitstimes.com/asia/se-asia/rename-pretzel-dog-to-pretzel-sausage-malaysias-islamic-body-tells-auntie-annes (accessed 14 August 2023).

Syafiq Hasyim. 2015. "Majelis Ulama Indonesia and Pluralism in Indonesia". *Philosophy & Social Criticism* 41, nos. 4–5: 487–95.

Vibes, The. 2022. "Muslims Forbidden from Saying 'Rest in Peace', Says FT Mufti's Office". 18 September 2022. https://www.thevibes.com/articles/news/71780/muslims-forbidden-from-saying-rest-in-peace-says-ft-muftis-office (accessed 14 August 2023).

Zainah Anwar. 1987. *Islamic Revivalism in Malaysia: Dakwah among the Students*. Petaling Jaya: Pelanduk Publications.

FINDING A SOULMATE THROUGH HALAL MEANS
Online Ta'aruf among Indonesian Muslim Youth

Wahyudi Akmaliah

INTRODUCTION

Most Indonesian Muslim youth are interested in finding their marriage partner through the practice of *ta'aruf*, traditionally viewed as an Islamic approach to selecting a spouse, a substitute for the secular practice of *pacaran* (dating). With digitalization permeating everyday Indonesian life, the emergence of multiple smartphone applications has transformed *ta'aruf* into an online activity. However, this transition to halal online dating extends beyond Indonesia and Southeast Asia, representing a phenomenon observed in Muslim societies globally. Examples of popular halal online dating services include Muzmatch, prevalent in the UK and Bangladesh, and Salam Swipe from Canada.[1] These platforms, with their varied features, are reshaping Muslim identity vis-à-vis the evolving dynamics of balancing inherited familial Islamic traditions with the need for adapting new values through the reinterpretation of Islamic sources. These digital platforms allow young Muslims to navigate the delicate balance of adhering to Islamic orthodoxy while engaging with the realities of contemporary life, especially in the area of Islamic courtship which occasionally generates tensions.

There are two key factors that have driven the emergence of halal online dating. The first is the rise of global capitalism, resulting in the changing global economic landscape and the growth of digital technology. The global interconnectedness between international corporations, national corporations, and state adaptation policy prompts practices like *ta'aruf* to align with global economic trends (Castells 2007, 2010). The impact on developing countries is particularly significant. As international and national corporations expand their capital, economically marginalized people find themselves facing increasing uncertainty (Standing 2011). In response, many individuals turn towards religious knowledge as a form of escape and a guidepost for life's journey. Simultaneously, they view religion as a source of solidarity, a mobilizing force referred to by some scholars as Islamic populism that rallies individuals against perceived enemies in the name of Islam (Hadiz 2016; Hikmawan 2022). Digital technology and media platforms connect individuals with shared beliefs and anxieties, connecting them across global, societal, communal and personal domains (Lim 2017). Responding to the demand for match-making applications, various religious traditions have proposed similar platforms that incorporate religious teachings for users (Nisa 2021, p. 233; Pasha 2015).

The second key factor pertains to social changes occurring in many Muslim countries facing internal and external problems. In the context of Indonesia, for instance, the downfall of Suharto's regime after a thirty-two-year reign created a power vacuum, allowing previously repressed Muslim groups to re-emerge and articulate their Islamic identity in the public sphere (Hadiz 2010; Hadiz and Robison 2004; Noorhaidi Hasan 2009; Heryanto 2014). These revitalized Muslim groups cater to young Muslim audiences, serving as their primary source of Islamic guidance. Many of their religious attitudes, the clothing they wear, and their religious orientations are influenced by transnational Muslim ideologies and movements such as Ikhwanul Muslimin (Muslim Brotherhood), Hizbut Tahrir Indonesia (HTI), and Salafi-Wahhabi ideology (Noorhaidi Hasan 2005; Iqbal 2017; Muhtadi 2012; Osman 2020). These new Islamic groups also adopt a Western popular culture approach to their Islamic preaching, initiated by young Islamic preachers (Akmaliah 2020b, 2020a; Kailani 2015, 2020).

Many scholars have discussed halal online dating from a range of perspectives. For instance, Sotoudeh, Friedland, and Afary (2017) conducted Facebook surveys in Muslim-majority countries with the aim of discussing young Muslims' interest in establishing intimate relationships and finding marriage partners. Amid the prohibition of physical intimacy due to religious norms and traditions, the study highlighted the role of dating applications in allowing Muslim youth to set up romantic dates and arranged marriages mediated by the Internet. Their study aligns with findings by Pourmehdi (2015) in Morocco, Chakraborty (2012) in India, Bunt (2009) in London, and Rochadiat, Tong, and Novak (2018) in America, each exploring similar themes among Muslim women. Meanwhile, Ali et al. (2020) examine halal online dating among British Muslims. They found that while most online dating platforms are incompatible with British Muslim culture and religious rules, halal online dating has changed their and their parents' perspectives. They no longer view it as prohibited and instead regard it as permissible. They do this by using Islamic sources to create subjective definitions and criteria for dating, ensuring it is halal and compatible with a shariah-compliant lifestyle. This development has made arranged marriages less popular. Building on Ali et al.'s work, de Rooij (2020) posits two points. Firstly, mobile applications for halal dating provide a reference point for European Muslims to strengthen their Islamic identity in non-Islamic environments, aiding their search for a spouse. Secondly, these applications facilitate romantic relationships within Islamic boundaries, eliminating the necessity for physical seclusion. By studying Muslim men in Germany, Hasan (2021), citing Asad (2009), places online halal dating as a part of Islamic discursive tradition. He situates online halal dating within the broader discourse of Islamic tradition, scrutinizing the motivation behind Muslim men's use of online matchmaking platforms, particularly their interpretations of Islamic tradition and their religious practices in everyday life.

Unlike prior works, this chapter examines the rise of halal online dating through the transformation of ideological doctrine, specifically focusing on the Tarbiyah activist movement's promotion of *ta'aruf*, and its popularization as a product of Indonesian popular culture. This study extends Nisa's (2021) research, which identified two main factors leading to the rise of digital platforms for Islamic teaching. First is the emergence of young Muslims in the 1970s who wanted to strengthen their religious practices in public, and second is the rise of the *hijrah* movement, which promoted a new lifestyle for Indonesian Muslim youth and encouraged them to look to the shariah as their primary source of guidance (Nisa 2021, pp. 233–34). This chapter examines the organizations driving the popularity of *ta'aruf* among Indonesian Muslim youth and analyses the competition among *ta'aruf* mobile application developers in positioning their halal online matchmaking process as "more Islamic". To do this, this chapter poses the following questions: What are the primary factors driving the popularity of *ta'aruf* among Indonesian Muslim youth? Are any organizations promoting *ta'aruf* as a part of an agenda to advance a shariah-compliant lifestyle? What implications does this development hold for Indonesian Muslim society, often perceived as the face of moderate Islam?

This chapter argues that the resurgence of new religious authorities has contributed significantly to introducing the term *ta'aruf* across several platforms, leveraging mediums such as books, movies, and social movements for knowledge dissemination. In the context of the global Muslim phenomenon towards halal online matchmaking and widespread digitalization in Indonesia, smartphone applications and social media groups—specifically on Facebook and Instagram—employ *ta'aruf* as a marketing strategy to attract Muslims to register and use their services. *Ta'aruf Online Indonesia* (TOI), a halal matchmaking application, distinguishes itself by asserting its platform as more Islamic than competing *ta'aruf* applications. While online *ta'aruf* has shaped public behaviour by promoting a more Islamic lifestyle, the popularity of *ta'aruf* has also posed challenges to activists of the Tarbiyah movement. These activists struggle to maintain or enlarge their sphere of influence among less observant Muslims and are therefore concerned over the preservation of their ideology.

MAINSTREAMING *TA'ARUF*: FROM THE TARBIYAH MOVEMENT'S PRACTICES INTO POPULAR CULTURE CONSUMPTION

The Concept of *Ta'aruf*, its Procedures, and Changing Patterns

The concept of *ta'aruf* originates from the Tarbiyah movement. Inspired by Egypt's Muslim Brotherhood, this movement began in the 1980s as a part of *da'wah* (proselytizing) efforts at the Bandung Institute of Technology (Institut Teknologi Bandung, ITB), initiated by the Indonesian Islamic Propagation Council (Dewan Da'wah Islamiyah Indonesia, DDII). To further this movement's mission to Islamize Indonesian society, two organizations were established; the National Front of Indonesian Muslim Students (Kesatuan Aksi Mahasiswa Muslim Indonesia, KAMMI) to bolster student activism in schools and campuses, and the Prosperous Justice Party (Partai Keadilan Sejahtera, PKS) to institutionalize their Islamist ideology at the regulatory and state level. The Tarbiyah movement organizes itself around the concept of *usroh* (family), highlighting the significance of famillial structures in their mission. However, *usroh* carries a deeper meaning beyond just family. It is the basic organizational unit in the movement's political struggle. Each *usroh* is comprised of around ten Tarbiyah members or *mutarabbi* (learners), led by a senior member referred to as the *murabbi* or *murabbiyah* (male and female mentors, respectively). These *usroh* groups hold weekly or fortnightly meetings called *liqa* to study Islam. Consequently, the movement is referred to as the Tarbiyah movement, with *usroh* members undergoing a process of *tarbiyya* (education) (Asyari and Abid 2016). Through their rigid organizational structure, the movement mandates strict procedures for establishing good Muslim families among the activists, a process referred to as *ta'aruf.* Thus, both *murabba* and *murrabiyyah,* along with the *Lajnah Munakahat* (Tarbiyah movement's committee or marriage bureau), serve as critical institutions in determining the marriage partners of the *mutarabbi,* even supplanting the parental role in the marriage process. In essence, establishing *usroh* was the main reason the Tarbiyah movement was established.

The term *ta'aruf* originates from Arabic and refers to the act of getting to know each other. It is mentioned in the Qur'an in Surah Al-Hujarat, verse 13, and has been interpreted in many ways. The Tarbiyah movement's exegesis of the verse is limited to getting to know each other within a social circle as a means to seek a spouse for marriage. Through this lens, *ta'aruf* evolves into a symbol, differentiating the Tarbiyah movement's Islamic identity from other Islamic groups, and acting as a counterpoint to the secular dynamics of dating. This unique interpretation also serves as the movement's mechanism to entrench their Islamic ideology into marriage practices. There are three key aims of the Tarbiyah movement, with the first being the transformation of self to embody ideal Islamic characteristics, as defined by the movement. This personal transformation precedes the second aim, which involves promoting marriage and fostering Muslim families among the aforementioned ideal Muslims. The third aim is the quest to Islamize both society and the state. This aim originates from Hasan Al-Banna, the founder of the Muslim Brotherhood, whose book *Majmū'at al-Rasāil* (*Collection of Treatises*) contends with the struggle to Islamize society (Asyari and Abid 2016; Machmudi 2008). Al-Banna proposes to Islamize society and state through a gradual four-stage process of changing the self, the family, the society, and ultimately the state. This gradual approach stands in sharp contrast to other Islamist movements that advocate for violent revolution as a means to achieve total change. Therefore, the family unit is the foundation for establishing Islamic values at the societal and state levels.

Since the family is seen as a fundamental unit, there is a rigorous process for internal marriage regulations. Specifically, when a *mutarabbi* wishes to marry, they must consult their *murabbi* or *murrabiyyah* and declare in advance their intention to marry. The *murrabi/murrabiyyah* then asks them to complete a marriage application form, similar in format to a curriculum vitae (CV). This form includes key personal details like their date and place of birth, education, employment, hobbies, physical appearance, a photograph, and vision for their marriage. The *murabbi/ murrabiyyah* will then submit the completed marriage application form to the *Lajnah Munakahat*, the marriage bureau of the Tarbiyah movement. After careful consideration, based on matching desired criteria and assessing *kufu* (suitability), the *ikhwan* and *akhwat* (prospective male and female spouses, respectively) initiate the *ta'aruf* process.[2] In the past, to prevent candidates—particularly men—from choosing potential spouses based solely on physical appearance, the marriage application form was stripped of certain details, including biographical data, address, and contact information. This step aimed to deter the man from seeking additional information beyond official channels. An *akhwat* could reject an *ikhwan's* marriage proposal and vice versa if they felt the criteria were unmet. After this, the marriage application is returned to the *Lajnah Munakahat* for a re-evaluation of the Tarbiyah candidate's potential (Asyari and Abid 2016, pp. 348–51; Savitri and Faturochman 2011, p. 63).

However, this *ta'aruf* process has differed across different generations of Tarbiyah activists. Savitri and Faturochman (2011, p. 64) indicate that the *ta'aruf* conducted among the first generation of Tarbiyah activists was more straightforward due to the structure of the movement which was still coming into formation. Rather than involving a mediator, marriage choices were primarily driven by personal interest among the activist members, such as mutual attraction and individual needs, alignment with Islamic values, and the ability to engage in *da'wah*. While they held no substantial negative views towards dating, they unanimously agreed against premarital sexual intercourse. Therefore, if the *ikhwan* was interested in an *akhwat*, he could directly propose (*khitbah*) to her, and vice versa. The close interactions among the activists facilitated the development of personal trust.

The dynamics shifted significantly when the movement became an Islamic political party, the Partai Keadilan (Justice Party), in 1999. Following a poor performance in the 1999 elections and failing to achieve the minimum representation of 2 per cent in the House of Representatives, the party rebranded itself as the PKS. The second generation of activists, in the form of the PKS, began to perceive marriage as a vehicle for the advancement of religion and support for *dakwah*. Contrary to the first generation, the second generation held opposing views on dating. The majority of marriages among them were facilitated by institutional mediation, making personal interactions uncommon. Amid these organizational changes, the marriage regulation among members became more structured, strictly adhering to institutional policy. For instance, when an activist member wishes to marry, they are required to submit a personal profile (marriage application form), including a photograph, to their *murrabi/murrabiyah*. The *murrabi* then forwards their profile to the religious elite structure, *Majelis Suro* (Suro

Assembly), acting as their marriage institution. This assembly convened to reach a consensus on suitable pairings among the marriage candidates. The outcome of this meeting was relayed to the *ikhwan* and *akhwat* through their respective *murrabi*. If both parties agreed with the proposed match, they proceeded to the next stage of *ta'aruf*. At this level, either the *ikhwan* or the *akhwat* can agree or disagree. If they agreed, a marriage proposal could be made involving their family members. Conversely, the process could be restarted from the beginning if there was a disagreement (Savitri and Faturochman 2011, p. 69).

For the third generation of activists, marriage aims included personal needs and became a part of *dakwah* (ibid., p. 67). Nevertheless, their view of dating remained similar to the second generation's. The evolution of the PKS from a closed, exclusively Muslim political party to an ideologically open one welcoming individuals from diverse backgrounds in 2021 has seemingly relaxed the organization's rigid institutional marriage regulations. This change also appears to have been driven by a desire to amplify their voice within the Indonesian public sphere, as well as a shift in ideology to accommodate a broader demographic, beyond their initial Muslim society and political elite membership.

Ta'aruf in the Form of Popular Culture Consumption

Outside of the Tarbiyah activist movement, the concept of *ta'aruf* is also adopted by other Islamic resurgence movements like the Salafi-based HTI and Jamaat Tabligh. These resurgence movements became more visible following the end of Suharto's regime. Their acknowledgement of *ta'aruf* as an integral part of the Islamic approach to family formation has contributed to the rise of halal matchmaking among Indonesian Muslims. However, the term's widespread usage among various Islamic resurgence movements and the proliferation of Islam is insufficient in explaining the considerable influence of *ta'aruf*. This chapter argues that we should observe the role of different organizations and institutions to understanding why *ta'aruf* has supplanted the term *pacaran* in the public sphere. In doing so, it proposes two reasons for the normalization of the term *ta'aruf* in everyday vernacular among Indonesian Muslims.

The first factor is the rise of Islamic publishing, fuelled by the growth of Islamic movements since the late 1970s and the strategic intent of the Suharto presidency during the 1990s to harness these publishers to support his administration. These developments led to the proliferation of publishers such as Mizan in Bandung, Gema Insani Press in Jakarta, and Solahuddin Press and the Institute for Islam and Social Studies (Lembaga

Kajian Islam dan Sosial, LKiS) in Yogyakarta to meet the demands of young Muslims. This trend escalated after the collapse of the Suharto regime, resulting in a power vacuum that allowed Islamic resurgence movements to strengthen their Islamic identity. While these movements varied in their visions for the *ummah* (global Muslim community), the publication of books and magazines served as a crucial medium of expression for these movements (Asyari and Abid 2016; Watson 2005). This development allowed the Tarbiyah movement to leverage their publishers, consisting of Pro-U Media in Yogyakarta, Lingkar Pena Publishing House in Jakarta, and Era Adicitra Intermedia in Solo, Central Java, to propagate their Islamic ideology, religious orientation and religious values. These publishers heavily promoted their notion of forming an ideal Muslim family centred on *ta'aruf*. Stylistically, most of these books emulated *Chicken Soup for the Soul*, an American self-help book series. The books referenced Islamic sources to address personal issues, anxieties and the challenges of navigating an un-Islamic lifestyle. These publishers also introduced *ta'aruf* into fiction, including novels and short stories, prompting other Islamic and secular publishers to emulate their approach to increase market share. For Islamic publishing, this trend is illustrated by Mizania (Mizan's publishing line targeted towards teenagers), and for secular publishing, by the rise of Kompas Gramedia Group (KKG), a Catholic-owned company (Asyari and Abid 2016, p. 354).[3]

The second driving force is the rise of Islamic-themed popular cinema. The success of the Islamic-themed publications across various genres, including those focusing on *ta'aruf*, incentivized filmmakers to adapt those stories into film. The bestselling Islamic book series written by Habibburahman El-Shirazi, *Ayat-Ayat Cinta 1* and *Ayat-Ayat Cinta 2*, sold over 100,000 copies and were watched by more than 3.7 million Indonesian Muslims after their adaptation into film. Hanung Bramantyo adapted the first novel into a film, while Guntur Soeharjanto adapted the second, bringing it to theatres. The first film introduced *ta'aruf* to Indonesian Muslims through the relationship between Fahri and Aisha. Fahri, an undergraduate studying at Al-Azhar University in Egypt, is portrayed as a humble, diligent, devout, and attractive Muslim man who adheres to shariah principles in his daily life. The narrative emphasizes his humanity and kindness towards everyone he interacts with, regardless of their background or religion. These admirable traits attracted women who sought romantic intimacy with him and envisioned him as their further partner. On the other hand, Aisha is depicted as an individual of striking appearance from a wealthy German family, recognizable by her headscarf and face veil.

Aisha's interest in Fahri was sparked when he offered his seat on the bus to a non-Muslim foreign woman. In the same scene, another man—dressed in religious attire—expressed his displeasure towards this woman, viewing her as a symbol of the West that frequently humiliated and discriminated against Muslims in Europe and the Middle East. Consequently, he refused to show her courtesy. Instead of endorsing this man's actions, Fahri criticized him, referencing Islamic and Western sources emphasizing the importance of treating all individuals with a sense of humanity. In light of this event, Aisha endeavoured to learn more about Fahri through her uncle, the most prominent *ulama* (Islamic scholar) in Egypt, and Fahri's mentor. Aisha successfully persuaded her uncle to approach Fahri and discern his interest in marriage, exemplifying the *ta'aruf* approach to a marriage proposal. This scene engrained in the minds of young Indonesian Muslims the Islamic approach to cultivating romantic relationships. The film's success prompted filmmakers and producers to adapt other books by El-Shirazy into film, such as *Ketika Cinta Bertasbih* (When Love Praises God), *Ketika Cinta Bertasbih II* (When Love Praises God II), *Dalam Mihrab Cinta* (Inside the Mihrab of Love), and *Cinta Suci Zahrana* (Pure Love of Zahrana).

Halal Online Matchmaking, Halal Industry, and Market Competition

The previous sections of this chapter primarily discussed the use of traditional media forms—consisting of movies and print culture (magazines, newspapers, and books)—when discussing the role of various organizations in promoting the concept of *ta'aruf* from 2006 to 2013. However, during this same time frame, the Internet and social media platforms such as Facebook and Twitter became popular in Indonesia, profoundly impacting social movements (Lim 2013). With this surge in the number of digitally savvy young Indonesian Muslims, old forms of media were no longer powerful enough as a tool for the Islamic resurgence movements to facilitate Islamic teaching. This reality reshaped the development of Islamic teaching in the public sphere. Taking into account the period between 2014 and 2022, this section discusses the proliferation of matchmaking smartphone applications featuring *ta'aruf* in their titles and how these platforms successfully attracted Indonesian Muslims seeking potential life partners. Among the various *ta'aruf* applications, this chapter focuses on TOI, which proclaims to be the most Islamic online matchmaking application.

Islamic Lifestyle in Indonesia
The digital world has seen a proliferation of online dating applications globally, leading to the emergence of halal online matchmaking. This surge in new mobile applications is not merely attributed to the desire to follow trends but is also a response to the changing media landscape, characterized by a shift from traditional to new media. Unlike traditional media consisting of television, radio, newspaper, and magazine—which require substantial resources to manage—these new applications provide cost-effective alternatives. In Indonesia, at least eight halal matchmaking applications have emerged, compatible with all smartphones in the country. These include Taaruf ID, Hijrah Taaruf, TOI, Taaruf Lalu Nikah, Tasyari (Taaruf Syar'i), and Media Taaruf-Jodoh Islami.[4] Social media platforms like Instagram also host halal matchmaking accounts, such as *taaruf. indo.id* and *taarufan_id*. Furthermore, several Facebook groups offer similar services, including Taaruf Islam Online, Taaruf Siap Nikah Islam International, and Menuju Taaruf dan Poligami. Online halal matchmaking also extends to websites such as *myQuran.com*, which since 2001 facilitates *ta'aruf* through a dedicated discussion forum section titled *Perkenalan dan Perjodohan* (Introduction and Matchmaking). This section expanded to include multiple subfora on *ta'aruf,* marriage, and household management, collectively serving as intermediaries to facilitate the matchmaking process among their Muslim members. The website subsequently underwent a name change to *rumahtaaruf.com*, reflecting its new specialization in facilitating the Islamic matchmaking process.

The emergence of online *ta'aruf* platforms is facilitated by an increased focus on fostering an Islamic or halal lifestyle among Indonesian Muslims. Given that Indonesia is home to the largest Muslim population in the world, it is a natural target for promoting such a lifestyle. The Global Islamic Economy Report 2018–19 revealed that Indonesia ranks among the top ten consumers in the halal industry across various product categories, including food, travel, and pharmaceuticals. In response to this report's findings, the Jokowi administration formulated targeted strategies within the "Indonesia Islamic Economic Masterplan 2019–24" to capitalize on the economic potential of the halal industry. The masterplan, conceived by the Ministry of National Development Planning (Bappenas), was followed by the establishment of Bank Syariah Indonesia (BSI), the country's largest state-owned shariah bank, aimed at fostering a conducive environment for the rapid development of the Islamic economy (Syafiq Hasyim 2022, pp. 9–11). Government institutions such as the National Economic and

Islamic Finance Committee (Komite Nasional Ekonomi dan Keuangan Syariah, KNEKS) have also supported the halal industry. Additionally, various digital platforms such as Tokopedia Salam, Bukalapak Syariah, Shopee Barakah, Layanan Syariah, and LinkAja have been established to cater to Muslims' consumption habits (Aldi and Ira 2020).

However, the government's efforts to support a halal lifestyle must be understood within the broader context of movements which have shaped the Islamic environment. One example is the *hijrah* movement, initiated by the leaders of various Islamic resurgence movements aiming to reshape public Islam in Indonesia through their teachings. While *hijrah* originally denotes the historical event in which Prophet Muhammad migrated from Mecca to Medina to avoid oppression by the Quraish tribe, the contemporary use of the term has come to refer to one's self-transformation to become a better Muslim (Akmaliah 2020a; Hikmawan 2022; Nisa 2017). In the effort to shape the discourse around Islamic lifestyle, Islamic resurgence groups have widely adopted this term, incorporating it in social media hashtags and offline taglines. Aware of their fewer resources compared to mainstream Islamic organizations, these groups held events within the Muslim United network and enlisted the help of popular preachers such as Hanan Attaki, Felix Siauw, Abdul Somad, Hamid Basalamah and Evi Effendi to expand their influence.

As a result of the Islamic lifestyle promoted by the *hijrah* movement, many Indonesian Muslim youth have been guided to perceive dating as un-Islamic, immoral and detrimental to their future. Initiated by La Ode Munafar, an activist of the Tarbiyah movement, this anti-dating discourse has been significantly reshaped into the *Indonesia Tanpa Pacaran* (Indonesia without Dating, ITP) movement.[5] After a gathering in 2014, Munafar endeavoured to set up a social media group for his readership, establishing a direct connection with his readers via instant messaging platforms such as WhatsApp and Line. On 6 October 2016, fan pages across various social media platforms—including Facebook, Instagram, and YouTube—were established to further disseminate his anti-dating discourse (Sari, Husein, and Noviani 2020, pp. 5–7). Through these platforms, Munafar raises issues such as the dangers of promiscuity, the rise in abortion rates, and the Islamic prohibition of premarital relationships between men and women. By raising these issues, he aims to create moral panic among the Muslim youth and convince them of the virtue of *ta'aruf*. Consequently, he has garnered a substantial following on social media (Nisa 2021, p. 245).

Various *Ta'aruf* Applications

All halal online matchmaking applications and websites adhere to a shariah-compliant mechanism in the spouse-seeking process. A standard marriage proposal within this mechanism includes a marriage application form, a photograph, and a clear vision and mission for the prospective marriage. These matchmaking applications vary in their sets of features, which act as moral differentiators, helping users evaluate the platforms' adherence to shariah. Many of these applications echo the design of the popular dating application Tinder. The user interfaces display the potential partner's photograph and geographical location, and users swipe to express their interest or disinterest. For successful matches, there is also a chat function available.

Certain Islamic resurgence movements have criticized the resemblance of *ta'aruf* applications to Tinder as un-Islamic, arguing that the process allows Muslim women to be excessively discerning in selecting their potential spouse. They contend that three issues arise from using photographs as a criterion in the *ta'aruf* process. Firstly, it could lower their devotion to God. Secondly, the potential for *khalwat* (when a man is found alone with a woman who is not his wife or immediate relative) increases due to direct communication via the chat function, especially considering the lack of intermediaries during this stage. Thirdly, without proper oversight from the application creator, users could misuse these halal matchmaking applications for nefarious purposes, such as seeking additional wives, committing adultery, and even money laundering.

Seeking adherence to Islamic principles, some matchmaking applications like TOI align with the interpretations of *ta'aruf* proposed by Islamic resurgence groups. TOI employs Instagram solely for marketing purposes. Users interested in the *ta'aruf* process must download their application and provide the necessary information for a potential match. Besides their personal information and their marriage vision, applicants can incorporate three questions in their profile for prospective matches to answer, responses to which help the applicant decide on future actions. If mutual interest arises, the applicants can arrange a meeting, which would be supervised by both a male and female religious teacher, termed *ustad* and *ustadzah* respectively. This stage, known as *nadzor* (the meet-up process), is followed by *khitbah* (marriage proposal)—a formal proposition sent to the couples' parents, demonstrating their commitment to the marriage.

The TOI application includes distinctive shariah-compliance policies, differentiating itself from Tinder and prior *ta'aruf* applications which are perceived as similar to Tinder. At least five factors significantly highlight TOI's adherence to the shariah compared to the previous ta'aruf applications. Firstly, unlike other halal online matchmaking applications, every applicant's picture is blurred. The picture only becomes visible once the two applicants have been successfully matched through their profiles. Secondly, the application upholds a user's privacy and prevents anyone from seeking additional personal information of others beyond the provided profile. They reinforce this by prohibiting screenshots and blocking Google searches of its users. Thirdly, TOI does not have direct messaging functionality, preventing prolonged or intimate conversations between users. Fourthly, the application limits the number of times applicants can send their profiles to others. This limitation serves to discourage frivolous interactions among the users. Finally, the application features exclusive educational videos for applicants to watch during the process, enabling them to learn about the Islamic marriage process within the context of ta'aruf.

TOI mandates a registration fee of IDR200,000 (S$20) to ensure that each applicant is genuinely committed. This fee contributes to the maintenance of the application, supports the administrative team, and funds the religious teachers who accompany the applicants during the nadzor process. Zaki, an administrative team member, acknowledges that this application operates within a capitalist industry and must compete with other applications for survival. Despite this, TOI strives to ensure higher shariah-compliance than its competitors. Despite the fee, many Indonesian Muslims continue to enrol. As noted by Zaki, TOI has been downloaded by 50,000 people, with 39,000 having completed the registration process. Of those registered, there have been 200 marriages between 2019 and 2023. Zaki also reports that approximately thirty-four potential couples reach the final nadzor stage each month. Overall, the app's usage is widespread, with users dispersed across ten cities.[6]

TOI employs three primary narratives in its promotional strategy. Firstly, TOI enlists religious teachers with strong religious authority to deliver Islamic teaching on shariah-compliant ta'aruf introduction through weekly Instagram streams. These religious teachers offer insights into Islamic knowledge and marriage principles, particularly regarding emotional management, maturity, and attitudes. Secondly, TOI shares success stories of members who have found their partners through the platform. By showcasing these success stories, TOI aims to persuade the public that its system and procedures are beneficial, especially for candidates who have not succeeded with other applications involving taa'ruf. Thirdly, TOI leverages on social media popularity by sharing and reposting posts from well-known preachers and celebrities discussing ta'aruf.[7] Recordings of these live streams are disseminated across various social media platforms including TikTok, YouTube, and other Instagram pages. These narratives help TOI position itself as the preeminent halal matchmaking application on the market and help to establish trust between the platform and its users.

Conclusion

This chapter has explored the transformation of ta'aruf from a practice within the Tarbiyah movement to a prevalent element of popular culture. Notably, apart from activists of the Tarbiyah movement, the concept is also promoted by an array of institutions and organizations, encompassing both religious and secular publishers, filmmakers, and producers. Given the sizeable halal industry in Indonesia, numerous institutions and organizations utilize the promotion of ta'aruf as a strategy to participate in this market. Other Islamic resurgence movements also adopted the concept to articulate their vision of an Islamic marriage. Consequently, the popularity of ta'aruf as a concept has led Indonesian Muslims to believe that it represents the appropriate Islamic approach to dating.

The increase in the number of Internet users in Indonesia, combined with the Islamization of the public sphere through the *hijrah* movement, has transformed *ta'aruf* from an offline to an online practice. As a result, halal online matchmaking has proliferated, leading to competition among various matchmaking application developers. These applications, therefore, are necessitated to devise innovative strategies for differentiation. TOI stands out by implementing numerous measures to position itself as the leading Islamic *ta'aruf* application on the market.

The popularity of *ta'aruf* gives rise to further discussion and development. Undoubtedly, the development of *ta'aruf's* online and offline popularity has supported Islamization in the public sphere. While some may agree with this, others may not agree with such developments, as it indirectly discriminates against Indonesian Muslims who may have different lifestyle preferences, or may interpret the concept of halal differently. In the case of relationships and marriage, some may choose to use the *pacaran* approach instead of the *ta'aruf* approach. For example, while Tinder has received a mixed reception among Indonesian Muslims, it is increasingly common for urban Indonesian Muslim youth from large cities to find their spouse via the application.

The growing popularity of *ta'aruf* also poses internal challenges for activists of the Tarbiyah movement. As explained earlier, the practice of *ta'aruf* helps to expand an organization's power through the regeneration of cadres. Thus, marriage is not only about establishing an Islamic family but also preserving Islamic ideologies and spreading their influence. However, if an activist of the Tarbiyah movement gets married to a member of another Islamic organization, both organizations may worry about the potential dilution of their ideological orientation. It would be even more problematic if the spouse with a different ideology is a Muslim man, given his prominent role within the framework of Indonesia's patriarchal society.[8]

Nevertheless, halal online matchmaking might provide the best opportunity for Indonesian Muslims struggling to find a spouse through traditional methods. Notably, these applications empower Muslim women to choose their spouses independently. Under a predominantly patriarchal structure and religious interpretation, it is often considered inappropriate for women to express romantic interest towards men first. The limited access to establish their romantic feelings for the person they love has worsened this condition. However, *ta'aruf* applications are transforming this narrative, providing a public platform for women to initiate their spouse-seeking journey. Furthermore, they present an opportunity to challenge traditional approaches to arranged marriage practices, which are still prevalent in many rural areas.

Notes

1. There are also other platforms such as Singlemuslim (2000) which was launched in the UK, LoveHabibi (2019) for European Arabs, Ishqr (2013) in the US, Minder (2015) in the US, Veil (2019) in Dubai, and Hawaya (2020) in Canada.
2. The terms *ikhwan* and *akhwat* are Arabic words which mean brothers and sisters. They are also used when communicating with strangers. Members of the Tarbiyah movement use them to differentiate their Islamic identity from others.
3. The other of two biggest Islamic publishing houses are part of the Agromedia group. These include Qultum Media and Quanta-Elez Media Komputindo, as well as the Islamic publishing wind of Republika.
4. Statistics indicate that many Indonesian Muslims have been downloading these applications and are also part of social media groups associated with the applications. For example, Taaruf ID has 1 million downloads, Hijrah Taaruf has 100,000 downloads, TOI has 40,000 downloads, Taaruf Lalu Nikah has 10,000 downloads, Tasyari (Taaruf Syar'i) has 5,000 downloads, and Media Taaruf-Jodoh Islami has 10,000 downloads. On Instagram, there are 10,000 followers in taaruf.indo.id, which has 18,000 followers and taarufan_id 405,000 followers. On Facebook, there are 180,000 members in the TA'ARUF ID, 19,000 members

in Taaruf Online, 319,000 in TA'ARUF SERIUS MENIKAH seluruh Indonesia, 263,000 members in the Taaruf Siap Nikah Islam International group, and 175,000 members in the Menuju Taaruf dan Poligami group. These statistics can be found on the respective social media pages of the applications. The links are available in the list of references.
5. The idea for this ITP movement came from one of his book titles, *Indonesia Tanpa Pacaran* (Munafar 2017).
6. In terms of geographical breakdown, there are TOI users in ten cities. These are Semarang (3,917 members), Bandung (2,714 members), Tangerang (2,358 members), Bekasi Bekasi, 2,351 members), Bogor (1,719 members), Surabaya (1,353 members), Depok (1,205 members), Aceh Barat (1,119 members), and Malang (693 members) (Taaruf Online Indonesia 2022).
7. Some of these preachers are Adi Hidayat, Handy Bonny, Hanan Attaki, Felix Siauw, and Oki Setiana Dewi. Additionally, some of the celebrities who support TOI are Arie Untung and Nata Reza.
8. The issue of getting married to members of different Islamic organizations has been discussed by Ustadz Amar Ar Risalah. See https://www.youtube.com/watch?v=ySjZJDlf1PM&t=199s

References

Akmaliah, Wahyudi. 2020a. "The Rise of Cool Ustadz: Islamic Preacher, Subculture, and the Pemuda Hijrah Movement". In *The New Santri: Challenges to Traditional Religious Authority in Indonesia*, edited by Norshahril bin Saat and Ahmad Najib Burhani, pp. 239–57. Singapore: ISEAS – Yusof Ishak Institute.

———. 2020b. "When Islamism and Pop Culture Meet: A Political Framing of the Movie 212: The Power of Love". *Studia Islamika* 27, no. 1: 1–33.

Aldi, Andika, and Azuma Ira. 2020. "Fenomena Gaya Hidup Halal Berdampingan Dengan Digital" [Halal Lifestyle Phenomenon alongside Digital Lifestyle]. *KNEK*, 3 September 2022. https://knks.go.id/berita/310/fenomena-gaya-hidup-halal-berdampingan-dengan-digital?category=1 (accessed 6 October 2022).

Ali, Nafhesa, Richard Phillips, Claire Chambers, Kasia Narkowicz, Peter Hopkins, and Raksha Pande. 2020. "Halal Dating: Changing Relationship Attitudes and Experiences among Young British Muslims". *Sexualities* 23, nos. 5–6: 775–92.

Annisa MP Rochadiat, Stephanie Tom Tong, and Julie M. Novak. 2018. "Online Dating and Courtship Among Muslim American Women: Negotiating Technology, Religious Identity, and Culture". *New Media & Society* 20, no. 4: 1618–39.

Asad, Talal. 2009. "The Idea of an Anthropology of Islam". *Qui Parle* 7, no. 2: 1–30.

Asyari, Suaidi, and M. Husnul Abid. 2016. "Expanding the Indonesian Tarbiyah Movement through Ta'āruf and Marriage". *Al-Jami'ah: Journal of Islamic Studies* 54, no. 2: 337–68.

Bunt, Gary R. 2009. *IMuslim: Rewiring the House of Islam*. Chapel Hill: The University of North Carolina Press.

Castells, Manuel. 2007. *The Power of Identity Narratives*. Oxford: Blackwell Publishing.

———. 2010. *The Rise of the Network Society*. Oxford: Blackwell Publishing.
Chakraborty, Kabita. 2012. "Virtual Mate-Seeking in the Urban Slums of Kolkata, India". *South Asian Popular Culture* 10, no. 2: 197–216.
de Rooij, Laurens. 2020. "The Relationship Between Online Dating and Islamic Identity among British Muslims". *Journal of Religion, Media and Digital Culture* 9, no. 1): 1–32.
Google Play. 2023a. "Taaruf ID: Cari Jodoh Siap Ni". 8 June 2023. https://play.google.com/store/apps/details?id=taarufapp.id (accessed 28 August 2023).
———. 2023b. "Hijra Taaruf: Muslim Dating". 3 August 2023. https://play.google.com/store/apps/details?id=com.app.hijra.taaruf (accessed 28 August 2023).
———. 2023c. "TLN—Ta'aruf Lalu Nikah". 22 August 2023. https://play.google.com/store/apps/details?id=com.wordpress.vyatri.tlnapp (accessed 28 August 2023).
———. 2023d. "Ta'aruf Online Indonesia". 22 August 2023. https://play.google.com/store/apps/details?id=id.taaruf.online (accessed 28 August 2023).
Hadiz, Vedi R. 2010. *Localising Power in Post-Authoritarian Indonesia*. Stanford: Stanford University Press.
———. 2016. *Islamic Populism in Indonesia and the Middle East*. United Kingdom: Cambridge University Press.
———, and Richard Robison. 2004. *Reorganising Power in Indonesia*. New York: Routledge.
Hasan, Farah. 2021. "Keep It Halal! A Smartphone Ethnography of Muslim Dating". *Journal of Religion, Media and Digital Culture* 10, no. 1: 135–54.
Heryanto, Ariel. 2014. *Identity and Pleasure: The Politic of Indonesian Screen Culture*. Singapore and Japan: NUS Press & Kyoto University Press.
Hikmawan, Saefullah. 2022. "Transformation of the Youth Resistance: Underground Music Scene and Islamic Politics in Post-Authoritarian Indonesia". PhD dissertation, Murdoch University.
Iqbal, Muhammad Asep. 2017. "Cyber-Activism and the Islamic Salafi Movement in Indonesia". PhD dissertation, Murdoch University.
Kailani, Najib. 2015. "Aspiring to Prosperity: The Economic Theology of Urban Muslims in Contemporary Indonesia". PhD dissertation, UNSW Sydney.
———. 2020. "Creating Entrepreneurial and Pious Muslim Subjectivity in Globalised Indonesia". In *Rising Islamic Conservatism in Indonesia Islamic Groups and Identity Politics*, edited by Leonard C. Sebastian, Syafiq Hasyim, and Alexander R. Arifianto, pp. 198–209. London and New York: Routledge Taylor and Francis Group.
Lim, Merlyna. 2013. "Many Clicks but Little Sticks: Social Media Activism in Indonesia". *Journal of Contemporary Asia* 43, no. 4: 636–57.
———. 2017. "Freedom to Hate: Social Media, Algorithmic Enclaves, and the Rise of Tribal Nationalism in Indonesia". *Critical Asian Studies* 49, no. 3: 411–27.
Machmudi, Yon. 2008. *Islamising Indonesia: The Rise of Jemaah Tarbiyah and the Prosperous Justice Party (PKS)*. Acton: ANU Press.
Media Taaruf Islami Official (@taaruf.indo.id). N.d. Instagram. https://www.instagram.

com/taaruf.indo.id/?igshid=NjIwNzIyMDk2Mg%3D%3D (accessed 28 August 2023).
Mohamed Nawab Mohamed Osman. 2020. *Hizbut Tahrir Indonesia and Political Islam: Identity, Ideology and Religio-Political Mobilization*. London and New York: Routledge.
Muhtadi, Burhanuddin. 2012. *Dilema PKS: Suara Dan Syariah* [Dilemma of PKS: Voices and Sharia]. Jakarta: Kepustakaan Gramedia.
Munafar, La Ode. 2017. *Indonesia Tanpa Pacaran*. Yogyakarta: Gaul Fresh.
Nisa, Eva F. 2017. "Creative and Lucrative Da'wa: The Visual Culture of Instagram Amongst Female Muslim Youth in Indonesia". *Asiascape: Digital Asia* 5: 68–99.
———. 2021. "Online Halal Dating, Ta'aruf, and the Shariatisation of Match-making among Malaysian and Indonesian Muslims". *Cyber Orient* 15, no. 1: 231–58.
Noorhaidi Hasan. 2005. *Laskar Jihad: Islam, Militancy, and the Quest for Identity in Post-New Order Indonesia*. New York: Cornell University Press.
———. 2009. "The Making of Public Islam: Piety, Agency, and Commodification on the Landscape of the Indonesian Public Sphere". *Contemporary Islam* 3, no. 3: 229–50.
Pasha, Shaheen. 2015. "Western Muslims Swipe Right to Find Their Match on 'Minder'". *Daily Beast*, 23 February 2015. https://www.thedailybeast.com/western-muslims-swipe-right-to-find-their-match-on-minder?ref=scroll (accessed 28 September 2022).
Pourmehdi, Mansour. 2015. "Globalisation, the Internet and Guilty Pleasures in Morocco". *Sociology and Anthropology* 3, no. 9: 455–63.
Rochadiat, Annisa MP, Stephanie Tom Tong, and Julie M. Novak. 2018. "Online Dating and Courtship among Muslim American Women: Negotiating Technology, Religious Identity, and Culture". *New Media & Society* 20, no. 4: 1618–39.
Sari, Yunita Trie, Fatimah Husein, and Ratna Noviani. 2020. "Hijrah and Islamic Movement in Social Media: A Social Movement Study of Anti-Dating Movement #IndonesiaTanpaPacaran". *DINIKA: Academic Journal of Islamic Studies* 5, no. 1: 1–26.
Savitri, Setiawati I., and Faturochman. 2011. "Politics and Marriage among Islamic Activists in Indonesia". In *Changing Marriage Patterns in Southeast Asia Economic and Socio-Cultural Dimensions*, edited by Gavin W. Jones, Terence H. Hull, and Maznah Mohamad, pp. 62–72. New York: Routledge.
Sotoudeh, Ramina, Roger Friedland, and Janet Afary. 2017. "Digital Romance: The Sources of Online Love in the Muslim World". *Media, Culture & Society* 39, no. 3: 429–39.
Standing, Guy. 2011. *The Precariat: The New Dangerous Class*. London and New York: Bloomsbury Academic.
Syafiq Hasyim. 2022. *The Halal Project In Indonesia: Shariatization, Minority Rights and Commodification*. Trends in Southeast Asia, no. 12/2022. Singapore: ISEAS – Yusof Ishak Institute.
Ta'aruf dan Sharing Islami. N.d. Facebook. https://www.facebook.com/groups/578954639631490/ (accessed 28 August 2023).

Ta'aruf Islami Siap Nikah Internasional. N.d. Facebook. https://www.facebook.com/groups/729227137578150/ (accessed 28 August 2023).
Ta'aruf Online. N.d. Facebook. https://www.facebook.com/groups/3294667900759215/ (accessed 28 August 2023).
Ta'aruf Serius Menikah (TSM) Seluruh Indonesia. N.d. Facebook. https://www.facebook.com/groups/744631186011115/ (28 August 2023).
Ta'aruf Siap Nikah. N.d. Facebook. https://www.facebook.com/TaarufSiapNikah (accessed 28 August 2023).
Temukan Jodohmu di Sini (@taarufan_id). N.d. Instagram. https://www.instagram.com/taarufan_id/?igshid=NjIwNzIyMDk2Mg%3D%3D (accessed 28 August 2023).

8
HALAL LIFESTYLE AND THE EVERYDAY POLITICS OF MUSLIM NON-STATE ACTORS IN BRUNEI

Siti Mazidah Mohamad

Introduction

In this day and age, digitally connected young people organize their religious activities and collective responses via new media technologies. As new media become part of our everyday lives, personal matters are widely surfaced and circulated on social media platforms and, to some extent, interlinked with everyday politics. Social media presence is more than just producing and consuming entertaining content and sharing mundane daily activities or personal thoughts; it also contributes to collective thinking and action shifts. Everyday politics and digital civic engagement in Brunei Darussalam cover themes framed around society's experiences and interests (Highfield 2016), such as racism (Black Twitter, Black Lives Matter, Asian Lives Matter) and feminism (women's rights and protections).

The growing online Muslim communities further explicate the digitalization of religious practices and the emergence of new religious landscapes. Examples of this development include the formation of the E-Ummah or Cyber Ummah community (Khamis 2018). Youth use these "alternative" spaces of engagement not only to share personal stories but also to police other Muslim bodies or trigger new religious movements and everyday activism on various concerns. Discourses on halal consumption and shariah-compliant lifestyles have also entered the social mediascapes. The politicization of the halal lifestyle comes from two fronts: the first, at the institutional level (top-bottom), focusing on halal production and consumption, market and trading, and certification and standards (Bergeaud-Blackler, Fischer, and Lever 2015; Yakin and Christians 2021); the second, relating to the more banal everyday politics surrounding halal or shariah-compliant lifestyle of individual Muslims and grassroots organizations. While cognizant of the intertwining state and non-state constructions of halal practices and their shaping of the halal lifestyle in society, this chapter examines Bruneian Malay Muslims' social media practices and shariah-complaint discourses at the micro-scale, everyday level. Their social media engagements can provide academics and relevant stakeholders with a deeper understanding of how they uphold socio-religious practices in relation to the dominant narratives at the state level.

I elucidate the everyday life, practices and concerns of the Malays and how they contribute to the emerging halal lifestyle in the country. This is done by drawing from several qualitative research projects I conducted between 2016 and 2022 on young people's use and engagement through social media platforms such as Instagram, TikTok and Reddit. In what follows, I offer Muslims' practices and digital presence before discussing the communal surveillance and policing of Bruneian Malay Muslims on social mediascapes. I frame this communal surveillance and self-vigilante moral policing as a form of youth activism that reinforces hegemonic practices of religious authority, maintains the interest and needs of the Malay/Muslim community, and shapes the Muslim youth culture in the country. Unlike Fischer's (2016) halal activism involving Islam, the state and the market, youth activism in Brunei is mostly grassroots-based with minimal state involvement, although I contend that their digital practices are directly or indirectly supportive of the state's interest. While the terms "halal" and "shariah-compliant" are rarely used, their actions in morally policing fellow Muslims and the practice of self-censorship somewhat support the country's aspiration to be a *Negara Zikir* (Zikir Nation) with strong *Melayu Islam Beraja* (Malay Islamic Monarchy, MIB) values. A halal lifestyle should not only be understood as food consumption but also cover emerging sectors such as the halal economy, pharmaceuticals, cosmetics and media and recreation. It must be extended to the everyday practices of the Muslim community. In the penultimate section, I offer a wider consideration beyond the vernacular form of everyday surveillance and policing; shariah-compliant social media practices in shaping the halal lifestyle in Brunei.

Muslim Practices and Digital Presence

Popular culture content such as short videos, skits, and Islamic-based memes produced and circulated online exhibit the everyday practices of Brunei Muslims. As social media sites mediate emergent Muslim cultures, several concerns are circulated on various digital platforms, portraying and defining what constitutes halal or shariah-complaint practices for Muslims. Among these, there are a few emerging concerns and interests not specific to the consumption of food and beverages but extend to Muslims' everyday life and social practices. Some examples are the modesty movement that focuses on Muslim fashion, particularly for ladies; the so-called "halal gap" between Muslim women and men in the context of premarital relationships; and the awareness regarding halal cosmetics such as dUCk cosmetics, SimplySiti, and Neelofa's henna/*inai* (nail polish). These issues are not only discussed offline but also penetrate social mediascapes.

Digital activism through various digital technologies and platforms has mobilized movements based on shared interests within and outside the region (Tatarchevskiy 2011; Velasquez and LaRose 2015; Barendregt and Schneider 2020; Smith and Halafo 2020). In 2011, the Arab Spring experienced in several countries in the Middle East was coordinated by young people through the use of social media. In some parts of the world, Muslim women participate in #*YourAverageMuslim* activism, which contributes to subverting stereotypes of Muslims—mainly Muslim women— as oppressed and backward (Islam 2019). Dakwah 2.0 or *da'wah* activism and religious practices are now commonly performed and consumed on digital platforms (Hew 2015; Slama 2017, 2018; Beta 2020). Southeast Asian Muslims are similarly pushing their agenda forward via everyday consumption and in digital spaces. In Malaysia, Indonesia, and to some extent, Brunei, Muslim women are moderately and subtly contesting the perception of the *hijab* as oppressive and backward, as well as addressing the misconception surrounding *hijab* practices. This contestation is conducted through their purchases of chic *hijab* brands and *hijab* styling practices and creating their own Muslim identities specific to their interests and concerns as modern middle-class Muslims (Baulch and Pramiyanti 2018, 2019; Beta 2019; Siti Mazidah and Nurzihan 2021; Siti Mazidah 2021). The diverse concerns and practices of Muslim youth in the digital space accompanying their social media practices (including influencing culture) provide valuable insights into their promotion of a halal lifestyle and discourse at the everyday level. The next section discusses how Malay Muslims' communal surveillance of social media users' online content maintains the dominant Muslim majority practices and narratives, treating these as unquestionable. This bottom-up behaviour also defines what constitutes a halal lifestyle and indirectly shapes societal norms even without the state's mandate.

COMMUNAL SURVEILLANCE IN BRUNEI: MAINTAINING THE STATUS QUO AND HALAL LIFESTYLE

Governing and regulating Muslim bodies and living everyday practices are ubiquitous in many Muslim societies, including Malaysia (Siti Mazidah 2019) and Pakistan (Aziz 2019). The regulating of *hijabi* bodies, particularly Muslim women's sartorial choices, and the general Muslims' public and private sphere arrangements, are seen at different socio-spatial scales: at the individual, communal (including home), and national spheres (Afshar 2008; Droogsma 2007; Hopkins 2007; Hochel 2013; Lily Zubaidah 2012; O'Toole et al. 2016; Williams and Nasir 2017). In Brunei, religious and cultural values are conflated, institutionalized, and embedded in Malay Muslims' everyday social and cultural practices under the state-endorsed MIB values. MIB is "simply the revival of Brunei's socio-political heritage, a cultural concept inherent within the Bruneian socio-political consciousness" (Umar 2013, p. 93) and it is practised as a way of life in workplaces and at home. It shapes Bruneian society and protects its core values (Muhammad Hadi and Muhammad Melayong 2020, p. 15). Malay Muslims are expected to be respectful to the head of state, government, and religion, and adhere to Brunei's socio-cultural customs (Siti Mazidah 2019b). These materialized under different social settings such as in private (the home) and public spaces, creating a socio-cultural and religious landscape unique to the context of Brunei.

In recent years, as Brunei saw a rapid rise in Internet and social media penetration, and access to digital technology intensified, communal surveillance and self-censorship based on MIB values have extended to digital spaces. Malay Muslims are now cognizant of how their everyday lives can be regulated in myriad ways, including through the community's expression of their expectations. Online presence becomes interpersonal and, as commonly understood, must be carefully managed to avoid misunderstanding and judgement by others (Siti Mazidah 2023). To some extent, such communal surveillance and policing include social media users calling out others' unacceptable behaviour and inappropriate content, reminding users to be decent and respectful in their everyday practices, and behaving according to what they consider to be society's expectations. Content deemed unsuitable for social media, regarded as a public space by these self-proclaimed vigilantes, such as the display of intimate affection, public airing of relationship problems, and "indecent" body displays could be raised, addressed, and flagged.

As social media content is circulated, exchanged, and reproduced widely and rapidly, enabling and enhancing visibility culture, social media users further amplify their presence and elevate their status through consistent, relatable, and authentic content (Marwick 2013; Abidin 2015, 2016). Users who are successful in raising their visibility and self-branding can potentially establish a solid and growing fan base on social media (Marshall 2006; Senft 2008, 2013; Marwick 2013; Abidin 2016, 2017; Khamis, Ang, and Welling 2016). Their elevated status accorded users "celebrity" status, like any other traditional celebrities (such as actors/actresses), though the former excel more in content, accessibility and relatability vis-à-vis their audience (Hearn and Schoenhoff 2016; Khamis, Ang, and Welling 2016). It is within this influencer-audience engagement that the dynamic interplay of this communal surveillance and policing grows. As these celebrated individuals are expected to be role models to society, their actions are highly scrutinized compared to ordinary individuals.

There have been cases where netizens have called out traditional celebrities and influencers who do not observe socio-cultural religious practices and the community's expectations. In 2019, a Malay Muslim male influencer was called out for uploading an Instagram video of himself nonchalantly touching a female influencer's hand while jokingly referring to his action as invalidating ablution (*membatalkan wudhu*). The public called him out and considered his actions offensive to Malay culture and religious norms. Recently, a social media user reminded another male influencer against publicly sharing his affection for his spouse on Instagram. The reminder was sent directly to his Instagram account, which he later shared on his profile to gather feedback from his followers. A few users agreed that such behaviour should not be shown in public (online) because it is culturally and religiously insensitive. Critics were concerned that the images could have been seen by young users on the site. Conversely, his supporters argued there was nothing wrong with a lawfully married couple displaying their affection online. Their comments about his actions reveal the common concerns and the socio-cultural and religious parameters that society lives within.

Bruneian Malay Muslims' social media profiles indicate that there is a moderate form of selective policing. There have been instances where the public turned a blind eye to what conservatives would consider being socio-culturally inappropriate and religious transgressions committed by influencers and non-influencers, such as the wearing of tight clothing or exposing certain body parts, as these are against keeping one's *aurat* or modesty in Islam. This somewhat liberal behaviour contradicts the general perception that Bruneians embracing MIB values are strict and intolerant. Understanding this selective policing of some transgressions requires a look into the country's context and society's everyday lived religiosities, especially among the young who happen to be the dominant users of social media sites. I account for at least two explanations for this selective policing. First, it is linked to young people claiming that they lack in-depth knowledge of Islam. Moreover, they are also unwilling to portray their Muslim identity, which could deter them from commenting on others' transgressions (Siti Mazidah 2023). Second, the Malay cultural values emphasizing humility and respect for others also contribute to this apparent moderate and selective policing on social media sites. In this collectivist society, confrontations are usually avoided and, if necessary, to be done moderately, carefully, or away from public scrutiny. Any form of moral policing (in the form of gentle reminders) is conducted privately via chat or inbox features.

In Brunei, this communal surveillance and policing have steadily progressed into cancel culture, which regulates influencers' practices. Although this online calling-out practice has become more common in the country, cancel culture on a larger scale is a fairly recent phenomenon. The act of cancelling is "an expression of agency, a choice to withdraw one's attention from someone or something whose values, (in)action, or speech are so offensive, one no longer wishes to grace them with their presence, time, and money" (Clark 2020, p. 3). The culture of cancelling public figures, celebrities, and brands for transgressive norms (Saint-Louis 2021; Clark 2020; Velasco 2020) has taken many forms. Calling out and cancelling culture has also been applied to other non-Islamic related issues, such as sexual harassment and other socio-cultural matters that offend public sensibilities. They are highly contextualized to local concerns, including the cancellation of individuals whom they perceive as displaying religious and socio-cultural transgressions. The intensification of digital platforms and technologies has led to the transfer of (religious) authority to the audience (Campbell 2007; Campbell and Teusner 2011). This points to individuals taking on an active role as religious/social police on behalf of the community and the state, similar to what the netizens in other countries—such as Malaysia—call the *halal-haram* police.

Self-Regulation in Negotiating Societal Surveillance and Policing

A significant part of this communal surveillance and policing is self-regulation, which takes the form of self-censorship. Mindful that members of their community are watching them online, users are often burdened by the constant need to portray themselves as good Muslims through captions, photos and videos shared on social media platforms. However, a growing number of young people, including influencers, are beginning to resist communal policing in several ways. First, they refuse to portray their Muslim identity. Young Bruneians' religiosities reveal that while more young Malay Muslims disclose their religious views and knowledge on social media sites, many are unwilling to share religious content, practices, and identity online (Siti Mazidah 2023). Their lack of in-depth knowledge about Islam, the fear of being called out for it, and the societal expectations that come with claiming and presenting oneself as a devout Muslim are some reasons for this refusal to share religious content and comment on others' offensive content. As one young Malay Muslim shared,

> I don't really see myself portraying myself as a religious figure on the Internet. There is no definite reason behind it. However, one of the reasons that I can think of is that to be someone who is "religious" I need to be someone who is perfect in every aspect. In the eyes of society, these religious people are regarded as [perfect beings], someone who doesn't make mistakes, someone who does good in every action, etc. One small mistake and these people are already *clicking on their phone, bashing the keyboard on these people's weaknesses.* We live in a judgmental society and are bound by it. In the end, I just keep a religious image of mine for myself to determine. (Discussant, male)

Some also uphold the basic principle that religion is a private matter. One influencer stated that "I try not to put religion into it (social media sites) just because dari awal [from the beginning] I always see religion as personal. Tsk like it is between you and God you don't need to involve (others)". In this case, portraying a neutral self is considered a strategy to protect oneself from the scrutiny of others.

Second, by displaying socio-culturally acceptable behaviours they can avoid communal surveillance and the potential complications that come with it. This is done by applying self-censorship and content filtering following the MIB values. One influencer learned the mistake of not adhering to community expectations and used her experience as a reminder, "yeah just—yeah MIB—just don't go viral again (ha)". Some concerns shared by young people about what online content to censor include,

> Any sexual content that is not in line with MIB and Islam (obviously as it is against the religion itself).
>
> Shaming & bullying, nudity, ill-intent posts etc. & basically anything that's against the norms & values of Brunei, from anything related to MIB, its cultures & society.
>
> Sexuality. Those Muslimah who show off their *aurat* [body parts Muslims are expected to cover] should be banned from Instagram.
>
> Inappropriate posts like what our so-called "influences" had posted before.
>
> Probably whatever is extreme that goes against the religion in Brunei, Islam.
>
> Anything extremely beyond MIB I guess.
>
> Sensitive content that may include crude, offensive or disturbing aspects of the Internet.
>
> Anything that is against MIB for example *melimping atas meja* [lying on the table] (a reference to a recent incident).

Content considered unacceptable includes common areas of concern such as nudity and pornography, and those specific to Brunei, including being critical of MIB values and offending Islam and society. Posts that offend the country's culture and image, Islamic values, and family problems are among the posts they know should not be shared (Siti Mazidah 2019). We have seen how the Bruneian Malay Muslims use different self-regulating mechanisms, self-censorship based on societal expectations and MIB values emphasizing socio-cultural and religious values, and the community's active surveillance and actions to address transgressions and misdemeanours. This self-regulation suggests their awareness of communal policing based on the MIB values embedded in their everyday lives. Only in some cases where individuals fail to self-censor, would they be called out and/or cancelled. This surveillance and policing are more individualized, and it has become a societal practice and does not involve government intervention or enforcement. Brunei's communal policing can be considered more moderate and individual-based in comparison to other forms of surveillance, such as digital vigilantism (Trottier 2017; Trottier, Gabdulhakov, and Qian 2020) and lateral surveillance (Andrejevic 2005, 2006) found in the United States, France, South Africa and the United Kingdom. In those instances, they practised more intense societal surveillance at various scales and involved coordinated actions of society and could be triggered by multiple issues such as breach of social norms, minor offences to larger-scale matters such as uncivil behaviour and corruption (Loveluck 2020).

This call-out and cancel culture can be contextualized as a form of youth activism, a form of social responsibility of the majority voices to address immoral and dishonest actions and maintain the status quo. They reveal the community's active role in regulating society in online and offline spaces. As Velasco (2020, p. 4) aptly writes, "the culture of cancellation has become an apparatus to enact an ideological purge". Although these calling out and cancelling measures enforced communal surveillance and policing and, to some extent, effectively maintained self-censorship in the country, there is no tangible impact on "cancelled" individuals. So far, the effect of this cancelling action is short-lived; the issues raised dissipate over time, which could be due to the nature of popular culture as fast-moving, where trends appear and disperse swiftly. Irrespective of the efficacy of the cancel culture, what is of utmost importance here is knowing that there is always the community guiding one's behaviour. Hence, it supports shaping the emerging halal lifestyle in the country.

Conclusion: A Halal Way Forward: Shariah-Compliant Social Media Content

The everyday politics of non-state actors via communal policing as grassroots youth activism offers an understanding of Muslims' everyday concerns about halal consumption and lifestyle. While they maintain their religious and socio-cultural practices and status quo in the country through communal surveillance and policing of the Malay Muslim community in digital spaces, they are supporting the state's aspiration of an Islamic state with strong MIB values. In this context, their digital practices substantiate the need to look beyond food production, consumption, and other economic activities to everyday discourses in shaping halal practices and lifestyles within and beyond the country.

In the previous sections, I contend that the dynamic interplay within the Bruneian Malay Muslim community via communal surveillance and policing is working towards protecting the community's interests. Beyond communal and lay people's practices, the context, actions, and concerns discussed in the previous sections implicate the state and the country's development. On this note, I want to return to the earlier point regarding selective policing. In the context of this selective policing, I question whether Brunei needs clearer guidelines to deal with transgressions on social media. A few young social media users I spoke to about regulating social media users welcomed the idea of social media regulation. In their words, a clear delineation of what is allowed and restricted (the dos and don'ts) will help Bruneians be more courageous in sharing creative content and worry less about the scrutiny and judgements of other Bruneians. For them, the lack of regulations impedes social media users from sharing their content freely due to the fear of judgements and unclear unwritten rules. At times, the wealth of unwritten rules that guide society (communal surveillance and policing) is considered a burden for the public to adhere to.

A local influencer has made several suggestions on how to guide fellow influencers in the country, covering the MIB philosophy and general ethical online practices. These suggestions include: "combating the teachings, elements, doctrine and everything that goes against the principle of Malay Islamic Monarchy in everyday life and 'filtering information before sharing any unauthorized facts, religious and government officials and others'" (Nazirul 2021, pp. 318–19). There are already existing social media guidelines in the country, but they are only drafted for government agencies. While there is no single social media regulation, existing laws are collectively and contextually applied to regulate relevant content sharing on social media, such as the Child Online Protection National Strategy Framework, Sedition Act (Chapter 24), Undesirable Publications Act (Chapter 25), Broadcasting Act (Chapter 180), Public Entertainment Act (Chapter 181), Computer Misuse Act (Chapter 194), Defamation Act (Chapter 192), and Internet Code of Practice (AITI 2018). The existing regulation and content management practices attest to the state's commitment to upholding social, cultural and religious practices and ensuring the well-being of its population.

If we listen to the suggestions given by these young people on having social media guidelines, what will need to be included? What would constitute shariah-compliant social media practices? Would it refer to actions specific to socio-cultural and religious contexts? To which demographics should these shariah-compliant social media guidelines be applied? Concerns with regulations have been debated within academic discourse and policymaking. One common issue in regulating users is the lack of freedom in unleashing creativity and infringement of freedom of speech (von Krogh 2016). How tight of a leash should the state have over social media practices? Would stringent policing paralyse the population's creativity in creating content and the nation's development? With all these challenges, would a soft approach be the best practice in shaping influencers' online sharing?

At this juncture, I contend that digital social literacy would be useful in educating influencers on the country's social, cultural and religious practices, norms and sensitivities. Taking note of the MIB values and lifestyle envisioned by the nation, there are five important features to consider. First, the form of language used in the content and caption. Second, modesty and public decency in behaviour and bodily display. Third, social interactions and communication. Fourth, ethical practice in the production, consumption, circulation and reproduction of social media content. Fifth, shariah-compliant economic activities and transactions. I do not intend to offer a prescriptive list of shariah-compliant social media practices in this chapter. What I have provided here are a few areas of concern sensitive to the country's context as an Islamic state, which the public has voiced on social media sites and everyday discourse. Bearing in mind that the country's religious and cultural practices are intricately tied, and from time to time cultural beliefs and practices triumph over religion, social media practices need to be contextually sensitive.

There remains an open space for future consideration of the best practices in dealing with their social media practice. If there is deliberation on this matter in the future, I would recommend a revision of the current social media guidelines. Finding a balance between regulation and freedom to create content would be imperative to maintain healthy social media practices and environments to mobilize social media users rather than paralyse them. In the context of Brunei, an Islamic state and a *Zikir* Nation, having some form of shariah-compliant social media practice based on the Muslim communities' everyday lives and practices would be useful. When fine-tuned to the country's Islamic and cultural contexts, social media practices adhering to Islamic teaching and guidelines and the country's socio-cultural values and aligned with the five elements of the *Maqasid Al-Shari'ah* (the national strategic objectives of development) would support the MIB's operational philosophy and achieve the *Zikir* Nation. As Brunei is focused on establishing strong economic, social and spiritual growth, this vision for development is apparent in the four principal policies of MIB (1984), *Wawasan* 2035 (Vision 2035, 2004),

Zikir Nation (2007), and *Maqasid Al-Shariiah* (2018) introduced by the government since its independence in 1984. With the non-state actors' indirect support of a shariah-compliant lifestyle, the state would be able to achieve its vision as an Islamic state with an Islamic form of governance unique to its context.

References

Abidin, Crystal. 2015. "Communicative Intimacies: Influencers and Perceived Interconnectedness". *Ada: A Journal of Gender, New Media, & Technology* 8: 1–16.

———. 2016. "Visibility Labour: Engaging with Influencers' Fashion Brands and #OOTD Advertorial Campaigns on Instagram". *Media International Australia* 161, no. 1: 1–15.

———. 2017. "#familygoals: Family Influencers, Calibrated Amateurism, and Justifying Young Digital Labor". *Social Media + Society* 3, no. 2: 1–15.

Afshar, Haleh. 2008. "Can I See Your Hair? Choice, Agency and Attitudes: The Dilemma of Faith and Feminism for Muslim Women Who Cover". *Ethnic and Racial Studies* 31, no. 2: 411–27.

Andrejevic, Mark. 2005. "The Work of Watching One Another: Lateral Surveillance, Risk, and Governance". *Surveillance & Society* 2, no. 4: 479–97.

———. 2006. "The Discipline of Watching: Detection, Risk, and Lateral Surveillance". *Critical Studies in Media Communication* 23, no. 5: 391–407.

Authority for Info-Communications Technology Industry of Brunei Darussalam (AITI). 2018. "Content Regulation". https://www.aiti.gov.bn/regulatory/content-regulation/ (accessed 25 March 2023).

Aziz, Fatima. 2019. "Performing as a Transgressive Authentic Microcelebrity: The Qandeel Baloch Case". In *Microcelebrity around the Globe: Approaches to Cultures of Internet Fame*, edited by Crystal Abidin and Megan Lindsay Brown, pp. 131–44. Bingley: Emerald Group Publishing.

Barendregt, Bart, and Florian Schneider. 2020. "Digital Activism in Asia: Good, Bad, and Banal Politics Online". *Asiascape: Digital Asia* 7, nos. 1–2: 5–19.

Baulch, Emma, and Alila Pramiyanti. 2018. "Hijabers on Instagram: Using Visual Social Media to Construct the Ideal Muslim Woman". *Social Media + Society* 4, no. 4. http://dx.doi.org/10.2139/ssrn.3353158

———. 2019. "Hijabers on Instagram: Visualising the Ideal Muslim Woman". In *Digital Transactions in Asia*, edited by Adrian Athique and Emma Baulch, pp. 260–84. New York: Routledge.

Bergeaud-Blackler, Florence, Johan Fischer, and John Lever. 2015. *Halal Matters: Islam, Politics, and Markets in Global Perspectives*. Oxon: Taylor and Francis.

Beta, Annisa. 2019. "Commerce, Piety and Politics: Indonesian Young Muslim Women's Groups as Religious Influencers". *New Media & Society* 21, no. 10: 2140–159.

———. 2020. "The Muslimah Intimate Public: Re-Considering Contemporary Da'wa Activists in Indonesia". *Asiascape: Digital Asia* 7, nos. 1–2: 20–41.

Campbell, Heidi. 2007. "Who's Got the Power? Religious Authority and the Internet". *Journal of Computer-Mediated Communication* 12, no. 3: 1043–62.
——, and P. Emerson Teusner. 2011. "Religious Authority in the Age of the Internet". *Christian Reflections (Virtual Lives)*: 59–68.
Clark, Meredith D. 2020. "DRAG THEM: A Brief Etymology of So-called 'Cancel Culture'". *Communication and the Public* 5, nos. 3–4: 88–92.
Droogsma, Rachel Anderson. 2007. "Redefining Hijab: American Muslim Women's Standpoints on Veiling". *Journal of Applied Communication Research* 35, no. 3: 294–319.
Fischer, Johan. 2016. "Halal Activism: Networking between Islam, the State and Market". *Asian Journal of Social Science* 44, nos. 1–2: 104–31.
Hearn, Alison, and Stephanie Schoenhoff. 2016. "From Celebrity to Influencer: Tracing the Diffusion of Celebrity Value across the Data Stream". In *A Companion to Celebrity*, edited by P. David Marshall and Sean Redmond, pp. 194–212. Chichester: John Wiley & Sons.
Hew Wai Weng. 2015. "Dakwah 2.0: Digital Dakwah, Street Dakwah and Cyber-Urban Activism among Chinese Muslims in Malaysia and Indonesia". In *New Media Configurations and Socio-Cultural Dynamics in Asia and the Arab World*, edited by Nadja-Christina Schneider and Carola Richter, pp. 198–221. London: Bloomsbury.
Highfield, Tim. 2016. *Social Media and Everyday Politics*. Cambridge; Malden: Polity.
Hochel, Sandra. 2013. "To Veil or Not to Veil: Voices of Malaysian Muslim Women". *Intercultural Communication Studies* 22, no. 2: 40–57.
Hopkins, Peter. 2007. "Young Muslim Men's Experiences of Local Landscapes after 11 September 2001". In *Geographies of Muslim Identities: Diaspora, Gender and Belonging*, edited by Cara Aitchison, Peter Hopkins, and Mei-Po Kwan, pp. 189–200. Aldershot: Ashgate.
Islam, Inaash. 2019. "Redefining #YourAverageMuslim Woman: Muslim Female Digital Activism on Social Media". *Journal of Arab & Muslim Media Research* 12, no. 2: 213–33.
Khamis, Sahar. 2018. "'Cyber Ummah' The Internet and Muslim Communities". In *Handbook of Contemporary Islam and Muslim Lives*, edited by Mark Woodward and Ronald Lukens-Bull, pp. 1–22. Cham, Switzerland: Springer.
Khamis, Susie, Lawrence Ang, and Raymond Welling. 2016. "Selfbranding, 'Micro-Celebrity' and the Rise of Social Media Influencers". *Celebrity Studies* 8, no. 2: 191–208.
Lily Zubaidah Rahim. 2012. "Governing Muslims in Singapore's Secular Authoritarian State". *Australian Journal of International Affairs* 66, no. 2: 169–85.
Lim, Joanne B.Y. 2013. "Video Blogging and Youth Activism in Malaysia". *International Communication Gazette* 75, no. 3: 300–21.
Lim, Merlyna. 2018. "Disciplining Dissent: Freedom, Control, and Digital Activism in Southeast Asia". In *Routledge Handbook of Urbanization in Southeast Asia*, edited by Rita Padawangi, pp. 478–94. United Kingdom: Routledge.

Loveluck, Benjamin. 2020. "The Many Shades of Digital Vigilantism: A Typology of Online Self-Justice". *Global Crime* 21, nos. 3–4: 213–41.
Marshall, David P. 2006. "New Media – New Self: The Changing Power of Celebrity". In *The Celebrity Culture Reader*, edited by David P. Marshall, pp. 634–44. New York: Routledge.
Marwick, Alice. 2013. *Status Update: Celebrity, Publicity and Branding in the Social Media Age*. New Haven: Yale University Press.
Muhammad Hadi, and Muhammad Melayong. 2020. *Malay Islamic Monarchy: The Journey*. Brunei: Brunei Historical Society.
Nasir M. Kamaludeen. 2016. *Globalized Muslim Youth in the Asia Pacific: Popular Culture in Singapore and Sydney*. New York: Palgrave Macmillan.
Nazirul Mubin Ahad. 2021. "MIB Beyond the Classroom: Local Influencers and their Impact on the Public Understanding of the State Philosophy". In *Globalisation, Education, and Reform in Brunei Darussalam*, edited by Le Ha Phan, Asiyah Kumpoh, Keith Wood, Rosmawijah Jawawi, and Hardimah Said, pp. 305–22. Switzerland: Palgrave Macmillan.
O'Toole, Therese, Nasar Meer, Daniel Nilsson DeHanas, Stephen H. Jones, and Tariq Modood. 2016. "Governing through Prevent? Regulation and Contested Practice in State–Muslim Engagement". *Sociology* 50, no. 1: 160–77.
Saint-Louis, Hervé. 2021. "Understanding Cancel Culture: Normative and Unequal Sanctioning". *First Monday* 26, no. 7. https://doi.org/10.5210/fm.v26i7.10891
Senft, Theresa. 2008. *CAMGIRLS Celebrity and Community in the Age of Social Networks*. New York: Peter Lang Publishing.
———. 2013. "Microcelebrity and the Branded Self". In *A Companion to New Media Dynamics*, edited by John Hartley, Jean Burgess, and Axel Bruns, pp. 346–54. Chichester: Wiley-Blackwell.
Siti Khadijah Ab Manan, Fadilah Abd Rahman, and Mardhiyyah Sahri. 2016. *Contemporary Issues and Development in the Global Halal Industry*. Switzerland: Springer.
Siti Mazidah Haji Mohamad. 2017. "Performance of Religiosity on a 'Techno-Religious' Space". *Advanced Science Letters* 23, no. 5: 4918–921
———. 2019a. "Everyday Lived Islam: Malaysian Muslim Women's Performance of Religiosity Online". *Journal for Islamic Studies* 37, no. 1: 74–100.
———. 2019b. "Self-Disclosure on Social Media in Brunei Darussalam". In *RSIS Monograph: Resilience in the Face of Disruption*, edited by Mely Caballero-Anthony and Margareth Sembiring, pp. 46–56. Singapore: S. Rajaratnam School of International Studies, Nanyang Technological University.
———. 2021. "Micro-celebrity Practices in Muslim-majority States in Southeast Asia". *Popular Communication* 19, no. 3: 1–15.
———. 2023. "Youth Religiosity and Social Media in Brunei". In *(Re)presenting Brunei Darussalam: A Sociology of the Everyday*, edited by Lian Kwee Fee, Paul J. Carnegie, and Noor Hasharina Hassan, pp. 51–67. Singapore: Springer.

———, and Nurzihan Hassim. 2021. "Hijabi Celebrification and Hijab Consumption in Brunei and Malaysia". *Celebrity Studies* 12, no. 3: 498–522.
Slama, Martin. 2017. "Social Media and Islamic Practice: Indonesian Ways of Being Digitally Pious". In *Digital Indonesia: Connectivity and Divergence*, edited by Edwin Jurriëns and Ross Tapsell, pp. 146–62. Singapore: ISEAS – Yusof Ishak Institute.
———. 2018. "Practising Islam through Social Media in Indonesia". *Indonesia and the Malay World* 46, no. 134: 1–4.
———, and Bart Barendregt. 2018. "Introduction: Online Publics in Muslim Southeast Asia: In Between Religious Politics and Popular Pious Practices". *Asiascape: Digital Asia* 5, nos. 1–2: 3–31.
Smith, Geraldine, and Anna Halafo. 2020. "Multifaith Third Spaces: Digital Activism, Netpeace, and the Australian Religious Response to Climate Change". *Religions* 11, no. 3: 1–16.
Tatarchevskiy, Tatiana. 2011. "The 'Popular' Culture of Internet Activism". *New Media & Society* 13, no. 2: 297–313.
Trottier, Daniel. 2017. "Digital Vigilantism as Weaponisation of Visibility". *Philosophy & Technology* 30, no. 1: 55–72.
———, Rashid Gabdulhakov, and Qian Huang. 2020. *Introducing Vigilant Audiences*. Open Book Publishers.
Umar Abdul Aziz. 2013. "Melayu Islam Beraja". *Journal of the Malaysian Branch of the Royal Asiatic Society* 86, no. 2: 93–97.
Velasco, Joseph. 2020. "You Are Cancelled: Virtual Collective Consciousness and the Emergence of Cancel Culture as Ideological Purging". *Rupkatha Journal on Interdisciplinary Studies in Humanities* 12, no. 5: 1–7.
Velasquez, Alcides, and Robert LaRose. 2015. "Youth Collective Activism through Social Media: The Role of Collective Efficacy". *New Media & Society* 17, no. 6: 899–918.
von Krogh, Torbjörn. 2016. " 'Self-Regulate, or We Will Regulate Your Content'. Are State Threats of Regulation Threats to Freedom of Speech?". In *Blurring the Lines: Market-Driven and Democracy-Driven Freedom of Expression*, edited by Maria Edström, Andrew T. Kenyon, and Eva-Maria Svensson, pp. 165–76. Göteborg: Nordicom.
Williams, J. Patrick, and Kamaludeen Mohamed Nasir. 2017. "Muslim Girl Culture and Social Control in Southeast Asia: Exploring the Hijabista and Hijabster Phenomena". *Crime, Media, Culture* 13, no. 2: 199–216.
Yakin, Ayang Utriza, and Louis-Léon Christians, eds. 2021. *Rethinking Halal: Genealogy, Current Trends, and New Interpretations*. Leiden: Brill.
Zhang Weiyu, and Emmanuel C. Lallana. 2013. "Youth, ICTs, and Civic Engagement in Asia". *International Communication Gazette* 75, no. 3: 249–52.

9

SPIRITUALITY AND COMMODITY
Drivers of Shariah Tourism in Singapore

Norshahril Saat

INTRODUCTION

Tourism is a robust sector in developed economies, and governments collaborate with private enterprises to cater to foreign tourists' needs. The meaning of tourism has also undergone significant changes for Singapore Muslims. In Islam, the movement of people from one place to another has always been part and parcel of community, cultural and religious life. Some of these travels are predicated on necessities, such as warfare (as refugees), migration (forced or voluntary) and religious obligations (such as the pilgrimage to Mecca). Muslims also travel for work and leisure (holidays). Examining how travel among Singapore Muslims has changed over the years is significant because it allows one to take stock of the impact of the Islamic resurgence movement of the 1980s, which scholars have identified as the reason for the attitudinal change of Muslims in Southeast Asia towards exclusivism or conservatism (Azhar 2014; Chandra 1987). Since the 1980s, Muslims (the majority of whom in Singapore are Malays) experienced improvements in their socio-economic life. The community's ascension into the Muslim middle and educated class corresponds to the changing appetite of needs, lifestyles, and requirements (Bourdieu 1984). The nexus between the expanding middle class and growing religiosity led to new demands and requirements, among others, for Islamic tourism or shariah-compliant travel.

Today, the haj (also called hajj) and *umrah* industry is the fastest-growing sector in the Malay-Muslim community. Based on the 2020 census, the Malay-Muslim community (also referred to as the Malays) makes up about 15 per cent of the 5.6 million Singapore population.[1] The haj is the fifth pillar of Islam, and it is obligatory for Muslims to perform the haj ritual to Mecca once in their lifetime. This chapter examines the evolution of the haj and *umrah* from a religious obligation into a flourishing industry in Singapore. During the colonial period, the city-state earned the reputation of being the centre of the haj pilgrimage, where travel to Mecca from outside Arabia was only feasible by sea, and Singapore played the role of the haj port in Southeast Asia. Today, as the mode of transportation has changed from sea to air, Singapore no longer plays that role. Nevertheless, the privatization of haj has made the ritual a business opportunity.

This chapter argues that two forces contributed to the growth of Muslim travel as an industry; the Muslim resurgence of the 1980s, and the rise of the Muslim middle class in Singapore. It also demonstrates three trends in Muslim travel. First, given the restriction in the number of haj pilgrims Singapore can accommodate every year due to the quota imposed by the Saudi Arabian government, many Singaporeans patronize the *umrah* season (minor pilgrimage) instead, which happens all year round. Second, the Malay middle class now incorporates *umrah* as part of Islamic tourism and is keen to explore other Muslim sites in the name of packages like *Jejak Rasul* (Tracing the Footsteps of Prophets) and Islamic heritage. Islamic tourism includes countries such as Turkey, Spain, Morocco, Bosnia and maritime Southeast Asia (Malaysia and Indonesia). Third, Islamic travel also includes countries that do not have a Muslim majority, including in Europe and Asia Pacific, and there are demands for shariah-compliant tour packages. These tour packages, however, are no different from the non-Islamic ones, except that they serve halal food and observe prayer times. Nevertheless, gaps remain in what is often termed shariah-compliant tourism. These packages remain pricier than non-shariah ones, with little emphasis on standards, environmental concerns and tackling inequality. The chapter contends that if shariah-compliant tourism wants to be known, it must adopt a holistic approach in cherishing Islamic principles and values and how these are operationalized, which can make it markedly different from so-called non-shariah-compliant products. In other words, its presentation of an Islamic alternative must go beyond scratching the surface. Most importantly, it must not demonstrate exclusivist tendencies that shun inter-civilizational learning.

Islamic Resurgence and Rise of the Muslim Middle Class

Scholars of Southeast Asian Islam refer to the 1970s and 1980s as the Islamic resurgence period. Numerous studies have demonstrated a significant shift in attitudes among Muslims in the region (Azhar 2014; Chandra 1987; Noor Aisha 2020; Norshahril 2012a; 2012b; 2014; Shaharuddin 2006). This period has also been identified as the Islamic revivalism period, the *dakwah* (missionary work) movement, or the reflowering of the Islam movement. The 1970s witnessed a shift in attitudes among Muslims and their conception of religious piety, particularly in Malaysia, Singapore and Indonesia. Of interest are the Muslims that live in the urban centres, where there is excessive rural-to-urban migration either for work (especially in factories) or for education (in campuses in Kuala Lumpur). This period coincided with the industrialization policies undertaken by then Prime Minister Mahathir Mohamad in Malaysia and President Suharto in Indonesia.

Global and local events shaped notable changes in the Islamic outlook among Southeast Asian Muslims. First and foremost, the Iranian revolution, which happened in 1979, shaped the political discourse of Islam in the region. There was greater interest among Muslim youth in Southeast Asia to apply Islam in its entirety to society, in line with Islam as *ad deen*, or a way of life. They were inspired by Ayatollah Khomeini—a 79-year-old cleric in Iran—who toppled the powerful, Westernized Shah of Iran. There was a greater interest that Islamic political governance led by an *ulama* (religious scholar) could be the saviour of the Muslim world suffering from colonialism, world wars, and fragmented leadership.

On the other hand, there was also the competing influence of the Saudi Arabian government, strengthened by their sizeable revenue of petrol dollars. Saudi Arabia represents Sunni Islam as opposed to its geopolitical rival Iran which represents Shi'ism. Southeast Asian Muslims are largely Sunnis, but their practice is not as puritan compared to Saudi Arabia's brand of Wahhabi-Salafism. Historically, Southeast Asian Muslims respected local cultural norms while remaining steadfast in religious principles. During this period, the influence of Wahhabi-Salafism prompted Southeast Asian Muslims to question their local cultures and to evaluate whether these were Islamic, despite Islam's principled respect towards local cultures.

During the Islamic resurgence period, there was a discursive shift in political, social, and cultural aspects of Malay life. For the first time, there was interest in political Islam and the creation of an Islamic state in Southeast Asia. These were championed by some political parties in Malaysia and Indonesia, though non-existent in Singapore. There was also a movement to establish an Islamic government based on shariah in Southeast Asia, particularly Indonesia and Malaysia. Some political parties in Malaysia championed Islamic laws in the form of *hudud*, which includes stoning, amputation and whipping as modes of punishment. They understood the literal meanings of punishments indicated in the Quran but not their underlying principles and contexts.

There were also visible changes in terms of the lifestyles of Muslims since then. A greater movement towards halal certification led to major fast-food restaurants like McDonald's, A&W and KFC seeking it. The call for a more shariah-compliant lifestyle was also extended to other facets of social life, including education, entertainment and culture. Central to the resurgence discourse was creating an Islamic alternative to Western life, which has been criticized as secular and lacking religious principles. There was also a marked change in terms of how people dressed. For instance, there was greater veiling among Muslim women, to the extent that some observers wrongly attributed it to the Arabization of Malays.

Over the last two decades, the Malay-Muslim middle class has expanded significantly. This is due to a higher percentage of them graduating from universities. According to the 2020 census, between 2010 and 2020, the percentage of Malay graduates almost doubled from 5.5 per cent to 10.8 per cent. The number of Malays with diplomas and professional qualifications increased from 9.8 to 16.9 per cent. In the same vein, the number of those attaining below secondary school leaving qualifications also declined (Department of Statistics 2021).

Similarly, Muslim spending power has also increased globally, which led them to travel more. Singapore Muslims have joined the pack as travellers, and some have also ridden on the expansion of halal travel by providing services to cater to global Muslim travel needs. Mohammad Hashim Kamali (2021) wrote about specialized tour agencies and websites that offer halal travel services, such as HalalBooking.com. He also differentiates halal tourism from Islamic tourism. According to Mohammad Hashim, halal tourism refers to activities, facilities, actions, and objectives according to Islamic teachings, and even non-Muslims can also participate in halal tourism. On the other hand, Islamic tourism involves *niyyah* (intention): earning God's pleasure or *ibadah*. If a Muslim goes to Mecca intending to steal, their pilgrimage no longer falls in the purview of Islamic tourism. There is a misconception of Muslim tourism that it only involves worship. However, it is practically similar to conventional tourism, with tourists shopping most of the time (Mohamad Hashim 2021).

Haj as an Industry

Muslim practices often necessitate travel. Some are obligatory, and others are encouraged. Two key examples are the haj and *umrah*. Additional forms of travel are encouraged for various purposes, such as *hijrah* (migration), *dakwah*, commercial activities, and learning or sojourn. The haj is the fifth pillar of Islam, one of the five obligatory acts of worship. The other four pillars are *shahadah* (the declaration of faith), *solat* (praying five times a day), *saum* (fasting during the month of Ramadan), and *zakat* (the payment of the annual tithe). The haj is obligatory for all Muslims if they can afford to take the journey, monetarily and physically. Additionally, the haj can be performed as often as possible in one's lifetime, though the first is obligatory (Majeed 1995). In other words, the haj is not compulsory for poor and sick Muslims. The annual haj pilgrimage can only happen once yearly and has to be conducted in Mecca (in modern-day Saudi Arabia) and not elsewhere.

Muslims are required to perform rituals at certain sites and commemorate the life of prophets Abraham and Muhammad. The primary rituals associated with the haj include the *wuquf* at Mount Arafah, where all pilgrims will gather to reflect and pray; the stoning ritual in Mina, the stop in Muzdalifah, circumambulation the Kaabah (*tawaf*); and the walks between mounts Safaa and Marwah (also referred to as the *saee*). Moreover, pilgrims must also adopt a state of ritual purity known as *ihram*, symbolized for men by putting on two pieces of unsewn towels. Those in the state of *ihram* are not allowed to put on perfume, shave, quarrel or conduct animal slaughter, among others. The Kaabah is a structure that holds significant importance for Muslims, as Muslims worldwide pray in its direction. Also known as Baitullah (or the House of Allah), it occupies a central place in Islamic worship.

The *umrah*, known as the lesser haj, can be conducted throughout the year. Most rituals performed during the *umrah* are similar to the haj, apart from some omissions. There is no *wuquf* in Arafah, the stoning of *jamrah* in Mina, and the stop in Mudzalifah. However, pilgrims performing umrah must still be in the state of *ihram*.

Most books on the haj and *umrah* focus on the ritualistic aspects, serving mainly as guides for pilgrims. However, some scholars discuss the philosophy of haj. One such book is Ali Shariati's *Hajj* (1974). For example, Shariati spoke of their principles and reasons rather than commenting on the dos and don'ts during the state of *ihram*.

> Now take off your clothes. Leave them at Miqat. Wear the Kafan which consists of plain white material. You will be dressed like everyone else. See the uniformity appear. Be a particle and join the mass; a drop, enter the ocean (Shariati 1974, p. 9).

There are certain things which you are expected to avoid while in the state of ihram. These include any sort of reminders of your business, position, social class, or race. In essence, all worldly matters belonging to the life before Miqat, are tabooed (ibid., p. 17).

The late Indonesian intellectual Nurcholis Madjid also reflected on his journey when he performed the haj ritual. Nurcholis contended that the haj should be performed once in a lifetime, though Muslims can repeat the *umrah* as often as they want. Nurcholis, in his reflections, argues that there should not be any social hierarchy in Mecca. He illustrated this by saying that a driver can speak to police officers as equals, and that Muslims must emphasize the spirit of equality while worshipping in holy sites such as Multazam (the door to the Kaabah), Maqam Ibrahim, Hijr Ismail and others (Nurcholis 1993).

The Haj and Singapore(ans)

Historically, Singapore had been the centre for haj pilgrims travelling from maritime Southeast Asia (today's Indonesia and Malaysia). Singapore was the hub for *kapal haji* (haj ships) since pilgrims outside Arabia could only travel to Mecca by sea (Green and Mohd Raman 2019). Anecdotes from these Southeast Asian pilgrims were often filled with messages of sacrifice and hardship. After all, the haj ritual is a festival that underscores the meaning of sacrifice. Mortality rates of the pilgrims journeying from Singapore to Mecca were also high, and most pilgrims were mentally prepared that they might not return to their families waiting at the Singapore harbour.

Singapore also became an important port for pilgrims. Many shops provided services for haj pilgrims, selling goods required for the haj rituals in Mecca, such as belts for the men to fasten their *ihram* clothes. When the Dutch colonial government restricted the number of pilgrims travelling to Mecca from Java, many also started circumventing this rule by travelling through Singapore. The pilgrims arrived in Singapore in disguise before going to Mecca. In this way, the Dutch colonial government could not track their intent to perform the haj.

Nevertheless, capitalism and marketing entered the haj discourse in the early twentieth century. Many respectable reformers in Southeast Asia were actively writing and teaching in Singapore, which served as the hub of haj and trade. Syed Shaikh Al-Hady was one such reformer. Influenced by the modernist movement at Al-Azhar University in Egypt, Al-Hady tried replicating those ideas in Southeast Asia. He contributed extensively to gender equality and pressed for scientific knowledge to be taught alongside religious knowledge. However, Al-Hady's reformistic ideals were also influenced by capitalism, such as the notion of self-help and market forces. Al-Hady was against Muslims seeing the haj merely as a ritual, arguing, "the purpose of the pilgrimage as intended by God is not to enable or to compel a person to put on a robe and the headgear, and to confer on him the title haji so that he can accept payments for praying upon the dead and for his supplication at the feast for the souls of the dead". Simultaneously, he made contradictory remarks reducing the ritual to a capitalistic, worldly pursuit. He stated, "We dare say that there has never been a greater exhibition on earth…than 'God's exhibition in Mecca,' that is, 'the pilgrimage'" (Shaharuddin 2014, pp. 88–89). This dichotomy reflects the complex interplay between religious tradition and the forces of capitalism during this era.

Developments in the mode of transportation, haj policies, and the growth of Muslim travel in the 1970s changed the nature of pilgrimage, leading to the emergence of the haj and *umrah* industry. Since the 1970s, air travel to Mecca has generally replaced sea travel. The number of haj pilgrims worldwide also surged during this time. By 1982, the Saudi Arabian government had the infrastructure to host 1 million haj pilgrims simultaneously. In 1984, the Saudi Arabian government introduced new policies to decentralize the organization of the haj. One such policy was the requirement for a body representing pilgrims from each country of origin, paired with a counterpart in Saudi Arabia, known as the Mutawwif of Southeast Asian Pilgrims (Muasassah). The Islamic Religious Council of Singapore (Majlis Ugama Islam Singapura, MUIS) became the representative for Singaporean pilgrims (Abdul Rahim 2018). Although haj administration is not explicitly mentioned in the Administration of Muslim Law Act (AMLA)—the legal basis of MUIS' authority towards all Muslims in Singapore—the statutory board took on a more active role in managing the haj due to several unfortunate incidents. Numerous instances occurred when pilgrims could not travel to Mecca at the last minute due to scams or poor management. In 1975, 300 haj pilgrims could not perform the haj and were left stranded at the Paya Lebar Airport as their agency could not get flight tickets. In 1978, 81 haj pilgrims were cheated after their agency misappropriated their deposit. In 1990, 200 haj pilgrims could not travel to Mecca at the last minute since their agency could not secure flights (Abdul Rahim 2018, p. 179). In response to these issues, Singapore adopted the "hybrid" model of haj administration. This model involves travel agents licensed and appointed by MUIS, under the

Association of Muslim Travel Agents, Singapore (AMTAS), to provide services for haj pilgrims.

For Singaporean Muslims today, the cost of performing the haj is about US$10,000 to US$15,000 per person, and the haj season only happens once in the Islamic calendar year. Notwithstanding, there are some financially challenged Malays who cannot afford to perform the haj in their lifetime. The primary obstacle for most Malays intending to conduct the ritual is not so much due to monetary cost but the quota imposed by the Saudi Arabia government. Singapore is granted a quota of 800 to 1,000 haj pilgrims to perform haj in Mecca every year. Consequently, many Malays regularly perform the *umrah*, a lesser or minor pilgrimage to Saudi Arabia, while waiting for their opportunity to participate in the major haj pilgrimage.

While MUIS oversees the administration of haj pilgrims in Singapore, the *umrah* sector is managed by the private sector. Unlike haj providers who require accreditation by MUIS and have their packages annually approved by the body, *umrah* operators have more autonomy. Before the COVID-19 pandemic, there were forty-six agencies under AMTAS, which has since reduced to thirty-three (Rosli 2022). Due to its year-round occurrence and more flexible programmes, the *umrah* sector is more challenging to manage than the haj. In the 1980s and the 1990s, *umrah* packages primarily included visits to Mecca and Medina. Mecca, housing the Grand Mosque Masjidil Haram, is where *umrah* pilgrims perform the necessary rituals. Conversely, Medina, a city five hours from Mecca, is home to Prophet Muhammad's tomb and the world's second-largest mosque, the Prophet's Mosque. It was also the seat of Muhammad's first government after his exile from Mecca (known as *hijrah*). Thus, Mecca and Medina became the obvious choice for *umrah* packages.

The third prominent pilgrimage site for Muslims is the Al-Aqsa Mosque in Jerusalem. Due to historical significance, the mosque, including the Dome of the Rock, is Islam's third holiest shrine after Mecca and Medina. Prophet Muhammad visited Jerusalem before his spiritual ascendency, known as Isra' and Mi'raj. Furthermore, Jerusalem was the initial direction of prayer for Muslims before it was changed to the Kaabah in Mecca. Despite its religious significance, Jerusalem is not as frequented because of ongoing political uncertainty and conflicts between Israel and Palestine. Additionally, unlike Mecca, Jerusalem lacks specific rituals related to pilgrimage. Still, Mecca, Medina and Jerusalem were what many commonly understood as spiritual travel before the popularization of shariah-compliant tourism.

Shariah-Compliant Tourism: *Jejak Rasul*

Haj in Singapore remains organized under a collaboration between MUIS and private entities, necessitated by the Saudi Arabian government's policy requiring states to elect representatives. However, the *umrah* is entirely operated by the private sector and has been subsumed under the broader umbrella of Islamic tourism. Private tour agencies compete with one another to provide services for pilgrims travelling primarily to Mecca and Medina in Saudi Arabia and to Jerusalem in Israel, with packages varying based on duration, destination, accommodation, and flight carriers.

Agencies also creatively market their packages to outdo one another, primarily relying on the commodification of religion. Fealy and White outline that religious commodification rides on the middle-class desire to obtain "moral certainty" through consuming religious products, with agencies adopting multi-level marketing to meet their needs (Fealy and White 2008, p. 4). Agencies openly indicated five-star hotels as part of their packages, driving up costs. To maintain price competitiveness, the agencies use hidden fees that are not stated upfront. For instance, agencies may advertise that the accommodation is close to the grand mosques, only one-to-two-minutes' walk away, implying easy access for worship. However, the hidden costs do not mention the guides (*mutawif*) who assist pilgrims in essential rituals such as encircling the Kaabah. First-time pilgrims unfamiliar with these rituals may have difficulties performing them due to unfamiliarity, but indicating this cost would drive up prices. Some agencies which choose not to hide this additional cost have their packages appear pricier. Conversely, some agencies market their services by featuring charismatic preachers or religious teachers (*asatizah*) with large followings. However, these *asatizah* do not always follow the pilgrims for *umrah*, often delegating such services to ground officials who are not adequately trained to lead rituals in the Grand Mosque.

Islamic tourism has grown into a saturated market, with many agencies offering packages. To diversify, agencies seek to explore new markets and adopt new strategies. One such innovative approach emerged in the 2000s when some Muslim-owned agencies adopted the programme *Jejak Rasul* or Tracing the Footsteps of the Prophets. *Jejak Rasul* was originally popularized by a Malaysian private television channel TV3 which ran a documentary with the same title. In 2021, the TV station ran the 27th edition of the programme, highlighting its popularity (Zaidi 2021). The host discovered places beyond Mecca, Medina, and Jerusalem, venturing into Syria, Jordan, and Egypt. The programme captured the attention of middle-class Malays in Singapore, who could view the documentary through a local channel. Consequently, many agencies began offering packages to other parts of the Middle East in the name of tracing the prophets.

However, the organization of *Jejak Rasul* tours has its constraints. The prophets' journeys are mapped based on Islamic perspectives, omitting a holistic historical approach that integrates insights from other civilizations. Moreover, such packages also shun non-Muslim places of worship because they are not considered places of Muslim prophets, often skipping churches or synagogues despite their historical significance in the Middle East. Other important historical sites are also avoided, either because they do not align with the tour agencies' conception of *Jejak Rasul*, because visiting them would inflate the costs of packages or both. For example, some agencies skipped Petra when visiting Jordan, arguing that no prophets had stepped foot there. The real reason for this is visiting Petra would require an additional day for the package and additional entrance fees to the scenic, historical and heritage sites. Petra is a world heritage site that was once the capital city of Nabatean. Among its stunning highlights is a city carved out of rocks and gorges. Moreover, the historical narrative presented in these tours tends to be one-dimensional. For example, in the Quran, there is the story of the cave of the seven sleepers, where seven pious men slept for 300 years before awakening to a changed world. Some believe the cave is in Jordan, but there are also contending views that it is elsewhere. Similar disputes exist regarding the location of Noah's Ark, prophets' tombs, and the dwellings of pious individuals. Consequently, these tours, while providing a historically driven spiritual journey based on theology, may overlook historical nuances.

Shariah Compliance in Non-Muslim Environments

The expansion of shariah-compliant tourism significantly advanced around the 2010s. By this time, the Malay middle class had expanded considerably, though a sizeable percentage of the Singapore underclass remained largely Malays. The number of university graduates and the proportion of PMETs (professionals, managers, executives and technicians) grew. Now, the appetite for travel goes beyond the Muslim countries of the Organization of Islamic Cooperation (OIC), as well as Muslim-majority countries such as Turkey, the United Arab Emirates (UAE) (particularly Dubai and Abu Dhabi), Qatar, Egypt and Morocco.

Interestingly, Iran is not a popular destination due to a lack of direct flights from Singapore, and also because of ideological differences. Iran is predominantly Shi'a, while Malays are mostly Sunni. Other Muslim-majority non-Middle East sites popular among Muslim travellers include Kashmir in Pakistan and Bosnia. This trend excludes Singapore's Muslim-majority neighbours of Malaysia and Indonesia, as Singaporeans also travel there for education, shopping, visiting families and friends, and work, rather than simply for religion. Malays either patronize Muslim-run agencies for their travel needs, or non-Muslim-owned agencies that provide shariah-compliant services.

Figure 9.1 shows the trend of the Global Muslim travel index. This map does not specifically refer to Singapore Muslim travel patterns but global Muslim travel patterns. Since data on Muslim travel remains a shortage, it also indicates the trends in Singapore. Southeast Asia remains a popular destination, along with Saudi Arabia, the UAE and Turkey. Other popular destinations include Egypt, Pakistan, Oman and Morocco.

There is also a growing trend for Malay middle-class travel to non-Muslim majority or non-OIC countries. The more popular destinations for Muslim travel are Australia, the United Kingdom, and France, followed by the United States, Canada, and South Africa (see Figure 9.2). These destinations may not represent the general trend for Southeast Asian Muslims due to the long distance. However, countries in the Pacific, such as South Korea and Japan, are also becoming popular destinations for Muslim travellers from Singapore.

To cater to the rising demand for shariah-compliant travel experiences, Muslim tour agencies have also stepped up their marketing efforts, promoting halal tourism to these non-Muslim countries. Generally, South Korean soft power has attracted youths to travel there. However, compliance with shariah principles mainly hinges on two issues: the provision of halal food and a commitment to observing prayer timings and spaces. Notably, shariah-compliant hotels are not a part of the package.

On the other hand, Singaporean tourism agencies see the opportunity to tap into global Muslim travel and position Singapore as a halal hub. In Singapore, informal "halal" streets have emerged, supplemented by guidebooks highlighting halal eateries. These resources extend beyond food and mosques, featuring halal spas and entertainment outlets, which defines halalness. Some halal spa packages employ marketing language like "hijab-friendly" to resonate with their target audience. In addition, the Singapore Tourism Board regularly publishes a Muslim visitor guide, and the booklet is also available for free download. The booklet shows the location of halal

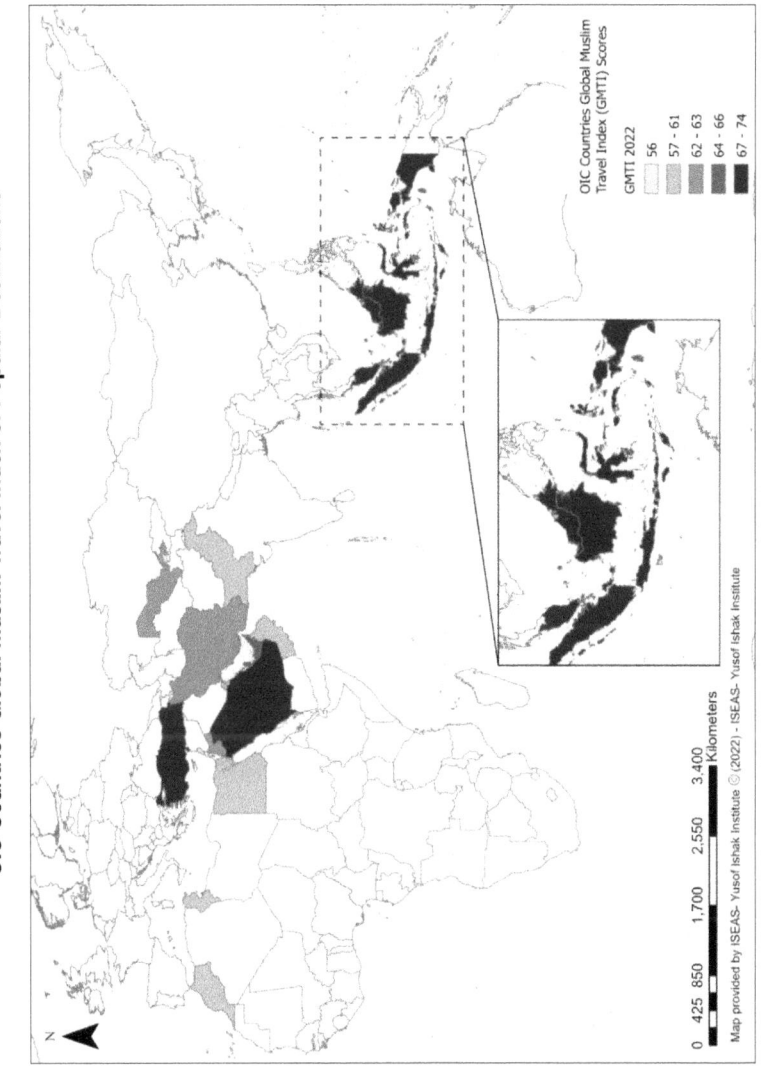

FIGURE 9.1
OIC Countries Global Muslim Travel Index of Popular Destinations

Source: CrescentRating (n.d.).

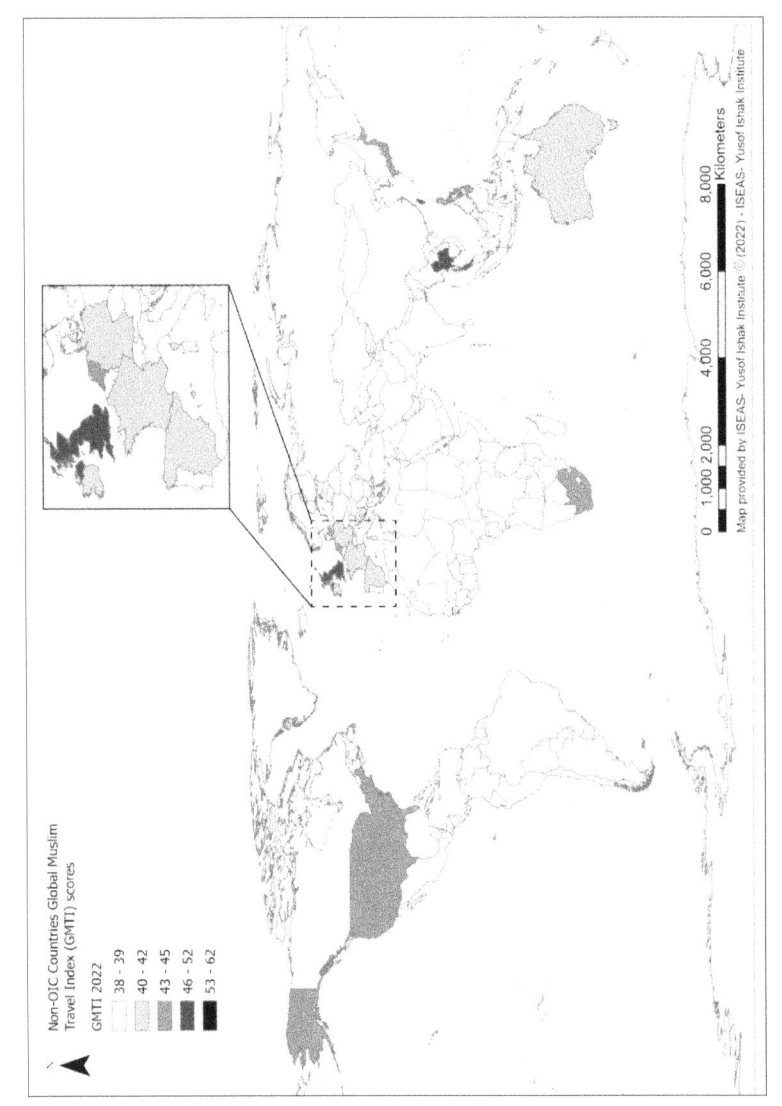

FIGURE 9.2
Non-OIC Countries Global Muslim Travel Index of Popular Destinations

Source: CrescentRating (n.d.).

food outlets and prayer places in Singapore's key tourist streets. The booklet also explains how individuals can identify establishments serving halal food: stores displaying the MUIS halal logo indicate that they are halal-certified by MUIS, and stores carrying a non-MUIS halal sign are not certified but still serve halal food (likely to be Muslim-owned). The booklet mentioned that Singapore is a Muslim-friendly destination by indicating: "Singapore has a vibrant and diverse multicultural community with accessible Muslim-friendly facilities such as Halal food and prayer spaces in popular areas. This guide helps you identify the different Halal-certified and Muslim-owned establishments around the city" (VisitSingapore.com 2020)

Travel itineraries catering to shariah-compliant travel will indicate "Muslim-friendly" on their website's advertisements. Looking deeper at their itineraries, the difference between Muslim-friendly and "unfriendly" establishments is the provision of halal food. Additionally, Muslim-friendly establishments also do not serve alcohol or liquor.

In Singapore, another growing trend caters to the evolving taste of the Muslim middle class, redefining traditional concepts of space and spirituality. In the past, spirituality was tied to mosques and sacred pilgrimage sites, including tombs. Today, contemporary practices have expanded the concept of spirituality, integrating it into new spaces such as halal cruises. Typically, such halal cruises include programmes such as congregational prayers and sermons.

The Commodification of Religion or Islamizing Commodity

Lukens-Bull (2008) writes about the commodification of religion and the "religification" of commodities. This trend does not only apply to Muslims but also to other faiths as well (Sinha 2008). There are two observable trends when speaking about shariah-compliant tourism. First is the commodification of religion, where Islamic rituals such as the haj, prayers and food are treated as commodities. There is excessive marketing and advertisement of these rituals, and one aspect of commodification is dividing these into tiers based on consumers' ability and willingness to pay (Lofton 2017). There is also significant branding involved in the commodification of shariah-compliant tourism. This commodification aligns with the emergence of halal labels on *tudung* and other markers of Muslim modesty (Bucar 2017).

Conversely, there is also the trend towards Islamizing commodities. The ethos of this trend is similar to the Islamizing project undertaken by revivalists in the 1970s and 1980s, which sought to apply Islamic principles to various domains, including laws, state, economics, sciences and music (Norshahril 2012b). During this period, Malay cultural practices were also under significant pressure to cease because they were deemed incompatible with the normative conceptions of religion. Under this trend, halal cruises and halal spas represent examples of religiously neutral practices and products given the Islamic label. Other examples include shariah-compliant dolls (Shirazi 2016).

Going forward, these trends will continue to shape the discourse on shariah-compliant tourism. However, to stay competitive in this niche market, providers of these services will have to innovate. Recent developments include a phenomenon described as the celebrification of tourism, where *umrah* packages now include celebrities. For example, *asatizah* such as Liyana Musfirah—who has reached celebrity status—started running some *umrah* packages. Aside from *asatizah*, other well-known personalities such as singer Hady Mirza and comedian Haryani Ismail, have also offered to be part of *umrah* packages. In Singapore, other innovative *umrah* packages have also emerged, including riding bicycles to sacred places, which leaves one to wonder whether the reasons are purely to save the environment or to mimic ancient modes of transportation where camel riding made travel possible. Another interesting offering is the combination of *umrah* with other interests like football. Singapore Muslims can now perform their *umrah* rituals in Saudi Arabia and proceed to spectate football in the United Kingdom (Rosli 2022).

Lately, tour agencies are not the only actors promoting shariah-compliant tourism. This discourse has expanded beyond marketing strategies to impact broader discussions on religiosity. Social media influencers have now popularized distinguishing halal travel from secular travel. Halal or shariah-compliant trips constantly make up the postings of these celebrities, showcasing how they overcome concerns about halal food, prayer schedule and modesty. These might be personal postings, but they impact the shariah lifestyle discourse despite being invented traditions.

Conclusion: Gaps in Shariah Tourism

Shariah-compliant tourism is a subset of the resurgence discourse to create Islamic lifestyles. Besides halal food and observing prayer times, which have become the main ingredients of shariah-compliant tourism, the other aspects of this tourism include marketing and branding strategies like shariah commodities and meeting expectations of shariah compliance. Given the extensive development of halal certification in the food and beverage industry (as demonstrated in some other chapters of this volume), it is clear there is no turning back or scaling down. The industry serves millions of Muslim consumers, and it caters to a necessity, food. Gradually, halal certification encroaches into other social and religious domains, including commodities, entertainment, children's toys and more (Shirazi 2016).

In conclusion, this chapter addresses some of the gaps in shariah-compliant tourism. These criticisms mirror those raised by scholars on other dimensions of shariah and the halal industry (Fischer and Jammes 2020; Hoesterey 2016; Mohamad Hashim 2021; Norshahril 2012a; Shaharuddin 2006; Shirazi 2016). Most of these criticisms revolve around the need for standardization in halal certification. On the theological front, criticisms of the shariah lifestyle often touch on exclusivism and how the lack of understanding impacts multicultural, modern and cosmopolitan societies. The majority of critical examinations, however, primarily focus on Islamic finance and the economy.

Nonetheless, gaps related to shariah tourism extend beyond standardization and theological debates. The discourse around shariah compliance must be measured against shariah principles in the form of its core values and principles. This comparison is not only restricted to haj, as the chapter has underscored. Overall, haj and *umrah* scams are few in Singapore and do not constitute a major problem, unlike in some Muslim countries. Furthermore, such incidents are actively addressed by MUIS. However, excessive marketing has created some misconceptions about the ideal haj package, including packages led by *asatizah* with Asatizah Recognition Scheme (ARS) certification, a form of occupational licensing before a religious teacher can preach directly. Possessing preaching accreditation does not necessarily denote competency in leading haj and *umrah* packages, as the latter requires familiarity with Mecca and Medina and networking with counterparts. Moreover, overemphasizing the theological dimensions of haj and *umrah* conceals poor, inefficient and careless planning. For example, the inability to secure accommodation or flights for pilgrims has been ascribed to "*takdir*" or fate, and pilgrims were asked to *sabar* (be patient) as these are part and parcel of pilgrim life. The inability of pilgrims to come to Mecca has been incorrectly equated to God not welcoming them to the holy lands.

Shariah tourism also does not explore complete learning or inter-civilizational engagement. For example, an excessive focus on tracing the prophet's footsteps limits exposure to other sites that are perceived as less significant from an Islamic perspective. A visit to Jordan centred on Islamic tourism will focus on tombs of prophets and pious people but neglect Petra, deemed overly touristy and less relevant to Islamic history. Petra also requires additional payment. Some packages may even deliberately shun churches and synagogues. For instance, some Muslims did not want to enter Jewish sites like the Wailing Wall. Moreover, historical, geographical and scientific explanations of sites are often inadequately explored and explained, sometimes reduced to magical and irrational explanations. Few Islamic tours visit locations such as Nazareth, where Jesus was born, to understand the birthplace of Jesus. Thus, there is often a lack of comprehensive understanding of the inter-civilizational experience; the approach is usually evangelical or *dakwah*-based, glorifying certain parts of Islamic history.

Shariah-compliant tourism also fails to address the higher costs involved. Comparing Muslim-friendly packages with other tour packages to places like Spain, the itinerary is almost similar, including visits to cathedrals and churches, but only offering halal food, and observing prayer timings as a differentiator.

Fortunately, shariah-compliant tourism remains more discursive than fully operational, implying that these gaps can still be rectified. Shariah-compliant tourism must address its environmental impact to feature itself as an alternative to conventional tourism. It has not addressed poor tourism standards and issues related to food wastage. Singapore has a movement towards Zero Waste, but such debates have not been integrated into shariah-compliant or conventional tourism. There is still wastage from halal buffets, including during Ramadan. Tourism must also be sensitive towards less privileged communities. To date, shariah compliance has primarily focused on rituals, symbolic elements and operational aspects: halal certification, slaughtering method, *hijab*, and halal ingredients. The guidance and leadership from authoritative bodies are crucial to prevent the emergence of new traditions that seek to exclude or partition halal tourism from the rest of the tourism industry.

Note
1. Not all Malays are Muslims, and vice-versa. Based on the 2020 Singapore Census, 0.4 per cent of Malays declare they do not have any religion, while 98.8 per cent of Malays are Muslims. 23.4 per cent of Indians also declare themselves as Muslims.

References
Abdul Rahim Saleh. 2018. "Haj Aspirations: A "Hybrid" of Public and Private Models for Singapore". In *Fulfilling the Trust: 50 Years of Shaping Muslim Religious Life in*

Singapore, edited by Norshahril Saat, pp. 179–98. Singapore: World Scientific and Majlis Ugama Islam Singapura.
Azhar Ibrahim. 2014. *Contemporary Islamic Discourses in the Malay-Indonesian World: Critical Perspectives*. Petaling Jaya: SIRD.
Bourdieu, Pierre. 1984. *Distinction: A Social Critique of the Judgement of Taste*. Cambridge: Harvard University Press.
Bucar, Liz. 2017. *Pious Fashion: How Muslim Women Dress*. Cambridge: Harvard University Press.
Chandra Muzaffar. 1987. *Islamic Resurgence in Malaysia*. Petaling Jaya: Fajar Bakti Sdn Bhd.
CrescentRating. n.d. "Global Muslim Travel Index". https://www.crescentrating.com/halal-muslim-travel-market-reports.html (accessed 21 October 2022).
Department of Statistics. 2021. *Singapore Census of Population 2020*. Singapore Census of Population 2020.
Fealy, Greg, and Sally White. 2008. "Introduction". In *Expressing Islam: Religious Life and Politics in Indonesia*, edited by Greg Fealy and Sally White, pp. 1–12. Singapore: Institute of Southeast Asian Studies.
Fischer, Johan, and Jérémy Jammes. 2020. "Introduction: Muslim Piety as Economy: Markets, Meaning and Morality in Southeast Asia". In *Muslim Piety as Economy: Markets, Meaning and Morality in Southeast Asia*, edited by Johan Fischer and Jérémy Jammes, pp. 1–28. London: Routledge.
Green, Anthony, and Mohd Raman Daud. 2019. *Kapal Haji: Singapore and the Hajj Journey by Sea*. Singapore: World Scientific.
Hoesterey, James Bourk. 2016. *Rebranding Islam: Piety, Prosperity and A Self-Help Guru*. Stanford: Stanford University Press.
Lofton, Kathryn. 2017. *Consuming Religion*. Chicago: University of Chicago Press.
Lukens-Bull, Ronald. 2008. "Commodification of Religion and the 'Religification' of Commodities". In *Religious Commodification in Asia: Marketing Gods*, edited by Pattana Kitiarsa, pp. 220–34. New York: Routledge.
Majeed, Fatima. 1995. *The Hajj: The Law and The Rationale*. Singapore: Ze Majeed's Publishing.
Mohamad Hashim Kamali. 2021. *Shariah and the Halal Industry*. New York: Oxford University Press.
Noor Aisha Abdul Rahman. 2020. "Religious Resurgence amongst the Malays and Its Impact: The Case of Singapore". In *Alternative Voices in Muslim Southeast Asia: Discourse and Struggles*, edited by Norshahril Saat and Azhar Ibrahim, pp. 33–66. Singapore: ISEAS – Yusof Ishak Institute.
Norshahril Saat. 2012a. "Countering Utopianism: Alatas and the Muslim Resurgence of the 1970s". *RIMA: Review of Indonesian and Malaysian Affairs* 46, no. 1: 105–25.
———. 2012b. "Islamising Malayness: Ulama Discourse and Authority in Contemporary Malaysia". *Contemporary Islam* 6, no. 2: 135–53.
———. 2014. "The Ulama, Thought-Styles, and the Islamic State Debate in Contemporary Malaysia". *Studia Islamika* 21, no. 1: 47–73.

Nurcholis Madjid. 1993. "Haji itu Transformasi Hidup" [Hajj is a Life Transformation]. In *Haji: Sebuah Perjalanan Air Mata* [Hajj: A Journey of Tears], edited by Mustofa Hasyim and Ahmad Munif. Yogyakarta: Yayasan Bentang Budaya.

Rosli A. Razak. 2022. "Permintaan Umrah Meningkat; GSA Baru Tawar Pengalaman Unik" [Demand for Umrah Increases; GSA Just Offered Unique Experience]. *Berita Mediacorp*, 16 October 2022. https://berita.mediacorp.sg/singapura/berita-permintaan-umrah-meningkat-gsa-baru-tawar-pengalaman-unik-699556 (accessed 21 October 2022).

Shaharuddin Maaruf. 2006. "Religion And Utopian Thinking among the Muslims in Southeast Asia". In *Local and Global: Social Transformation in Southeast Asia: Essays in Honour of Professor Syed Hussein Alatas*, edited by Riaz Hassan, pp. 315–31. Leiden; Boston: Brill.

———. 2014. *Malay Ideas on Development: From Feudal Lord to Capitalist*. Petaling Jaya: SIRD.

Shariati, Ali. 1974. *Hajj*. Free Islamic Literatures.

Shirazi, Faegheh. 2016. *Brand Islam: The Marketing and Commodification of Piety*. Austin: University of Texas Press.

Sinha, Vineeta. 2008. "'Merchandizing' Hinduism: Commodities, Markets and Possibilities for Enchantment". In *Religious Commodification in Asia: Marketing Gods*, edited by Pattana Kitiarsa, pp. 169–85. New York: Routledge.

VisitSingapore.com. 2020. *Your Muslim Visitor Guide to Singapore*. https://www.visitsingapore.com/content/dam/desktop/global/about-singapore/traveller-information/guides/muslim-visitor-guide-singapore.pdf (accessed 9 June 2023).

Zaidi Mohamad. 2021. "Jejak Rasul Bawa Sisi Berbeza" [Jejak Rasul Shows a Different Side]. *Berita Harian* (Malaysia), 16 April 2021. https://www.bharian.com.my/hiburan/selebriti/2021/04/807346/jejak-rasul-bawa-sisi-berbeza (accessed 21 October 2022).

10

MARKETING AN "ISLAMIC LIFESTYLE" IN SINGAPORE
The Case of Islamic-Inspired Products in Kampong Gelam

Sharifah Afra Alatas and Nadirah Norruddin

INTRODUCTION

A 2021 report by the *Straits Times* on economic expansion and the growth of the middle class in Southeast Asia suggests that "the percentage of people in the region categorized as middle-class is expected to more than double from 24 per cent today [2021] to 51 per cent in 2030—or from 135 million people to 334 million people". It further said that "by 2022, the ASEAN middle class is expected to wield over US$300 billion in disposable income (Michalak and Mealy 2021). Muslim communities in individual Southeast Asian countries have not been excluded from this growth, and there is also a growing Muslim middle class in the region. They can be found in countries with a Muslim majority, such as Malaysia and Indonesia, but also in countries with a Muslim minority, such as Thailand and Singapore.

Singapore's Muslims constitute 15.6 per cent of the population, most of whom are Malay (Department of Statistics Singapore 2020). Over the years, there have been discussions about the socio-economic growth of the Malay/Muslim community and how Singapore's Malays/Muslims have become more affluent and wealthier. In 2002, then Minister-in-charge of Muslim Affairs, Yaacob Ibrahim, remarked that "there is an emerging Malay/Muslim middle class with the resources to do things for themselves" (Ministry of Information, Communications and the Arts 2002). In 2019, he expressed concerns that there could be a class divide within the community and warned that "we can't afford for the middle class to peel apart from the entire Malay/Muslim community" (Lai 2019). From these statements, it is clear that the Malay/Muslim middle class has lain firmly within Singapore's growing middle class.

However, entry into the middle class does not just result in a change in one's consumption habits or socio-economic position. It could also mean a change in one's approach to religion. As Abdur Rozaki et al. put it, the interaction between religion and socio-economic class means that "Islam is not merely a set of values but also a set of principles legitimating the way to socialize, image branding, self-marketing either for personal needs, or the needs of communities in projecting religious identities in the public sphere" (Abdur Rozaki et al. 2019, p. 7).

One of the consequences of this growing Muslim middle class is the increase in demand for consumer goods and services which comply with the shariah. In the 1980s, this demand manifested in the form of the provision of services such as Islamic banking and insurance, educational institutions, and halal certification for food. More women also began to cover their hair with a *tudung* or *hijab*. However, over the decades, demands have changed, and anything from facial products to electronics can be slapped with a halal label. Furthermore—and in line with the assertion above—the community's demands are no longer about a product's or service's shariah compliance. Instead, their demands are about living an "Islamic lifestyle" in line with a certain image or identity. According to Oxford Languages, lifestyle can be defined in two ways: (1) "the way in which a person lives"; and (2) the denotation of "advertising or products designed to appeal to a consumer by association with a desirable lifestyle".

With these definitions in mind, this chapter will examine Kampong Gelam—a historical district in Singapore—as a case study of an emerging "Islamic lifestyle". More specifically, it serves as a survey of the Islamic-inspired products that are sold in the district. In doing so, we explore how these products are illustrative of the moulding or marketing of a particular lifestyle among middle-class Muslim consumers. The growth and marketing of such a lifestyle are reflective of the commodification of religion. This is manifested in the sacralization of mundane, everyday products, and at the same time, the desacralization of heritage and religion. We also discuss the possible consequences of this phenomenon not only for the Muslim community specifically but also for Singapore's larger multicultural society.

History of Kampong Gelam

Kampong Gelam has a centuries-long history. Prior to the British colonization of Singapore in 1819, the district was home to the Malay royal family. However, the signing of a treaty between the British East India Company and the Sultan and Temenggong of Johor in 1819 set the wheels in motion for changes to the district. With the signing of the treaty, Singapore became home to a trading post, and Kampong Gelam was designated as an ethnic enclave for Malays and Arabs. As commercial activities continued to expand, so too did the population. The district eventually became home to a multi-ethnic community, comprising Chinese and Indians, in addition to Arabs and other Malay immigrants from Malaysia and Indonesia.

In the past, each street in Kampong Gelam was identified by the types of trade or communities that inhabited the area. For example, Bussorah Street used to be known by three different names: Kampong Kaji for its significance as a departure point for the haj pilgrimage, Jalan Sultan for housing royal families, and Kampong Tembaga after the coppersmiths who plied their trade at the lower end of the street (National Heritage Board et al., n.d.). Meanwhile, Arab Street used to be populated by Javanese migrants and pilgrims and was referred to as Kampong Jawa by Malay speakers, Jawa Koi in Hokkien, and Flower Street in Tamil (ibid.).[1] As a whole, the district was once a flourishing area where the streets were lined with bookshops, perfumeries, songkok makers, rattan weavers, blacksmiths and tombstone makers. The artisans and tradespeople hailed from different parts of the region, from China to Java. The multi-ethnic and multi-religious enclave of Kampong Gelam was thus a showcase for the eclectic combination of cultural forms and influences.

On 15 April 1910, British municipal commissioners renamed streets in the area after prominent cities of the Muslim world. These included Bussorah Street, Muscat Street, and Kandahar Street. There are two lasting impacts to renaming the streets as such. Firstly, naming the streets after mainly Middle Eastern cities replaces the diversity of people and trades that flourished in the area. Vernacular place names such as Kampong Jawa or Kampong Tembaga thus serve as memories of days gone by, and the streets are no longer reflective of the different parts of the Muslim world from which people came. Secondly, replacing vernacular place names with Middle Eastern cities imprints a strong Arab identity on the area.

Nevertheless, new industries have emerged since the mid-2000s. Older craftsmen and trades have either gone out of business due to low demand or were displaced by trendy restaurants and boutiques. Today, there are a dozen shops selling goods and knick-knacks from Turkey and the Middle East. There were also once shisha cafes along Bussorah Street and Haji Lane, thus manufacturing an image of Middle Eastern culture in Singapore.[2] However, these businesses are not necessarily new as religious items and imported goods have always been part of Kampong Gelam due to its nature as a port town and an embarkation point for Muslim pilgrims in the archipelago. However, the commercialization and commodification of items from areas that are recognized as Muslim is a developing phenomenon that needs to be considered.

Today, Kampong Gelam's distinct and unique physical landscape has drawn crowds from the world over. Due to the diversity of businesses and trades, the district holds a spectrum of associations for different groups of people from past to present, young and old. On a website advertising the area, it is referred to as a "mecca for culture, entertainment, food and arts" (One Kampong Gelam n.d.). The area's colourful narratives and redevelopment are an inviting call for entrepreneurs who are keen to explore the halal market in Singapore. This is illustrated by the upward trend of stores, boutiques, and halal restaurants and cafes around the area which attract a niche audience of pious and trendy Muslim youth looking for halal alternatives to Western lifestyle goods and services. Apart from form and function, Muslims may be more encouraged to consume a product that appears to enhance piety, aid religious rituals, and/or allow them to follow the path of Prophet Muhammad. As such, there are two important factors taken into consideration when making consumption choices: (1) that the goods are safe and halal for consumption; and (2) that they bestow blessings, also referred to as *berkat* or *barakah* (Nilan 2008, p. 45). As will be discussed in this chapter, the goods found in Kampong Gelam are marketed as products which fulfil such considerations.

Kampong Gelam is therefore a site that showcases an "Islamic lifestyle" despite conjuring contrasting images to different groups of people across time. The present-day landscape signals the continuation of colonial map-making as the area is now established with a strong Middle Eastern influence. A focal point of Kampong Gelam is Muscat Street, as it forms a gateway to Sultan Mosque. A trading hub from the 1800s to the early 1900s, Muscat Street was always buzzing with traders and Muslim devotees who frequented the mosque for their daily prayers.

Kampong Gelam was gazetted as a conservation area on 7 July 1989. The areas that are demarcated as protected or which carry the designation "heritage site" appear to be more authentic in the eyes of visitors, as they are secured from further physical damage or loss of cultural value. In November 2012, a multimillion-dollar collaboration between Singapore's Urban Redevelopment Authority and the Muscat Municipality of Oman to revamp Muscat Street was completed (*Straits Times*, 9 November 2012). The highlight of the project is the granite arches with decorative Omani carvings which were built at both ends of the street. It is complemented by eight murals depicting significant items in Omani history and culture such as a dagger and ship. The redevelopment was a highly momentous occasion as it signalled strong and active state efforts to produce a Middle Eastern landscape, in contrast to what was previously a strongly Javanese-inhabited area.

Governments are responsible for sponsoring and shaping tourist assets, fashioning and promoting narratives, and portraying images of a country both to its own citizens and to tourists. With the existence of the murals and arches, as well as street names, it is ingrained in the psyche of visitors to Kampong Gelam that the district holds a distinctly Middle Eastern—and therefore—an "Islamic" character.

Islamic-Inspired Products

Oud (Agarwood) Scent

As discussed above, one of the industries that has been historically present in the Kampong Gelam area is the perfume industry. With a total of three branches, the most popular perfume business in the vicinity is Jamal Kazura Aromatics. While they first set up shop in 1933 as a general trade store run by the family, by the 1970s they evolved into a perfume business which specializes in creating a wide variety of non-alcoholic Arabic perfumes which are made from ingredients such as sandalwood, frankincense, and most significantly, oud, also known as agarwood. Over the years, oud-scented perfume has become undeniably popular among Muslims and is readily available in areas which are predominantly occupied by Muslim-owned businesses.

However, the use of oud has evolved to the extent that it is used in daily-use products such as wet wipes (Figure 10.1), deodorant, air fresheners, body and hand wash, and humidifier oil.[3] Some of the perfumes and air fresheners which contain oud are also marketed as reminiscent of Islamic holy sites such as the Prophet's Mosque in Medina, or the Great Mosque in Mecca, Saudi Arabia. For example, some of the products are named "Rindu Raudhah" (Figure 10.2), which refers to a sense of longing for the *raudhah*, an area in the Prophet's Mosque near Prophet Muhammad's tomb.

Food

There is also a food industry which has evolved according to the demands of Muslim consumers. One of the food products that is highly consumed

FIGURE 10.1
Arabic Perfume Wet Wipes

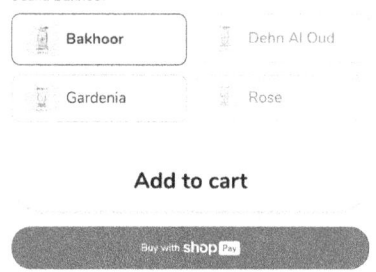

Source: Swing Muslim Lifestyle Store.

FIGURE 10.2
"Rindu Raudhah" Products

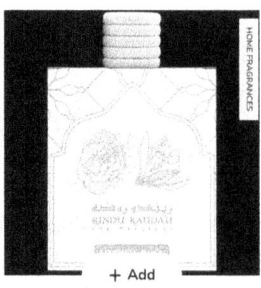

Source: Swing Muslim Lifestyle Store.

by Muslims is *sidr* honey, which has become so popular to the extent that it is available in honey straws. The other product would be black seeds (commonly known as *habbatus sauda*). These black cumin seeds have become highly popular as an alternative remedy for various medical diseases due to a saying of the Prophet Muhammad which states that the seeds are a remedy for all ailments except death (*Sunnah.com*, n.d.). The seeds are commonly available on their own or in the form of capsules. However, it is not uncommon now to find the seeds in honey (Figure 10.3), and they are even available in the form of a body wash (Figure 10.4).

Aside from specific food products, some of the restaurants in the Kampong Gelam vicinity are also reflective of a developing "Islamic lifestyle". A walk through Kampong Gelam easily reveals that the area is populated with restaurants selling Turkish or Arab cuisine. Among these restaurants are also a few restaurants which sell Malay food. However, not all the Malay restaurants specialize in Malay cuisine. Upon closer inspection of the menus at some of these restaurants, the cuisine of the food they serve tends to be mixed even though they market themselves as Malay restaurants. One such example is Padi. Located on Bussorah Street, Padi's website states that they offer "authentic Malay food". While their menu certainly indicates an array of Malay food, it is not the only type of cuisine they offer. For example, their dessert menu includes Turkish and Arab favourites such as baklava

FIGURE 10.3
Black Seed Honey

Source: Swing Muslim Lifestyle Store.

FIGURE 10.4
Black Seed Body Wash

Hab Shifa Black Seed Revitalizing Body Wash

Source: Swing Muslim Lifestyle Store.

and kunafe, while their main menu also includes Turkish and Arab dishes, in addition to Western dishes (Figure 10.5).

A short conversation with one of the employees at the restaurant revealed that the diversity of the menu is deliberate, as they wish to cater to large families with members of different generations who dine there. Based on their observations, younger generations tend to be more inclined to Western cuisine, while the older generations are inclined to Turkish and Arab food. Another restaurant with a similar marketing tactic is LePak @ Rayz, which is located just a few doors down on the same street.[4] With an undeniably Malay-sounding name, their menu is similar to Padi's, and they market themselves as offering Malay Arabian or MalArab cuisine (Figure 10.6). They also offer Western and Chinese dishes.

Hygiene and Personal Care

As evident from the oud-scented body wash and deodorant, the desire to lead an "Islamic lifestyle" even permeates one's personal care products. This is evident from the fact that hygiene goods that are packaged and marketed as shariah-compliant are readily available in lifestyle stores around Singapore.

FIGURE 10.5
Padi's Dessert Menu

DESSERT

PISANG GORENG $5.50
with kicap cili api

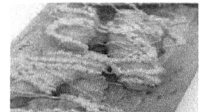
PISANG GORENG CHEESE $8.50

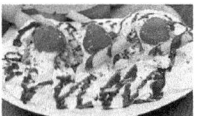
PISANG GORENG SPLIT $17.90
with vanilla ice cream topped with
whipped cream, chocolate syrup and
cherries

PISANG GORENG CHOCOLATE $8.50

KUNAFE $12.90
KUNAFE WITH ICE CREAM $14.90

BAKLAVA (3PCS) $11.90

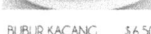
BUBUR PULUT HITAM $6.50   BUBUR KACANG $6.50

Source: Padi @ Bussorah.

FIGURE 10.6
Lepak @ Rayz's "MalArab" Cuisine

Source: Facebook.

One such example is the *daun bidara* bath soap (Figure 10.7), which—in addition to its cleansing properties—claims to rid one of black magic and the evil eye. In traditional Malay medicine, *daun bidara*, or the jujube plant (*Ziziphus Mauritian*) is known to provide relief for individuals plagued by unexplainable diseases related to charms and sorcery. Moreover, the *daun bidara* has also been cited in *hadith* (narrations of Prophet Muhammad), attesting to its potency. The availability of this product signals demand from consumers who seek specific items that are not readily available in pharmacies or convenience stores. It also demonstrates that consumers are easily swayed by such Islamic-inspired products, even if their effectiveness is not backed by scientific evidence.

There are also products meant for oral hygiene. For example, there are *miswak* products. A *miswak* is a twig made from the arak tree (*Salvadora persica*) which is native to the Middle East. It is used as a natural toothbrush and is often regarded as one of the first forms of oral hygiene. However, the *miswak* has added significance for Muslims, as Prophet Muhammad was said to have spoken about its benefits and even used it himself. For Muslim consumers, its association with the Prophet thus lends an

FIGURE 10.7
Daun Bidara Bath Soap

Source: Halal Lifestyle SG.

added layer of credibility to the product. Furthermore, there is scientific evidence which emphasizes the benefits of using a *miswak*. Apart from the toothbrush itself, there are other products derived from the arak tree, such as *sewak* toothpaste and mouthwash. One of the toothpaste products is marketed as approved by the US Food and Drug Administration (FDA). According to the US FDA, any approval from them means that "the agency has determined that the benefits of the product outweigh the risks for the intended use" (FDA 2022). This seal of approval lends legitimacy to the safety of the product. As for the mouthwash, there are some Muslims who may seek alternative goods to allay their fears of consuming certain prohibited products, such as alcohol in readily available mouthwash products in the mass market.

However, what is interesting to note is that in a separate description of the *sewak* toothpaste and mouthwash as part of a "Fight COVID Gift Pack" (Figure 10.8), the mouthwash is described with the following benefits: "antiseptic, anti-inflammation, anti-bacterial, kill more than 60 per cent germs, increase immunity against virus, healing properties, chemical-free, fluoride-free." While most of these characteristics apply to regular mass-produced mouthwash products, it is striking that a product which reportedly kills more than 60 per cent of germs is marketable in contrast to the former which reportedly kills 99 per cent of germs.

FIGURE 10.8
Fight COVID Sewak Gift Pack

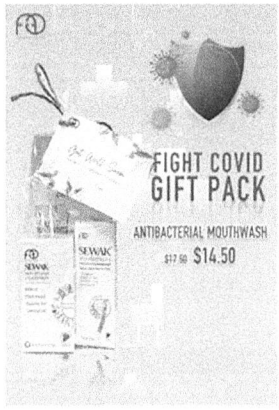

Source: Swing Muslim Lifestyle Store.

Another hygiene product is the *sejadah* and fabric spray (Figure 10.9), which is an anti-odour spray for prayer mats and other products made out of fabric. The spray is available in four different scents, including an Oriental oud and roses scent. However, seeing that the spray serves the same purpose as other fabric sprays, and can be used on other fabric products such as sofas, beds, and carpets, one may question the necessity of such a product, and whether it plays any function in honouring religious practice, or in this case, prayer. Furthermore, in contrast to regular fabric sprays, the spray is not marketed as anti-bacterial, and is simply meant to be a refreshing mist. Moreover, it is an expensive product, going for S$14.90 for a 140 ml bottle, whereas an 800 ml bottle of regular Febreeze spray goes for S$5.95.

Yet another range of personal care products—specifically for Muslim women—are the products meant for their *hijab*. These are the *hijab* awning starch and the *hijab* wash from the brand Niqa. While the *hijab* wash is simply meant for cleaning the *hijab*, removing stains, and making sure it smells fresh, the awning starch serves the purpose of keeping the awning of the *hijab* in shape. Both these products are also sold together in a Niqa travel pack, alongside an instant stain remover. When marketed specifically as a travel pack, the product could have a specific type of Muslim woman

FIGURE 10.9
Sejadah and Fabric Spray

Source: Halal Lifestyle SG.

in mind. She could be a middle-class consumer who is mobile, always on the go, and loves travelling. Amid her busy schedule, she places utmost emphasis on the appearance of her *hijab*.

Stationery and Knick-Knacks
Stationery and other related knick-knacks with a religious twist have also become more popular as part of an emerging "Islamic lifestyle". For example, Swing Muslim Lifestyle Store carries stationery products such as bookmarks (Figure 10.10), notebooks (Figure 10.11), planners, and sticky notepads with an "Islamic" theme. These products may have religious expressions such as *"Bismillah", "Insha Allah",* and *"Masha Allah"* printed on them, short verses from the Quran, excerpts from the *hadith*, or general expressions with religious connotations, such as "dream *doa* do". There are also other knick-knacks such as keychains, mousepads, badges, car decals, and tote bags with similar religious expressions. Yet again, these products are designed with a specific demographic in mind and are more of a symbol of conspicuous consumption. Not only do they have a religious twist, but they are also pleasing to the eye, designed with attractive fonts, patterns and colours. Furthermore, they have the added feature of religious expressions. By imbuing a religious character in otherwise mundane goods, such products take on an entirely different meaning for Muslim consumers. While consumers may believe that these products bring them spiritual

FIGURE 10.10
Wooden Bookmarks with Quranic Verses

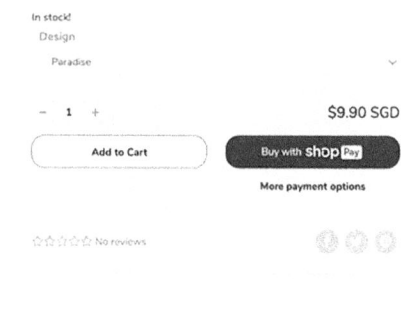

Source: Swing Muslim Lifestyle Store.

FIGURE 10.11
Notebook with Hadith

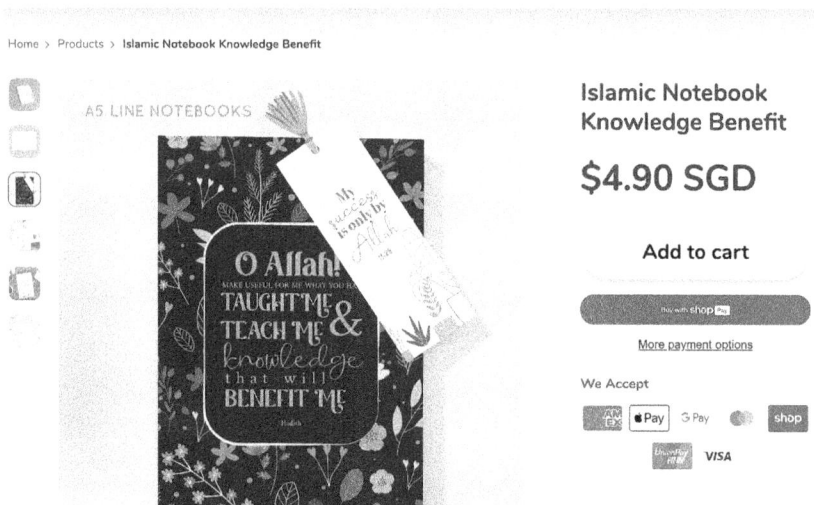

Source: Swing Muslim Lifestyle Store.

benefits, it is worth pointing out that such products are a manifestation of the commodification of religion for capitalistic reasons. By imbuing a religious character in otherwise mundane goods, such products take on an entirely different meaning for Muslim consumers.

Quran and Accompanying Services and Tools
There have also been developments in the way Qurans are produced. For example, they are designed in such a way that a reader is able to read the Quran thematically. These themes are identified either through pages that are printed in different colours, or through sticker tags on the edges of the pages. While Swing Muslim Lifestyle Store sells both these types of Qurans, there are also businesses which offer the tagging service itself. For example, Deen Dunya, an "Islamic Lifestyle Store" which has its flagship store in Kampong Gelam, allows customers to order a regular Quran, and to top up the purchase with the tagging service, which they can have in either English or Malay (Figure 10.12). Additionally, for a few extra dollars, they may wish to customize the Quran by adding their name to its cover. Apart from Deen Dunya, there are other stores in Singapore which offer

FIGURE 10.12
Quran Tagging with Add-On Name-Customization Service

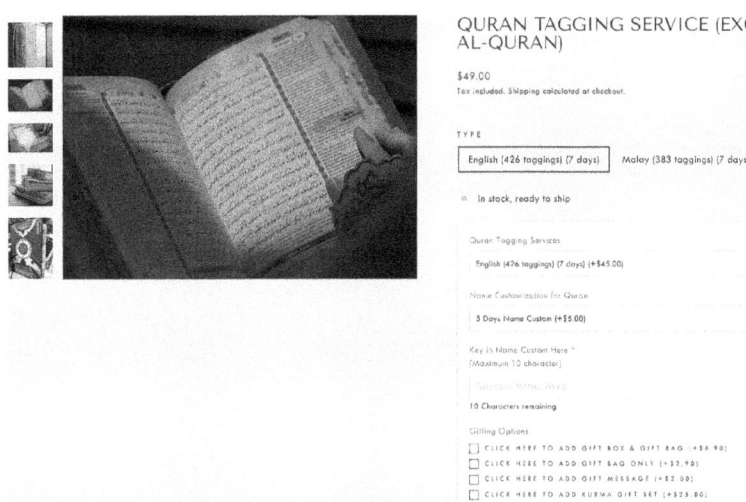

Source: Deen Dunya.

the tagging service, such as Al-Hiqma Souq, and the online store Al-Quran Tagging.Sg.

Apart from the tagging and thematic organization, Qurans are also available separately for men and women. For example, the Quran available for sale in Swing Muslim Lifestyle Store that is marketed for men and which also has tags (Figure 10.13) is described as one which "describes men's affairs, such as prayers, attitudes, roles, and life stories of male figures in the Quran, such as the prophets". Similarly, the Qurans that are available for women are designed in such a way that they emphasize the themes that are relevant to women and tell the stories of prominent female figures. What is also interesting to note is that in the description of the product, it is stated that the Quran was checked and approved by the Malaysian Ministry of Home Affairs (Kementerian Dalam Negeri, KDN). There is also a sticker of the Malaysian Coat of Arms on the Quran, which proves this certification. This certification may be necessary for some consumers to ensure the validity of the translation and interpretation provided in the Quran, thereby providing a source of relief for them.

When reading the Quran, it is not uncommon for some to use a pointer instead of using one's finger to guide them through the words.

FIGURE 10.13
Quran for Men

Al-Quran Tagging Zip : Al Amin Edition (199 Tags)

Source: Swing Muslim Lifestyle Store.

With the advancement of technology, some may also play an audio recitation simultaneously while reading. However, there have been further technological advancements, and there is now a new type of tool to assist with the recitation of the Quran. Also approved by KDN, this new tool is a digital pen which plays an audio recitation of the Quran simply by touching any part of the page of the Quran that the pen is sold with. For example, if one were to use the pen to touch the beginning of a particular verse, the pen would play the audio of the chosen verse. The digital pen is available at Swing Muslim Lifestyle Store and is sold as a set together with a Quran and a few other books on Islam, such as on prayer and daily supplications. However, this is only a "standard" set, as there is also a "VIP Edition" (Figure 10.14) which comes with additional items, such as an organizer bag, an exclusive box in which to keep all the items, index cards, a set of earphones, a warranty card for the pen, a USB cable and charger for charging the pen, and a bag to keep them. Effort has thus been put into designing an exclusive set of the digital pen and Quran.

FIGURE 10.14
Quran Digital Pen, VIP Edition

Source: Swing Muslim Lifestyle Store.

For Kids

Apart from products which are marketed specifically towards men and women respectively, there are also products which are made specifically for children. Aside from adults, children (and their millennial parents) are a big consumer market to be tapped into. Similar to the *hijabi* dolls which are available for young Muslim girls, there are numerous products available for children of all ages which are part of a growing "Islamic lifestyle". These products introduce Islam into children's daily lives, beyond their engagement in religious rituals. For example, "Kaabah Bricks" is a Lego-inspired toy that allows one to reshape the bricks of a Kaabah to form animals that are featured in the Quran (Figure 10.15). It also familiarizes children with different parts of the Kaabah, and the set comes with a book which tells the story of Prophet Ibrahim, who built the Kaabah. The toy is therefore both fun and educational for young Muslim children. There are also puzzles which teach children about important landmarks and stories in Islamic history. For example, there is a 3D model puzzle of the Prophet's Mosque which also comes with a book about the mosque, and a pop-out

FIGURE 10.15
Kaabah Bricks Set

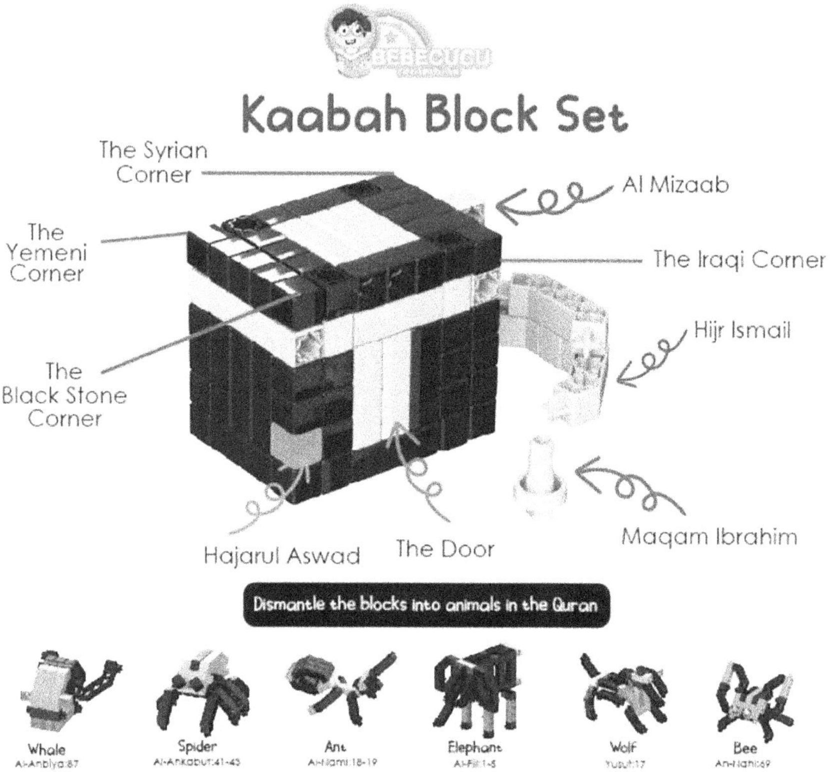

[Kaabah Block Set diagram with labels: The Syrian Corner, Al Mizaab, The Yemeni Corner, The Iraqi Corner, Hijr Ismail, The Black Stone Corner, Hajarul Aswad, The Door, Maqam Ibrahim. Below: "Dismantle the blocks into animals in the Quran" — Whale (Al-Anbiya:87), Spider (Al-Ankabut:41-43), Ant (An-Naml:18-19), Elephant (Al-Fil:1-5), Wolf (Yusuf:17), Bee (An-Nahl:69)]

Source: Swing Muslim Lifestyle Store.

map telling the story of the twenty-five prophets who are mentioned in the Quran. There are also colouring sets which teach children about the pillars of Islam, or which illustrate verses from the Quran, which can be coloured in.

These products are illustrative of the culture of inculcating the consumption of "Islamic" products from a young age. It is therefore worth asking if such a culture will have an indelible impact on future generations and their consumption patterns. It is not unlikely that this may happen, as nostalgia is a fundamental aspect of identity construction. Growing up and playing with certain toys incites pleasant memories, causing one to seek similar items in the future for themselves and their children. Consequently, "the resulting desire for things of the past has made nostalgia a major driver in the contemporary marketplace generally, and particularly for children's toys" (Brookfield 2012, p. 62). Ultimately, toys are "adult creations that are presented to children" (Baxter 2016, p. 12).

Evolving Trends

The rising popularity of the products introduced above is illustrative of evolving trends among Muslims in Singapore. For example, in the late 2010s, a number of local scholars and community leaders were concerned about the trend of Arabization, or the tendency to be inclined to Arab culture at the expense of local culture. However, some scholars pointed out that Arabization itself should not be a threat; the worry was that Singaporeans' interest in Arab culture and the perception that it was the more authentic "Islamic culture" would result in them becoming exclusivist in their religious understanding and social interaction with both Muslims and non-Muslims (Norshahril 2018). There were also concerns about ideological influence from the Middle East, such as in the form of ideologies like Wahhabism, Jihadism, or that of the Muslim Brotherhood.

At present, Arabization may not be as big a concern as it used to be. Instead, trends have evolved, and increasing concern has arisen as a result of the preoccupation with shariah compliance, or the necessity of having halal logos on various types of products. For example, halal-certified eyeglasses were launched in Indonesia in 2019. In Malaysia, proposals were made to have separate trolleys for halal and non-halal products in supermarkets (*Malay Mail,* 19 January 2016), and the state of Kelantan announced in 2021 that they plan to build a shariah-compliant aquatic centre to host the Malaysia Games (Sukma) in 2026 (*The Vibes* 2021). Interestingly, the director of the company which produced the eyeglasses in Indonesia said that "halal certification will also add value and enhance the branding of our products in the eyes of the Indonesian people" (*Jakarta Post,* 6 November 2019). This therefore illustrates how important halal branding has become.

However, what is observable now is that the concern is no longer about explicit halal branding or shariah compliance, but that it is about lifestyle. As discussed at the beginning of this chapter, a lifestyle does not just refer to the way a person lives, but also to the creation of products which are made to appeal to consumers who wish to keep up with current trends—or lifestyles. It is this latter definition which applies to the growing demands for the products discussed above. It is a conscious process of production and marketing in which everyday products such as toiletries and stationery are made to have an "Islamic" image, to the extent that the consumption or possession of such products leads to the cultivation of a particular lifestyle or identity concerning what it means to be a middle-class Muslim consumer. The desire for an "Islamic lifestyle" has its roots in the Islamic resurgence of the 1980s, which also saw the expansion of a Muslim middle class within the context of increasing urbanization and industrialization, and the subsequent concerns that arose as a result of these phenomena.

The widespread availability of such goods in both physical and online stores indicates that there is substantial demand for such products. However, similar to the other products discussed above, these goods are costlier than other similar products which are mass-produced, and are therefore indicative of a middle-class consumer base. When contrasted with the ideals of moderation and self-restraint in Islamic teachings, the emergence of conspicuous consumption poses a paradoxical situation as piety becomes closely tied to consumerist behaviour, and sometimes even extravagance.

Furthermore, the perceived and carefully crafted identity of Kampong Gelam as the site of an "Islamic lifestyle" also leads to discussions on what should or should not be permitted in the area. For example, the contestation between Kampong Gelam's trendy façade and its "Islamic" character was manifested in a belly dancing debacle that occurred in the area in December 2022. A belly dancer was spotted performing for diners at Derwish Turkish Restaurant located along Bussorah Street, mere steps away from Sultan Mosque. The performance sparked ire among some members of the local Muslim community who felt that it was in poor taste due to the restaurant's location and the wider sanctity of the area (Ong 2022).[5] The response of the community thus underlined the public's perception of Kampong Gelam's distinctly Islamic spirit with Sultan Mosque as a distinct signifier of this image. Similarly, it is not uncommon to hear of calls to ban the sale of alcohol in the area, as well as general grievances about Kampong Gelam's identity as a "hipster" area.[6]

Conclusion

The discussion above ultimately leads to the observation that there is a process or phenomenon of sacralizing profane or mundane objects. This occurs through the commodification of sacred or religious symbols. This explains the existence of products such as building blocks to build and dismantle the Kaabah, or notebooks, bookmarks and sticky notepads with religious expressions or verses of the Quran printed on them. At the same time, there is a desacralization of religious space through the replacement of heritage with capitalist enterprise, as in the case of the Kampong Gelam district. Although sacralization and desacralization are processes that occur in reverse to one another, they are both tied together by the same phenomenon, which is the commodification of religion, whether in the form of symbols or spaces.

Additionally, beyond the Islamic-inspired products themselves, the general atmosphere of the Kampong Gelam area and the fact that it is meant to be a heritage site solidifies the idea that it is not just a confusingly Arabized area, but a place that embodies this particular "Islamic lifestyle". This leads to questions about what forms of heritage or lifestyle we seek to preserve or promote, or what we are doing with the sites that we designate as conservation sites. Furthermore, the growth of this lifestyle is not just restricted to Kampong Gelam. As discussed above, shops similar to Swing Muslim Lifestyle Store are available in other areas in Singapore where there are large numbers of Muslims, and the products are also readily available online.

This gives rise to further questions about whether there should be concerns about this development. On the surface, it might appear as though there is nothing harmful about having a beautiful notebook with a Quranic verse on it, or air fresheners which smell like the tomb of Prophet Muhammad. However, on a deeper level, this could be harmful in the long term, as the continuous desire for such products and the continued commodification of religious symbols could lead to a loss of spirituality. One may also ask: to what end? Are there other products which these producers might seek to sacralize? And would the continued production and consumption of such goods meant for Muslims lead to any distance between the Muslim community and other communities? Furthermore, could it lead to eventual ringfencing of what it means to be Muslim or to live an "Islamic lifestyle"?

Notes
1. Javanese women had flower shops along the five-foot way, giving rise to the Tamil name.
2. As a result of its adverse health effects, the government enforced a ban on the distribution and consumption of shisha in 2014.
3. Links to the products of which pictures are not provided in the main text can be found in the list of references at the end of the chapter. While many of the products discussed here are available at Swing Muslim Lifestyle Store, the authors are in no way criticizing the store for their selection of products.

4. They recently rebranded and are now Lepak @ Sultan.
5. The restaurant apologised and clarified that a regular patron organized the dance in appreciation for a party the restaurant had hosted earlier. They went on further to resolve the misunderstanding regarding her outfit: "Our patron who had performed had worn a fitted skin-coloured vest draped on the outside in a belly-dancer costume. It would be unthinkable for us to allow a scantily dressed dancer in front of the shops, knowing our proximity to the mosque."
6. Since the early 2000s, there have been calls from Muslims shop owners in Kampong Gelam to ban the sale of alcohol in the area. This movement gained momentum in 2012, and a Facebook page named "Alcohol Free Kg Glam Conservation Area" was created. See also Hidayah Amin's (2022) letter to the *Straits Times* on the promotion of Kampong Gelam as a hipster neighbourhood.

References

Abdur Rozaki, Suhadi, Bayu Mitra A. Kusuma, Abd. Aziz Faiz, Wiwin S. Aminah Rohmawati, M. Ali Usman, and Wening Fikriyati. 2019. *The Trajectory of Middle Class Muslim in Southeast Asia: Religious Expression in the Public Sphere of Indonesia, Malaysia, and Thailand*. Yogyakarta: Institute of Southeast Asian Islam.

"Alcohol Free Kg Glam Conservation Area". Facebook. https://www.facebook.com/kgglamalcoholfree (accessed 5 June 2023).

Baxter, Jane Eva. 2016. "Adult Nostalgia and Children's Toys Past and Present". *International Journal of Play* 5, no. 3: 230–43.

Brookfield, Molly. 2012. "From American Girls into American Women: A Discussion of American Girl Nostalgia". *Girlhood Studies* 5, no. 1: 57–75.

Deen Dunya. "Quran Tagging Service". https://deendunya.co/products/quran-tagging-service (accessed 26 May 2023).

Department of Statistics Singapore. 2021. "Census of Population 2020 Statistical Release 1: Demographic Characteristics, Education, Language and Religion". Singapore: Department of Statistics, Ministry of Trade and Industry. https://www.singstat.gov.sg/-/media/files/publications/cop2020/sr1/cop2020sr1.ashx (accessed 26 May 2023).

Halal Lifestyle SG. "Belafi Sejadah & Fabric Spray". https://halal-lifestyle.sg/product/sweetdreams-spray (accessed 26 May 2023).

———. "What Is Daun Bidara Bath Soap?". Facebook. 18 June 2021. https://www.facebook.com/watch/?v=158697182945139 (accessed 26 May 2023).

Hidayah Amin. 2022. "Why Promote Kampong Glam Historic District as Hipster Neighbourhood?". *Straits Times*, 25 March 2022. https://www.straitstimes.com/opinion/forum/forum-why-promote-kampong-glam-historic-district-as-hipster-neighbourhood (accessed 5 June 2023).

"Is It Really 'FDA Approved'?". FDA. https://www.fda.gov/consumers/consumer-updates/it-really-fda-approved (accessed 26 May 2023).

Jakarta Post, The. 2019. "Ministry Launches Indonesia's First Halal-Certified Corrective

Glasses". 6 November 2019. https://www.thejakartapost.com/news/2019/11/06/ministry-launches-indonesias-first-halal-certified-corrective-glasses.html (accessed 27 May 2023).

Lai, Linette. 2019. "Yaacob Ibrahim Warns of Potential Class Divide in Malay Community". *Straits Times*, 10 October 2019. https://www.straitstimes.com/singapore/yaacob-ibrahim-warns-of-class-divide-in-malay-community#:~:text=Yaacob%20Ibrahim%20warns%20of%20potential%20class%20divide%20in%20Malay%20community,-Professor%20Yaacob%20Ibrahim&text=SINGAPORE%20-%20There%20is%20a%20risk,to%20help%20the%20rest%20succeed (accessed 26 May 2023).

"LepakatSultan". *Facebook*. https://www.facebook.com/LepakAtSultan (accessed 18 May 2023).

Malay Mail. 2016. "Ministry Mulls Guidelines to Segregate Halal, Non-Halal Trolleys in Supermarkets". 19 January 2016. https://www.malaymail.com/news/malaysia/2016/01/19/ministry-mulls-guidelines-to-segregate-halal-non-halal-trolleys-in-supermar/1043957 (accessed 27 May 2023).

Michalak, W. Michael, and Marc Mealy. 2021. "Go 'Glocal' to Grow in Asean". *Straits Times*, 11 January 2021. https://www.straitstimes.com/opinion/go-glocal-to-grow-in-asean (accessed 26 May 2023).

Ministry of Information, Communications and the Arts. 2002. "Speech by Assoc Prof. Yaacob Ibrahim, Acting Minister for Community Development and Sports, Minister-in-charge of Muslim Affairs, at Department of Malay Studies Seminar, 'The Malay/Muslim Community in Singapore: Bridging Gaps and Widening Options (Are We Boat Builders?)', Held at AS7, National University of Singapore on 18 April 2002, at 4.00pm". Singapore Government Press Release, Media Division, Ministry of Information, Communications and the Arts, 2002. https://www.nas.gov.sg/archivesonline/data/pdfdoc/2002041802.htm (accessed 25 May 2023).

National Heritage Board et al. N.d. "Kampong Glam: A Heritage Trail". Singapore: National Heritage Board, Moulmein-Kallang GRC and Whampoa SMC CCCs, Malay Heritage Centre, The Malay Heritage Foundation. https://www.nhb.gov.sg/~/media/nhb/files/places/trails/kampong%20glam/kgglamtrail.pdf (accessed 23 May 2023).

Nilan, Pamela. 2008. "Muslim Media and Youth in Globalizing Southeast Asia". In *Media Consumption and Everyday Life in Asia*, edited by Youna Kim, pp. 45–58. New York: Routledge.

Norshahril Saat. 2018. "Arabisation and the Threat to Singapore Culture". *Today*, 14 August 2018. https://www.todayonline.com/commentary/arabisation-and-threat-singapore-culture (accessed 27 May 2023).

One Kampong Gelam. n.d. "Immerse Yourself in the Unique Experiences of Kampong Gelam". https://visitkamponggelam.com.sg/ (accessed 5 June 2023).

Ong Su Mann. 2022. "Kampong Glam Restaurant Apologises to Muslim Community for Belly Dance Performance Near Sultan Mosque by 'Almost Naked' Dancer". AsiaOne, 27 December 2022. https://www.asiaone.com/singapore/kampong-glam-restaurant-apologises-muslim-community-belly-dance-performance-near-sultan (accessed 5 June 2023).

Padi @ Bussorah. "Menu". https://quandoo-assets-partner.s3-eu-west-1.amazonaws.com/partner/uploads/7edf57d9-7990-464e-82e6-7f437be1efae/MD-document-3bf0ecfb-d68a-492d-b2fe-8d35255b790b.pdf (accessed 18 May 2023).

Straits Times, The. 2012. "The Charm of Oman in Kampong Glam". 9 November 2012.

Sunnah.com. N.d. "Sahih al-Bukhari 5687: (7) Chapter: (To Treat with) Black Cumin (Nigella Seeds)". https://sunnah.com/bukhari:5687 (accessed 26 May 2023).

Swing. N.d. "30 Yemeni Sidr Honey Straws (1 Pack)". https://swingstore.com.sg/products/30-yemeni-sidr-honey-straws-1-packed?_pos=3&_sid=861422167&_ss=r (accessed 26 May 2023).

———. N.d. "Al-Quran Tagging Zip: Al Amin Edition (199 Tags)". https://swingstore.com.sg/products/al-quran-tagging-zip-al-amin-edition-199-tags?_pos=1&_sid=9b6d7d082&_ss=r (accessed 26 May 2023).

———. N.d. "Al-Quran Muslimah: Rainbow Pages (A5)". https://swingstore.com.sg/products/al-quran-muslimah-rainbow?_pos=1&_sid=edc4e55c7&_ss=r (accessed 26 May 2023).

———. N.d. "Habbatul Barakah Black Seed Honey—160g". https://swingstore.com.sg/products/habbatul-barakah-black-seed-honey-160g?_pos=2&_sid=67829eaad&_ss=r (accessed 26 May 2023).

———. N.d. "Islamic Notebook Knowledge Benefit". https://swingstore.com.sg/products/islamic-notebook-knowledge-benefit?_pos=1&_sid=5590b1132&_ss=r (accessed 26 May 2023).

———. N.d. "Kaabah Bricks Set". https://swingstore.com.sg/products/kaabah-block-set?_pos=1&_sid=4370acd43&_ss=r (accessed 26 May 2023).

———. N.d. "Niqa Travel Pack". https://swingstore.com.sg/products/niqa-travel-pack (accessed 26 May 2023).

———. N.d. "Oud Deo—200ml (3 Scents)". https://swingstore.com.sg/products/oud-deo-oriental-200ml?_pos=1&_sid=376ab8580&_ss=r&variant=40056150163521 (accessed 26 May 2023).

———. N.d. "Oud Hand & Body Wash—500ML (6 Scents)". https://swingstore.com.sg/products/oud-hand-body-wash-500ml (accessed 26 May 2023).

———. N.d. "Swing Mini Badge (24 Designs)". https://swingstore.com.sg/products/swing-badge-assorted-designs?_pos=1&_sid=f1802e3c3&_ss=r (accessed 26 May 2023).

———. N.d. "Swing Sticky Notepad (13 Designs)". https://swingstore.com.sg/products/swing-sticky-notepad-assorted?_pos=1&_sid=05649278f&_ss=r (accessed 26 May 2023).

———. N.d. "Quran Digital Pen Tajwid (A4/A5)". https://swingstore.com.sg/products/a4penqurantajwid?_pos=1&_sid=cc242fc9d&_ss=r (accessed 26 May 2023).

———. N.d. "Quran Digital Pen Tajwid VIP Edition (A4/A5)". https://swingstore.com.sg/products/quran-digital-pen-tajwid-vip-edition-a4-a5?_pos=1&_sid=78b74b5e4&_ss=r (26 May 2023).

———. N.d. "Wooden Bookmarks (13 Variants)". https://swingstore.com.sg/products/wooden-bookmarks?_pos=1&_sid=a5bca62cd&_ss=r (accessed 26 May 2023).

———. N.d. "Ziva 10—Oriental Arabic Perfume Antibacterial Wet Wipes". https://swingstore.com.sg/products/ziva-10-oriental-arabic-perfume-antibacterial-wet-wipes?_pos=1&_sid=abd039808&_ss=r (accessed 26 May 2023).

Vibes, The. 2021. "Kelantan to Build Shariah-Compliant Aquatic Centre for 2026 Sukma". 30 September 2021. https://www.thevibes.com/articles/sports/43167/kelantan-to-build-shariah-compliant-aquatic-centre-for-2026-sukma (accessed 27 May 2023).

Visit Kampong Gelam. "Immerse Yourself in the Unique Experiences of Kampong Gelam". https://visitkamponggelam.com.sg/ (accessed 23 May 2023).

BRANDING ISLAM IN SINGAPORE
Between Representation and Commodification of Muslim Piety

Sheikh Mohamad Farouq and
Nailul Farah Mohd Masbur

Introduction

In 2017, Nike introduced the Pro Hijab, its first *hijab* designed for Muslim female athletes, which has been met with mixed views. While some have lauded the brand for moving towards greater inclusion that accordingly dismantles practical and cultural barriers to empower the agency of Muslim women, the move has also triggered varying degrees of suspicion, claiming it to be a part of the growing trend of the global fashion industry that views Muslim women to be its latest consumer niche. Large retailers have positioned themselves as socially conscious havens for Muslims. However, operating on a profit motive rather than a moral imperative, they attempt to legitimize their aims to tap into the multibillion-dollar potential of the Muslim consumer market (Moore 2018). This conundrum highlights the classic struggle between agency and structure in which there is a need to empower the agency of Muslim women in the face of hegemonic structures such as patriarchy and Islamophobia that target and regulate the expressions of Muslim women. However, the alternative structures afforded to them equally impede emancipatory efforts by selling an imagined feeling of inclusivity that often does more harm than good (Karakavak and Özbölük 2022). This is because it imagines Muslim women as a homogeneous oppressed mass that requires saving. Moreover, this tokenistic inclusion distracts us from engaging in more profound and demanding conversations about meaningful social reform to create an inclusive society centred on ethical imperatives.

Against this backdrop, this chapter explores two key factors contributing to the commodification of piety: neoliberalism and Islamophobia. These phenomena serve as a broader conceptual background to understand the trends discussed in the latter sections of the chapter. It is essential to note that this chapter does not intend to project a normative discourse evaluating the attitudes of religious actors using a legal barometer. Rather it focuses on an exploratory study of how market actors have capitalized on Muslim piety to serve their respective interests rather than benefiting the Muslim community. Interestingly, this phenomenon is not unique to Muslim majority societies but also operates within spaces where Muslims are the minority, such as in Singapore.

Conceptual Background: Neoliberalism and Islamophobia

The Deceitful Inclusion Strategies of Neoliberalism

Neoliberalism originated from the concept of promoting free choice in the market, encompassing the freedom to produce, sell and buy. Initially confined to economics, it gradually expanded its influence to encompass all spheres of life, becoming the doctrine that views market exchange as an ethical framework for all human action. It is crucial to recognize that neoliberalism extends beyond being simply an economic theory; it is a cultural project that subtly and pervasively organizes contemporary life (Harvey 2007). Therefore, in a society that operates within a neoliberal framework, the ability for individuals to attain upward mobility necessitates competitiveness, adherence to financial performance standards, and the capability to deliver tangible outcomes. These terms are commonly encountered in corporate environments, where individuals are expected to strive for progress and success continuously.

Similarly, the Muslim market is not immune to the cultural project of neoliberalism. The term "Muslim market" refers to the potential spending power of approximately 1.8 billion Muslim consumers worldwide. Over the last decade, there has been a strong interest in this market due to the emergence of a growing Muslim middle class and increasing demand for halal products and services within Muslim geographies and beyond. "The State of the Global Islamic Economy 2022 Report" projected the global halal economy to be a multi-trillion dollar industry encompassing many sectors of Muslim life (Salam Gateway 2022). This bodes well with the functioning of a neoliberal system.

The ramifications of neoliberalism on the Muslim market beget a new narrative, which posits that Muslims can be integrated into mainstream society only if they become economic actors. This pontification presents a seemingly emancipatory narrative where the attainment of happiness and security is purely contingent on achieving material success in the form of economic prosperity, fame or influence (Barylo 2016). In this regard, the modest fashion industry is not just an extension but a product of neoliberalism. This raises a couple of critical questions. First, can modest fashion be truly liberating if companies such as Nike produce Muslim-friendly products but have a history of exploiting workers, including underpaid and overworked women and young girls in the global south? (McVeigh 2017). Second, can women on the margins realistically achieve the kind of success dictated by the neoliberal market? Or is this success only attainable for a privileged few? Moreover, what happens to those who refuse to assimilate into this inflexible version of a successful/modern Muslim due to their ethical beliefs?

Interestingly, neoliberalism does not force people to adopt the dominant norms but instead suggests that assimilation is necessary for acceptance and happiness. It is a manifestation of what psychologist Hussein Bulhan refers to as meta colonialism, wherein the influence of colonialism continues to influence the thoughts, behaviour, and identities of colonized peoples even more than the earlier forms of colonialism (Bulhan 2015). The flags of empires may be gone, but the structures and modes of thinking remain. This induced assimilation can also be understood as a response to a climate of fear engendered by the infamous war on terror. According to Mamdani, the war on terror created a new language to typecast and control Muslim political identities. The good-bad Muslim differential was employed to distinguish between "modern, Westernized Muslims" and "primitive, violent Muslims", in order to cultivate the former and target the latter. As a consequence, Muslims are compelled to prove their "goodness" through an acceptance of values that may be ontologically at odds with the ethical impulses of Islam and support the policing of "bad Muslims" (2005, pp. 371–72). This consequently denies Muslims the possibility of formulating an alternative narrative that is based on their lived experiences, which reinforces parochial tropes on Muslimness perpetuated by the Islamophobia industry (Lean 2012).

Understanding Islamophobia
In the context of Islamophobia, discussing this phenomenon's relationship with neoliberalism is essential before moving into further detail. This chapter

contends that Islamophobia should not be viewed merely as anti-Muslim sentiments but as a form of racialization that is simultaneously reductive and malleable (Sayyid 2014). The reductive aspect of Islamophobia manifests in the construction of diverse Muslim communities around the globe as a homogeneous group, characterized by essentialized tendencies towards certain behaviours such as misogyny, violence, incivility, and fanaticism. This reductionist approach reinforces the notion that Muslims must be civilized and assimilate with reductive values associated with progress and modernity, often at the expense of cultural sensitivity. All these are necessary to fit in the image of a good or successful Muslim which was manufactured post-9/11.

The intersection between neoliberalism and Islamophobia reveals a powerful dynamic. Neoliberalism, as the hegemonic ideology, and racialized Islamophobic tropes present Islam, the Muslim world, and Muslims as fundamentally incompatible with the neoliberal values of success. Through the neoliberal lens, experiences of Islamophobic hostility and discrimination are seen as simply the "failure" of the Muslim individual to abide by the ideals of neoliberal society. Thus, there is a natural pull for Muslims to assimilate, be visible, and liberate themselves from these racialized imaginaries but only through the dictates of neoliberalism. This has consequently enabled a new knowledge and proselytizing economy that caters to a rising Muslim middle class seeking to negotiate piety with a modern lifestyle. A notable phenomenon within this context is the emergence of "social media religious influencers", a term coined by Annisa Beta to describe individuals who creatively fuse their interests in spiritual growth with economic gains to engage primarily with young followers online and offline (Beta 2019, p. 7). The following section will elaborate on this topic by analysing a few case studies from Singapore that illustrate the commodification of piety and symbolism to serve the market's interests.

Case Study Analysis

This section will examine specific manifestations of neoliberalism and Islamophobia in Singapore by analysing paid partnerships between Muslim microcelebrities and business corporations. This analysis focuses on microcelebrities or virtual influencers who have commodified their personal brand on social media.

Each subject in this analysis possesses a distinct and visibly Islamic public brand that attracts the attention of many Singaporean Muslims. Their influence is evident from their considerable following on social media. Their personal branding, or the branding of their social media persona, has been used as commercial leverage into Singapore's niche Muslim market through monetizing their social media posts. Paid partnerships occur when the microcelebrity's commercial influence aligns with the business corporations' needs. Since this influence is rooted in their personal branding, engaging in financial collaborations requires these influencers to commodify not only their personal branding but also their piety.

This commodification poignantly illustrates how Muslim piety is permitted in the public sphere when it aligns with the market forces of neoliberalism and conforms to the palatable image prescribed by the Islamophobic industry. As such, by analysing these paid partnerships, this chapter will be able to study how neoliberal and Islamophobic structural forces interact with a Muslim's piety in the Singaporean context.

It is important to note that the arguments presented in this chapter are not directed towards the subject, but rather reflect the broader issue of capitalism's impact on human autonomy. This impact is characterized by the outsourcing of ethical considerations to market forces, as exemplified by Shoshana Zuboff's concept of "surveillance capitalism". It highlights the ways in which Big Tech such as Meta extracts personal data to create new forms of economic value, often without the knowledge or consent of users whose data is being collected (Zuboff 2019).

We selected three case studies of paid partnerships established on the social media platform Instagram. Each case study will include the following components:

A. Analysis of the microcelebrity's personal branding;
B. Analysis of the business corporation involved in the partnership, including its branding, business practices, and motivations for entering the Muslim market vis-à-vis Brand Islam, a "highly successful marketing strategy" that develops and markets "inutile and mundane objects" as Islamic commodities by attaching religious significance to them (Shirazi 2016, pp. 1–7);[1]
C. Analysis of the paid partnership; and
D. Examination of the ethical considerations associated with the partnership.

Case Study 1: Partnership between Masturah Khalid and H&M
The first case study is the 19 April 2022 paid partnership between Masturah Khalid and H&M on Instagram.

A. *Personal Branding Analysis*

Masturah Khalid is a fashion influencer primarily active on Instagram (@masturahkay). She joined the platform in December 2010 and, as of August 2023, has over 12,700 followers. Her high following guarantees her significant appeal and influence, thus solidifying her position as a Singaporean microcelebrity.

Masturah's Instagram page primarily showcases a pastel aesthetic and content comprising meticulously crafted self-portraits and short videos highlighting her fashion choices and daily activities, focusing on fashion and an upper-middle-class lifestyle. The selection of backdrops and activities consistently alludes to a privileged lifestyle associated with a modern, independent woman. In general, Masturah's visual content subliminally promotes the perception that happiness is inherently connected to material success.

Masturah's content can be categorized into two phases: pre-*hijab* and post-*hijab*. Despite maintaining consistency in aesthetics and content focus, a notable change between these phases is an increased number of paid partnerships that commodify her piety or brand as a *muslimah* (Muslim woman). During her pre-*hijab* phase, her partnerships generally did not involve the commodification of her piety as a Muslim. Sponsored content relating to her Muslim identity was limited to Eid/Hari Raya wear, which lacked explicit elements of piety such as modesty or texts calling to Islam, but did contain elements of Malay culture.

> Who else can't wait to raya differently this year? Imagine all the kuehs & cakes you can have to yourself on the first few days now isn't that just splendid. You can do your last minute shopping over @fashionvaletcom with my code "MAYMASTURAH" for discounts. Best time to buy now or during raya because that's when prices are all slashed, sisters. #FVootd #masturahkayxFV I'm wearing @fiziwoo's kebaya sipadan set (Masturah Khalid 2020).

In contrast, several of her post-*hijab* sponsored content incorporates elements of her piety, such as the ritual act of *sahur* (a pre-dawn meal before fasting commences) during Ramadan.

> During Ramadan, fasting from dawn to dusk only means that conservation of energy is important to get through the day, especially when I'm working full time. I'm forever thankful @foodpandasg for helping me save even more time and energy to get by. I get to top up my snacks/food (for sahur) and also food for my fur babies, last minute without even having to leave

the house. I spend time with my family & also do extra personal content work every weekend and I'm loving how I get to pick up food on the way and enjoy the discounts that come with it too! That's a double win for me. Thank you @foodpandasg for having my back always. #foodpandaclub #foodpandasg (Masturah Khalid 2022a).

It is important to note that wearing the *hijab* is a form of visual piety as it signifies the wearer as a Muslim woman. Hence all paid partnerships that commodify her brand as a *hijabi* (woman who wears *hijab*) *muslimah* indirectly commodify her piety. However, Masturah's posts still refrain from explicit calls to Islam (*dakwah*). This absence, whether deliberate or accidental, also contributes to her personal branding.

In summation, Masturah's personal branding during her partnership with H&M portrays her as a *hijabi* fashion influencer who is moderately pious, modern, and materially successful. Hence, it can be deduced that her muted Islamic identity and willingness to commodify her piety have given her access to the neoliberal public space.

B. Partnered Business Analysis

H&M is a multinational retail corporation headquartered in Sweden, with over 4,700 stores spanning 75 geographical markets. Although H&M follows a fast fashion business model which prioritizes profit maximization at the expense of numerous ethical considerations, the company maintains a marketing image that portrays itself as an ethical brand.

H&M's ethical branding initiatives revolve around promoting diversity (Asare 2020) and sustainability (DeAcetis 2021). However, it is crucial to critically assess the meaningfulness and impact of these efforts, considering the possibility of superficiality and inconsistency. H&M's diversity campaign remains within the confines of marketing. While their campaigns visually portray inclusivity by featuring people from diverse cultural and racial backgrounds and, to a lesser extent, offering clothing lines that cater to diverse needs, such as modest wear for Muslim women, the company remains embroiled in cases of labour exploitation in its supplier factories in the Global South. Despite the release of a report by the Centre of Alliance of Labour and Human Rights in December 2015 which exposed H&M's exploitative labour policies, the company has exhibited inconsistent (*Al Jazeera*, 11 January 2023) and inconclusive efforts to implement changes that ensure the protection of its workers (Guilbert 2018).

The corporation also faces ongoing allegations of greenwashing, which refers to false marketing regarding sustainability practices. Furthermore, it remains the second-largest fast fashion business, actively encouraging overconsumption and contributing to retail wastage (Jordan 2022). Hence, a clear disconnect exists between H&M's branding efforts and business practices.

At the time of the paid partnership with Masturah Khalid, H&M continued to operate as a profit-driven multinational corporation embroiled in various cases involving ethical violations.

C. Paid Partnership Analysis

On 19 April 2022, Masturah Khalid uploaded a sponsored post in collaboration with H&M, promoting their 2022 Ramadan collection. The post features a brief video clip in which Masturah showcases several items from the collection while providing a short text promoting the clothing line (Figure 11.1).

FIGURE 11.1
Masturah Khalid's Paid Partnership Reel for H&M's 2022 Ramadan Collection

Note: "Did someone say colour? H&M Ramadhan collection is now available on H&M's SG website & Zalora! Which is your favourite? Thank you H&M for these beautiful pieces" 🤍🤍🤍
Source: Masturah Khalid (2022b).

This 2022 Ramadan collection comprises flowy and colourful tops, skirts, and long dresses. It is more apt to describe the collection as modest than Islamic, as the ethical principles in Islam are not necessarily contingent on specific clothing products or designs. These principles exist as guidelines for good character and virtuous behavioural choices. In this regard, H&M's Ramadan collection is a set of neutral clothing products that are Muslim-friendly but do not inherently represent Islam or the piety of Muslims. However, H&M superficially attached them to a period (Ramadan is a month in the Islamic calendar) with Islamic religious significance and chose a head-covering—hence visually obvious—Muslimah to promote them. These are Brand Islam marketing choices, a deceitful marketing strategy employed to presumably invoke psychological sentiments towards Islam in the bid to encourage consumerism among Muslims.

Furthermore, the collection's release is limited to specific markets with a significant Muslim consumer base. In Singapore, it is only available in H&M Singapore's online store and the online platform Zalora. Zalora is an online shopping platform which provides modest clothing options and is popular among Singapore's Muslim middle class. By partnering with Masturah Khalid as a brand ambassador and collaborating with Zalora, H&M has strategically penetrated and tapped into Singapore's Muslim middle-class market.

H&M's partnership with Masturah is a strategic decision, likely driven by the alignment between their business and personal branding. As mentioned, Masturah's personal brand revolves around being a moderate *hijabi muslimah*. While her outfits are modest, they are not explicitly Islamic, as they are visually attractive and do not completely mask the shape of her figure. Masturah's choice to model this style on a public platform does not strictly adhere to Islamic dressing principles for women in public, which emphasize presentability with muted and shape-masking attire. As a fashion influencer, Masturah has also created high visual accessibility to her personal life and physical appearance. This inherently compromises Islamic principles that promote a modest and private lifestyle, emphasizing a sense of shyness. Moreover, Masturah's commodification of her beauty and fashion choices contradict these principles. Masturah also inadvertently promotes material overconsumption by promoting fast-fashion commodities which contradict Islamic principles of moderate to low material consumption (Abdul-Matin 2012).

Based on this analysis, it can be deduced that Masturah's partnership with H&M, as an economic agent operating within the neoliberal market, involves choices that do not necessarily align with Islamic principles that shape ethical consumer behaviour and representation.

D. Ethical Considerations

The pervasiveness of neoliberalism magnifies its capacity to manufacture our epistemological framework that is fixated on material rewards and satisfaction (Sardar 2022, p. 4). To overcome the ease of impulsive ethical outsourcing to market forces, frequent exercise of conscious and intentional ethical considerations is needed. Accordingly, after analysing this paid partnership, we propose the ethical considerations listed below.

As a microcelebrity, Masturah has a unique influencing capacity. This presents her with the choice to act solely based on self-prosperity, be solely a beacon of positive influence, or alternatively, choose a balance between the two. In the case of this paid partnership, as observers, we cannot presume Masturah's intent. However, since the choices of microcelebrities bear weight over the Muslim community, it is important to continue exploring their ethical responsibilities and encourage them to be more intentional in their decision-making processes. Between the choices of economic prosperity, Muslim representation, and the promotion of an ethically questionable brand and a consumerist lifestyle, where does Masturah's responsibility lie and what should Masturah prioritize?

This analysis presents us with a bleak reality. It appears that in a capitalist society, Muslim women will only be allowed visibility and respect if they are economic agents and are not overly Islamic. It is doubtful that H&M would have partnered with Masturah had she worn a *niqab* (face covering), outwardly engaged in *dakwah*, or did not regularly post self-portraits. Hence, despite the opportunity for representation, the piety of Muslims remains suspect. Muslims are presented with the choice of either obliging to neoliberalism and containing their piety within a commodified and altered boundary or being pushed to the outskirts of society by Islamophobia.

Case Study 2: Paid Partnership between Fatin Afika and Deen Dunya

The following case study is the 18 December 2021 paid partnership between Fatin Afika and Deen Dunya.

A. Personal Branding Analysis

Fatin Afika (@fatinafika) is an *ustazah* (female religious teacher) influencer primarily active on Instagram. She joined the platform in December 2011 and, as of August 2023, boasts over 17,100 followers. The high follower count establishes her as a Singaporean microcelebrity.

The central focus of Fatin's branding revolves around her status as an *ustazah* which grants her religious authority within the Singaporean Muslim community. Analysing her social media content, Fatin's brand of *dakwah* can be characterized as "feel-good Islam". This particular style of *dakwah* emphasizes self-development and focuses on uncontroversial and uncomplex aspects of Islam (Abdullah 2021, p. 151).

> Oh Allah, don't make this dunia our biggest concern. — A beautiful doa, to seek Allah, to not make this worldly affairs our biggest concern. Bcos by doing that, you will just burn a hole in your heart. It's not worth it to do that to yourself for something that is temporary. Indeed, the eternal life, paradise, is not easy. But is definitely worth to fight for. May we constantly have the drive to fight for what matters most (Qul ameeeen) (Fatin Afika 2020).

The enduring popularity of this brand of *dakwah* can be attributed to its palatability across diverse Islamic ideological bents, its easily consumable nature which requires minimal intellectual study, and its fulfilment of the psychological needs of Singaporean Muslims living in a fast-paced capitalist society. The popularity of this brand of *dakwah* partially explains Fatin's popularity among young Singaporean Muslims.

Beyond Fatin's brand of *dakwah*, her popularity can also be attributed to her image as a young, modern and fashionable *ustazah*. By applying Abidin's (2018) theory of microcelebrities to analyse her image branding, Fatin's online presence contains a combination of "everydayness" and qualities of exceptionalism reflected in the content and aesthetic of her social media page. The inclusion of amateur photos and videos capturing moments spent with friends and family, accompanied by diary-like reflections in her captions, fosters a sense of familiarity and trust among her followers.

> Another bestie getting hitched! Getting emotional bcos …. Imagine witnessing each other's milestone for 18 years? 18 years worth of friendship & still counting, masyaAllah. May Allah ease your affairs … Btw, Delicious pizzas are from@mijhub.sg @ashrafcfe.mij (Fatin Afika 2021b).

The qualities of exceptionalism lie in the content which is reflective of her authoritative position as an *ustazah*, the popularity of her personal styling (reflected in her capacity to commercially partner with several fashion brands such as TudungPeople, Deen Dunya, and Sweet Rose Couture), and the visually captivating bright pastel aesthetic of her Instagram page. The combination of "everydayness" and exceptionalism increases her ability to connect with followers while allowing her to maintain an elevated status. This is likely to contribute to attracting and retaining the attention of her predominantly young middle-class followers.

During her paid partnership with Deen Dunya, Fatin's personal branding portrayed her as a moderate, young, modern and attractive *ustazah*. She successfully created a personal brand reconciling a modern middle-class Singaporean lifestyle with a moderate Muslim lifestyle. These qualities, which likely aligned with Deen Dunya's branding and Fatin's influential presence, presented an opportunity for Fatin to commodify her piety and personal branding as a popular Islamic religious teacher.

B. Partnered Business Analysis

Deen Dunya is a local Singaporean brand specializing in Islamic worship commodities and Muslim lifestyle products. Their products' quality, aesthetic appeal, and pricing match the consumption pattern prevalent among Singaporean middle-class Muslims, positioning them as their primary target market. Deen Dunya sells its items through a physical and online store, with its Instagram page (@deen.dunya.sg) boasting over 25,400 followers.

Deen Dunya's branding approach centres on reconciling Islamic principles with modern lifestyles. This concept is reflected in their range of high-quality, exquisitely designed, and beautifully packaged products that encompass both inherently Islamic items such as the Quran and Islamic books, as well as Islamically packaged commodities like modest-wear apparel. A careful inspection of the items leads to the deduction that these items are luxury commodities rather than necessities (Deen Dunya 2023). By enhancing the quality of ordinary Islamic or Muslim-friendly items and marketing them as products essential to the Islamic lifestyle, Deen Dunya has commodified Islamic piety and engaged in the branding of Islam.

Deen Dunya's branding strategy also integrates elements of *dakwah*. Their online campaigns and content incorporate quotes from the Quran or prophetic traditions. Like Fatin, they adopt a "feel-good Islam" approach in their *dakwah* branding. An example of how they utilize *dakwah* elements can be seen in their 4 February 2023 Instagram marketing post of prayer garments. The post features a short visual clip of a beautiful *muslimah* model wearing the product, accompanied by the text.

In the midst of chaos and uncertainty, finding peace within is essential. What better way to do that than by elevating your spiritual practice with our latest, stunning prayer wear (Deen Dunya 2023).

They have strategically utilized "feel-good Islam" *dakwah* to market their product. The marketing campaign also used captivating visuals and upbeat music to attract and retain consumers. Deen Dunya's overall marketing and branding strategy is to interweave Islamic elements with modern marketing strategies, such as beautiful models, vibrant colours, and short videos backed with upbeat music. To optimally navigate the neoliberal market, Deen Dunya has strategically commodified Islamic products and piety and packaged them as luxurious and modern Islamic lifestyle items.

In our analysis, we observe an alignment in Deen Dunya and Fatin's branding, from their *dakwah* and product branding to their aesthetic branding. The alignment in branding and commercial benefits, we presume, led to Deen Dunya, and Fatin deciding to enter an economic partnership.

C. Paid Partnership Analysis

On 18 December 2021, Fatin Afika and Deen Dunya uploaded a video clip to promote Deen Dunya's product, a prayer set. The video showcased Fatin using the prayer set during acts of worship at the Haram, the Holy Mosque in Mecca, Saudi Arabia, with the Kaabah and fellow Muslims worshipping in the background (Figure 11.2).

Fatin's choice of location and performance are both significant Islamic symbols. These symbols evoke strong emotional reactions from the Muslim population. By employing these Islamic symbols in a marketing campaign that promotes the sale of worship items, Fatin and Deen Dunya have commodified their piety and the piety of Muslims, leveraging Brand Islam to attract Muslims into becoming economic agents. In Islam, acts of worship and the Haram hold sacred status and are discouraged from being overly displayed for public attention. Hence this marketing strategy, despite its potential success, has indirectly compromised the Islamic principle of privatizing acts of worship and the sanctity of the Haram as a sacred space meant for Muslims to deepen their connection with God.

The items marketed in this partnership were female prayer wear, prayer beads, and a prayer mat. While these items hold inherent Islamic significance as worship commodities, their high-quality construction, appealing design, and appealing packaging position them as luxury items, and marketing them encourages material consumption. This paid partnership also strategically utilized Fatin's membership in the *asatizah* (plural for religious teachers)

FIGURE 11.2
Fatin Afika and Deen Dunya's Paid Partnership Reel

Note: "This prayer set from @deen.dunya.sg makes it easy for me to just 'grab & go' to perform my ibadah throughout my stay here in the masjidil haram ..."
Source: Fatin Afika (2021a).

fraternity and "feel-good Islam" *dakwah* to penetrate and retain their access to the Singaporean Muslim middle-class market. By targeting the piety of Muslims and encouraging them to become economic agents, Deen Dunya and Fatin Afika successfully accessed the neoliberal market.

The paid partnership also subliminally transmits the message that Muslims can reconcile their Muslim identity with active participation in modern society by becoming economic agents and enjoying luxurious material goods. Despite the possibility of creating the marketing campaign without this intent and deliberation, Deen Dunya and Fatin Afika, as Muslims, have made compromises to access and optimally navigate the neoliberal and Islamophobic market.

D. Ethical Considerations

It is challenging for Muslims, as a minority group, to attain economic prosperity in Singapore. This plants into the psyche of Singaporean Muslims the urgency to optimize all forms of economic opportunities. However, this circumstance does not negate the problematic nature of Brand Islam. It remains ethically questionable for Deen Dunya to repackage inherently

Islamic items into luxury items to encourage "guiltless" consumption. It also remains ethically questionable for Deen Dunya and Fatin Afika to commodify sacred Islamic symbols, the relationship between Muslims and God, and Fatin's position as an *ustazah*, to influence her followers to become economic agents.

On the other hand, Deen Dunya and Fatin also leveraged their influencing capacities to make calls to Islam and create space for Muslim representation. This manifested in the dual act of leveraging on piety for economic opportunities and leveraging on economic opportunities to actualize piety. Thus, Deen Dunya and Fatin can be regarded as actors negotiating with structural boundaries, and as actors who have conformed to the boundaries.

The capacity to engage the structure signifies the influence Muslim economic enterprises and microcelebrities have over the Muslim community. Making it pertinent for them to carefully examine the opportunities presented to them by the market. Influential Muslim actors must exercise their agency and consider the consequences of their choices in order to maximize optimal results for the community, rather than compromise even further, the position of Muslims in society. This capacity also makes it important to continue examining the ethical responsibilities held by Muslim economic enterprises and *asatizah* microcelebrities.

Case Study 3: Paid Partnership between Mizi Wahid and Maybank Islamic

The last case study is the 11 October 2021 paid partnership between Mizi Wahid and Maybank Islamic.

A. Personal Branding Analysis

Mizi Wahid (@miziwahid) is an established *asatizah* influencer primarily active on Instagram. He joined the platform in December 2011 and, as of August 2023, has secured more than 142,000 followers. Compared with the other microcelebrities analysed in this chapter, Mizi Wahid boasts the largest audience.

Like Fatin, Mizi Wahid's branding also centres around his role as an *ustaz* (male religious teacher), and his *dakwah* branding aligns with the "feel-good Islam" approach. However, in contrast to Fatin, Mizi maintains a more authoritative position, which can be attributed to the qualities of exceptionalism present in his branding. Firstly, his seniority within the *asatizah* fraternity contributes to his unique authoritative standing. Having been an active religious teacher for a long period, he has established himself as a respected figure within the Singaporean Muslim community. His exceptional societal position is further strengthened by the design of his content. He primarily posts structured and informative *dakwah* content that is easily consumable.

> God has a perfect plan for your life. No matter how rough things are, or how tough things get—learn to trust in His flawless ways, and His perfect timing. And while waiting, know that your prayers can make a big difference. Pray. Wait. Trust. (Mizi Wahid 2021a).

While personal posts are limited, they are designed as *dakwah* posts and still reflect his role as an *ustaz*. His Instagram page also employs a muted and serious aesthetic, with predominantly black, white and brown hues. Hence, his personal branding, which includes his societal position and the content design, psychologically instils a perception of authority.

Mizi Wahid also strategically partners with popular figures such as Malaysian influencer Neelofa and actress Lisa Surihani. Apart from celebrity status and influence, these figures have also incorporated *dakwah* into their branding. These partnerships often take place within the context of physical *dakwah* events. Hence, Mizi Wahid can attract a significantly larger following from neighbouring Malaysia and retain and secure his authoritative brand as a reliable senior *ustaz*.

During the paid partnership with Maybank Islamic, Mizi Wahid's personal branding as a well-respected and senior *ustaz*, his association with renowned Malaysian celebrities, and his "feel-good Islam" *dakwah* branding were well established. This branding, which secured him a high followership, allowed Mizi Wahid to penetrate the neoliberal market, as it aligns with the needs of major business corporations such as Maybank Islamic. The financial collaborations that ensued are ultimately the result of Mizi Wahid's commodification of his piety and *ustaz* status.

B. Partnered Business Analysis

Maybank Islamic is the Islamic banking and finance arm of Malayan Banking Berhad (Maybank). Based in Malaysia, it is the largest Islamic bank in Southeast Asia. Despite operating within a broader, inherently exploitative system, Maybank Islamic markets itself as a shariah-compliant and Islamically ethical banking and finance system.

Presently, the conventional banking and finance industry, governed by principles of capitalism, dominates the global economic system. This system is inherently exploitative due to its emphasis on unbridled individualism.

However, individuals and society are fundamentally connected. Hence, maintaining a balance between personal and public welfare is necessary to ensure the collective good. In contrast, due to its individualistic nature, the capitalist market responds only to the subjective wants of individuals in power, leading to the manipulation of the system. The constant pursuit of self-interest by powerful individuals causes gross imperfections and distortions in the global economy. This prevalence results in extreme inequalities that "distort society's productive and consumptive priorities", unbalancing the economic system and making it exploitative (Ahmad 2003, pp. 185–88). This exploitative capitalist economic system is the antithesis of Islamic morality, inspiring continuous debates and discussions defining and challenging permissible intersections for Muslims.

Maybank and other commercial banks strove to define a permissible intersection and enter the Muslim market by developing an alternate system with Islamic branding. Initially, this system aimed to adhere to Islamic ethical and legal principles. However, this adherence is both inconclusive and inconsistent. The distinctive element of Islamic economics ethics is the integration of individual "freedom with responsibility and efficiency with justice" (Ahmad 2003, p. 194). This integration would establish a balance in ensuring the protection of individual and societal welfare, propelling the subjective desires of powerful individuals into objective needs. However, the reality observed within the Islamic banking and finance industry is the convergence of the Islamic system with the conventional system instead of the necessary divergence dictated by Islamic ethics. Rather than ensuring the development and promotion of products which adhere to Islamic ethical principles, Islamic banks adhere to capitalist principles by mainly promoting products and systems that maximize profitability and efficiency and undermine individual responsibility and social justice. There is a disproportionate emphasis on Islamic banking and finance products that are legally permissible within Islam due to their interest-free nature but remain Islamically unethical as they retain exploitative characteristics (AlHammadi, Alotaibi, and Hakam 2020, p. 1175).

Maybank Islamic presently offers a range of financial products, including *murabaha* (mark-up sale/sale at a margin), *qard* (loan), and *mudarabah* (profit and loss sharing contracts). However, their online list of products displayed a higher number of *murabaha* over *mudarabah* products (Maybank Islamic Berhad 2022a). The former are essentially modifications of conventional banking and finance products, developed to circumvent the usage of interest, making it Islamically legal but still retaining capitalist qualities. Its focus remains the maximization of profit for shareholders, with little emphasis on Islamic ethical characteristics, such as ensuring social justice and individual responsibility. The marketing of the products also overemphasizes their profitability and Islamic legality while providing minimal to no information on their ethical qualities (Maybank Islamic Berhad 2022b). This practice illustrates the convergence of Maybank Islamic's system with the conventional system rather than towards a uniquely Islamic system adhering to Islamic ethical principles. Thus, despite using an Islamic branding targeting the piety of Muslims, Maybank Islamic's products remain questionably Islamic.

In summation, during the paid partnership with Mizi Wahid, it is apparent that Maybank Islamic is leveraging Islam as a branding strategy to penetrate the Muslim market. However, it is inconclusive whether their products truly adhere to Islamic economic principles or circumvent Islamic legal requirements to maximize profits and adhere only to capitalist neoliberal principles.

C. Paid Partnership Analysis

On 11 October 2021, Mizi Wahid posted a short *dakwah* video clip on Instagram about *sadaqah* (charity) in partnership with Maybank Islamic. The reel commenced with the logos of Maybank Islamic and a picture of Mizi Wahid, accompanied by the text "promoting good deeds" and the title "*Sadaqah* Removes Difficulties". The remaining 90-second is Mizi Wahid discussing *sadaqah*. Hence, the video serves as a *dakwah* initiative sponsored by Maybank Islamic.

The video clip did not promote any products from Maybank Islamic but subtly incorporated the Islamic concept of *sadaqah* within the broader branding of Maybank Islamic. It delivers a perceptual message that Maybank Islamic is an Islamically ethical organization that promotes social justice through charitable acts. This messaging was further strengthened by the accompanying text in the reel's description.

> Sharing this *tazkirah* (reminder) video would be one of your *sadaqah* for today and together with Maybank Islamic for this *Maulidur Rasul* (Birth of the Prophet) we'll be sharing useful reminders and the importance of giving back while we reminisce the blessed life of our beloved Prophet Muhammad PBUH. His kindness is a beautiful inspiration (Mizi Wahid 2021a).

This messaging, irrespective of Maybank Islamic's actual business practices, products or ethical stance, portrays the corporation as one that prioritizes

FIGURE 11.3
Mizi Wahid's Dakwah Reel in Partnership with Maybank Islamic

Source: Mizi Wahid (2021a).

economic and social justice, aligning with the guidance of Prophet Muhammad. Hence Maybank Islamic's decision to partner with Mizi Wahid to deliver this specific content is a deliberate strategic effort to position itself as a trustworthy and Islamically ethical business entity.

Beyond commodifying the *dakwah* content, Maybank Islamic, through the paid partnership, also commodifies Mizi Wahid's authoritative position and piety as an *ustaz*. Mizi Wahid's branding grants him significant influence over the Muslim community, particularly on Islamic-related issues. Despite not promoting specific products from Maybank Islamic, his partnership with the bank serves as a wholesale endorsement of the corporation. Through Mizi Wahid's influence, Maybank Islamic can perceptually shape the Muslim community into believing that its products are compliant with Islam. Hence, by commodifying Mizi Wahid's branding, Maybank Islamic solidified its intended branding and successfully accessed the Muslim market.

Through a 90-second video clip, the paid partnership effectively establishes a strong Islamic branding for Maybank Islamic, regardless of its business practices. This collaboration allows Maybank Islamic to penetrate the Muslim market. This partnership poignantly illustrates the effectiveness of Brand Islam as a commodification tool to access the consumer potential of the Muslim community. Moreover, this partnership demonstrates how neoliberal forces permit the expression of Islamic piety and identity when they show economic agency.

D. Ethical Considerations

In this analysis, we observed another ethical conundrum. As an *ustaz*, Mizi had commodified his authoritative Islamic position for economic benefits, but in doing so, he had also provided space for Muslim piety. Nonetheless, the gravity of his choices cannot be ignored. As Mizi is an authoritative figure, it is important to question whether his decision to partner with Maybank Islamic was the result of a thorough investigation into its practices and adherence to Islamic ethical principles that envision human well-being as an end in itself, rather than as a means to achieve economic gains. It is equally crucial to question the acceptability of banking and finance entities which facilitate partnerships that instrumentalize the influence of *asatizah* such as Mizi Wahid to penetrate the Muslim market. The choices made by *asatizah* like Mizi have significant consequences for the Muslim community in Singapore. Thus, as religious leaders, it is incumbent on them to engage in informed considerations that critically examine the trade-offs of partnerships driven by market forces that view bodies as quantifiable commodities.

Probing the Limits of Representation

The case studies illustrated the different ways neoliberal and Islamophobic market forces influence the agency of Muslims. In each case, the subject had to commodify elements of their piety, and participated in Brand Islam to gain visibility and representation. Hence it is apparent that Muslims are constantly challenged to negotiate their convictions with pressure to assimilate into society.

Representation matters as it allows those on the margins to feel validated and empowered. It helps increase their self-esteem, and, particularly for Muslims in a climate of suspicion and fear, representation has the immense power to challenge, shape, and transform the status quo (Kidd 2016). However, as discussed in this chapter, it should not be unfettered but instead examined against the power structures that monopolize the image of "proper" representation. Thus, society must rethink how it views representation and belonging and challenge hegemonic attempts to typecast Muslims into a singular identity to serve the interests of the market and state. In this regard, it is crucial to mobilize our collective capacity to think of an alternative paradigm that would provide Muslims with the freedom to frame their representation and self-identity that is not based on fear or commodification.

Conclusion: Deconstructing Doxa, Critical Consciousness and Identity-Making

In his analysis of the relationship between power and culture, the French sociologist Pierre Bourdieu coined the term *doxa* to describe the internalization of a set of values and power structures that are accepted as self-evident in a particular society. It reflects the collective obliviousness to the status quo, reinforcing existing power structures responsible for the unequal social divisions (Deer 2008, pp. 19–20). This has a significant impact on identity-making, wherein it limits the space for reflexivity and the formulation of an alternative identity that is not contingent on the prevailing *doxa*. The arguments presented above have demonstrated the influence exerted by state and market forces in delineating the parameters of "success" and "goodness" that a Muslim must conform to accept as part of the mainstream. Moreover, the subjects lack the reflexivity to question the hegemony of the prevailing *doxa* as the status quo is implicitly accepted to be natural and not consequential. For example, in a society where neoliberalism is accepted as a dominant philosophical project, it is difficult to envision an alternative system that regards human nature as sacrosanct and not a commodity that can be profiteered. In this regard, challenging the *doxa* is necessary for social change and enabling new ways of thinking. This entails a certain degree of critical consciousness that recognizes the inequities in society and actively transforms these structures to enable human flourishing and justice (Freire 2017).

Building on the concept popularized by Paulo Freire, Watts, Diemer, and Voight (2011) conceptualization of critical consciousness is useful in transforming the dominant *doxa* on an individual and collective level. It comprises three distinct yet interrelated components: critical reflection, political efficacy, and critical action. In this respect, it would allow Muslims to reverse any "*doxic*" attitude and define their identity based on their terms. However, any change should start with a critical reflection of the dominant *doxa* that entails a social analysis and moral rejection of the structural inequities that have limited human agency and well-being. In particular, the *asatizah* in the Muslim community, who are traditionally seen as the moral gatekeepers of the Muslim community, should embody a social consciousness in their dissemination of religious messages. For example, a discussion on Islamic finance or "shariah-compliant" products should not be devoid of an analysis of the planetary implications of the capitalistic system. Unfortunately, the subject in one of the case studies fails to reflect on this and, as a result, implicitly reproduces the structural inequities despite being couched in religious language. What immediately follows after reflection is the enabling of individuals and the collective to feel politically efficacious, in which they are more likely to engage in activities that would advocate for social transformation. In this sense, one can only change their social conditions if they are first aware of the structural injustices. Consequently, with the increase of reflection, critical action and social change follow (Watts, Diemer, and Voight 2011, p. 47).

However, as discussed above, the market and state forces do not allow space for this reflection to occur. Thus, subjects are induced to internalize and reproduce the *doxa*, which impacts individual consciousness and collective representation.

This chapter has thus shed light on the confluence of neoliberalism and Islamophobia in the process of commodifying Muslim piety. This phenomenon serves as a contextual framework to critically examine the motivations of modern Muslim representation that is exploited by market forces. It debilitates our ethical compass as it is based on hegemony, individualism and insatiable desire. However, this chapter contends that only critical reflection of the dominant *doxa* would help Muslims reclaim their "technologies of the self" to negotiate Islam and everyday precarity with self-confidence and start defining their identities based on who they are and their values rather than who they are not.

Note

1. Shirazi denotes the rise of Brand Islam as the product of capitalism commercializing Islam to stimulate consumerism among Muslims.

References

Abdul-Matin Ibrahim. 2012. *Green Deen: What Islam Teaches About Protecting the Planet*. Leicestershire: Kube Publishing Ltd.

Abdullah, Walid Jumblatt. 2021. *Islam in a Secular State: Muslim Activism in Singapore*. Amsterdam: Amsterdam University Press.

Abidin, Crystal. 2018. *Internet Celebrity: Understanding Fame Online*. United Kingdom: Emerald Publishing.

Ahmad, Khurshid. 2003. "The Challenge of Global Capitalism: An Islamic Perspective". In *Making Globalization Good: The Moral Challenges of Global Capitalism*, edited by John Dunning, pp. 181–209. New York: Oxford University Press.

Al Jazeera. 2023. "Global Fashion Brands Exploiting Bangladesh Workers: Study". 11 January 2023. https://www.aljazeera.com/news/2023/1/11/fashion-brands-paid-less-than-production-cost-to-bangladesh-firms (accessed 6 February 2023).

Alhammadi, Salah, Khaled O. Alotaib, and Dzikri F. Hakam. 2020. "Analysing Islamic Banking Ethical Performance from Maqāṣid al-Sharīʿah Perspective: Evidence from Indonesia". *Journal of Sustainable Finance & Investment* 12, no. 4: 1171–93.

Asare, Janice Gassam. 2020. "How H&M Has Completely Revamped their Diversity and Inclusion Training". *Forbes*, 18 March 2020. https://www.forbes.com/sites/janicegassam/2020/03/18/how-hm-has-completely-revamped-their-diversity-and-inclusion-training/?sh=347024105df0 (accessed 6 February 2023).

Barylo, William. 2016. "Neo-liberal Not-for-Profits: The Embracing of Corporate Culture by European Muslim Charities". *Journal of Muslim Minority Affairs* 36, no. 3: 383–98. https://doi.org/10.1080/13602004.2016.1216626

Beta, Annisa R. 2019. "Commerce, Piety and Politics: Indonesian Young Muslim Women's Groups as Religious Influencers". *New Media & Society* 21, no. 10: 2140–59.

Bulhan, Hussein A. 2015. "Stages of Colonialism in Africa: From Occupation of Land to Occupation of Being". *Journal of Social and Political Psychology* 3, no. 1: 239–56.

DeAcetis, Joseph. 2022. "H&M Drives Innovation in Sustainability with 2021 Style". *Forbes*, 9 November 2022. https://www.forbes.com/sites/josephdeacetis/2021/05/06/hm-drives-innovation-in-sustainability-with-2021-style/?sh=17fbc5c05346 (accessed 6 February 2023).

Deen Dunya (@deen.dunya.sg). "In the Midst of Chaos and Uncertainty, Finding Peace within Is Essential". Instagram, 4 February 2023. https://www.instagram.com/reel/CoOYc-Vhh3F/?utm_source=ig_web_copy_link (accessed 10 March 2023).

Deer, Cecile. 2008. *Doxa*. In *Pierre Bourdieu: Key Concepts*, edited by M. Grenfell, pp. 119–30. Stocksfield: Acumen Publishing.

Fatin Afika (@fatinafika). 2020. "A Beautiful Doa, to Seek Allah, to Not Make This Worldly Affairs". Instagram, 23 October 2020.

———. 2021a. "This Prayer Set from @Deen.Dunya.Sg Makes It Easy for Me to Just 'Grab & Go' to Perform My Ibadah Throughout My Stay Here in Masjidil Haram". Instagram, 18 December 2021.

———. 2021b. "Another Bestie Getting Hitched!". Instagram, 15 August 2021. https://www.instagram.com/p/CSl1A-rBW3U/?utm_source=ig_web_copy_link. (accessed 10 March 2023).

Freire, Paulo. 2017. *Pedagogy of the Oppressed*. London: Penguin Books.

Guilbert, Kieran. 2018. "H&M Accused of Failing to Ensure Fair Wages for Factory Workers". *Thomson Reuters Foundation*, 24 September 2018. https://news.trust.org/item/20180924122505-h2rtz/ (accessed 6 February 2023).

Harvey, David. 2007. "Neoliberalism as Creative Destruction". *Annals of the American Academy of Political and Social Science* 610: 22–44.
Jordan, Daisy. 2022. "Is H&M Ethical and Sustainable?". *Wear Next*, 24 February 2022. https://wear-next.com/news/is-hm-ethical-and-sustainable/ (accessed 6 February 2023).
Kidd, Mary Anna. 2016. "Archetypes, Stereotypes and Media Representation in a Multi-Cultural Society". *Procedia—Social and Behavioral Sciences* 236: 25–28.
Karakavak, Zerrin, and Tuğba Özbölük. 2022. "When Modesty Meets Fashion: How Social Media and Influencers Change the Meaning of Hijab". *Journal of Islamic Marketing*. https://doi.org/10.1108/jima-05-2021-0152
Lean, Nathan. 2012. *The Islamophobia Industry: How the Right Manufactures Hatred of Muslims*. London: Pluto Press.
Mamdani, Mahmood. 2005. *Good Muslim, Bad Muslim: America, the Cold War and the Roots of Terror*. New York: Harmony.
Masturah Khalid (@masturahkay). 2020a. "Who Else Can't Wait to Raya". *Instagram*, 19 May 2020. https://www.instagram.com/p/CAX1faTh_yk/?igshid=NzZhOTFlYzFmZQ%3D%3D (accessed 10 March 2023).
———. 2022a. "During Ramadan, Fasting from Dawn to Dusk Only Means That Conservation of Energy Is Important to Get Through the Day, Especially When I'm Working Full Time". *Instagram*, 30 April 2022.
———. 2022b. "Did Someone Say Colours? H&M Ramadhan Collection Is Now Available in on H&M's SG Website & Zalora!". *Instagram*, 19 April 2022. https://www.instagram.com/reel/CciMofQh8d-/?utm_source=ig_web_copy_link (accessed 10 March 2023).
Maybank Islamic Berhad. 2022a. "Deposits/IA". https://www.maybank.com/islamic/en/deposits/deposits_listing.page (accessed 11 March 2023).
———. 2022b. "Term Accounts". https://www.maybank.com/islamic/en/deposits/islamic_term_listing.page (accessed 11 March 2023).
McVeigh, Karen. 2017. "Cambodian Female Workers in Nike, Asics and Puma Factories Suffer Mass Faintings". *The Guardian*, 25 June 2017. https://www.theguardian.com/business/2017/jun/25/female-cambodian-garment-workers-mass-fainting (accessed 13 March 2023).
Mizi Wahid (@mizi_wahid). 2021a. "Dealing with Life's Problems?". *Instagram*, 11 October 2021. https://www.instagram.com/p/CU36fOKByxA/?utm_source=ig_web_copy_link (accessed 10 March 2023).
———. 2021b. "Sorry I Haven't Posted Details About the Giveaway Yet". *Instagram*, 26 August 2021. https://www.instagram.com/p/CTCokL7hbS6/?utm_source=ig_web_copy_link (accessed 11 March 2023).
Moore, Rick Clifton. 2018. "Islamophobia, Patriarchy, or Corporate Hegemony? News Coverage of Nike's Pro Sport Hijab". *Journal of Media and Religion* 17, nos. 3–4: 106–16.

Salam Gateway. 2022. "State of the Global Islamic Economy 2022 Report". https://www.salaamgateway.com/specialcoverage/SGIE22 (accessed 11 March 2023).

Sardar, Ziauddin. 2022. *Emerging Epistemologies: The Changing Fabric of Knowledge in Postnormal Times*. Virginia: International Institute of Islamic Thought.

Sayyid, Salman. 2014. "A Measure of Islamophobia". *Islamophobia Studies Journal* 2, no. 1: 10–25.

Shirazi, Faegheh. 2016. *Brand Islam: The Marketing and Commodification of Piety*. Austin: University of Texas Press.

Watts, Roderick J., Matthew A. Diemer, and Adam M. Voight. 2011. "Critical Consciousness: Current Status and Future Directions". *New Directions for Child and Adolescent Development*, no. 134: 43–57.

Zuboff, Shoshana. 2019. *The Age of Surveillance Capitalism: The Fight for a Human Future at the New Frontier of Power*. London: Profile Books Ltd.

12

THAI MUSLIM WOMEN'S NEGOTIATION WITH SHARIAH THROUGH FOOD AND CLOTHING

Amporn Marddent

INTRODUCTION

We do not have to put a halal logo or apply for the halal certificate. Wearing a *hijab* is enough! It already means a lot and it's better than using the crescent and star icon at food cupboards.
    Hasnah, personal communication, 24 April 2022

In the evolving landscape of Thai Muslim society, women entrepreneurs are employing innovative means to assert their identity and navigate the business world. Hasnah's statement above reflects how the *hijab*, a headscarf donned by Muslim women, serves as an important marker of religious identity, allowing Muslim women in Thailand to conduct business in the Muslim community successfully. This became particularly salient during the economic downturn following the COVID-19 pandemic. Notably, Phuket, a province that has been a prominent tourist destination since the 1980s, experienced high unemployment rates during the pandemic despite its popularity (Wannaphong 2013). In Thailand, the tourism sector ranks as the fifth highest source of income and thus constitutes a primary driver of the country's economy. Before the global declaration of the coronavirus pandemic, Phuket's economy relied mainly on the service sector (NESDC 2019). However, the pandemic wrought severe economic consequences across Thailand. Measures implemented by the government, including domestic and international travel restrictions, social distancing guidelines, and the temporary closure of small businesses, exacerbated the economic strain (Baum and Nguyen 2020).

In 2021, the Office of the National Economic and Social Development Council (NESDC) examined the strategies which workers and small and medium enterprises (SMEs) in the tourism sector employed to adapt during the pandemic. Among those workers is Hasnah who operates a micro halal enterprise through a family-owned food stall. A key element of Hasnah's business approach involves using the *hijab* during operation hours. As a symbol of Muslim identity, the *hijab* assures customers that the food is halal and safe for Muslim consumption. This assurance is crucial given that food stalls selling basically to Muslims are not required to obtain halal certification.

In Thailand, the concept of "halal" has undergone a significant transformation, shifting from its fundamental religious roots to a system intertwined with capitalism, engaged in halal tourism and commercialization. Critics within the Muslim community point out that what was once a religious structure has been mobilized and manipulated by religious authorities. Regardless, the Thai government continues to support the Halal Standard Institute of Thailand, an exclusive statutory religious organization governed by the Central Islamic Committee of Thailand (CICOT). Comprising of experts in Islamic jurisprudence, food scientists, government representatives, and collaborators, CICOT is responsible for verifying and endorsing halal certification, aligning its regulations with international halal standards, and communicating these halal standards to Provincial Islamic Committees across the country. These Provincial Islamic Committees must adhere to CICOT regulations and are responsible for halal-related matters within their regions (Wannasiri et al. 2019). This system presents a challenge to many small Muslim-owned businesses due to the high certification cost. Additionally, they must navigate the complex process of aligning their products with halal standards, a practice called "sacralizing their commodities" (Rinallo, Scott, and Maclaran 2012). Drawing on Fisher's study (2005), this term reflects the intricate relationship between halal and capitalism, highlighting concerns about the commodification of halal. This chapter reveals how women business owners in particular strive to apply religious notions in their businesses, seeking to reconcile faith with the demands of a capitalist economy.

Hasnah, along with other lower-middle-class Muslim women, face limited access to financial capital and private investment channels. As a result, they have discovered an alternative means of pursuing their entrepreneurial goals: using the *hijab* as a universal symbol of Islamic identity. Through their micro halal food businesses, they aspire to achieve financial prosperity and profit. Despite forgoing official halal certification, these women conscientiously adhere to Islamic dietary guidelines. They use halal storage and materials, ensuring that the food and related products they produce can be readily accepted in halal food markets.

With this context in mind, this chapter explores how Muslim women in Southern Thailand negotiate their entrepreneurial activities with shariah principles. Specifically, it provides an understanding of the local "halalization" process, in which women business owners harmonize their religious beliefs with their commercial endeavours. The chapter further analyses how small business owners seek to align their practices with halal principles within a given social space by illuminating how these women's religious identities shape their participation in local economic development.

Methodology and Context of the Research Site

This study investigates the dynamic of halal in micro business, focusing on everyday practices within the specific context of southern Thailand. Together with the cultural characteristics of the region, the *hijab*, serving as a physical identity marker for Muslim women, is central to my analysis. In conducting this research, I employed multi-sited ethnography, particularly in Phuket and Pattani. Marcus (1995) delineated how multi-sited ethnographic research can be designed, emphasizing the ethnographer's responsibility to establish connections among various sites or within the overall argument of the ethnography. In aligning with this approach, I was able to comprehend how lower-middle-class women who run their small halal food businesses are positioned as actors within the global halal economy.

To gain insight into the subjective experience of Muslim women entrepreneurs in southern Thailand, I selected two locations for participant observation. The specific case studies of Muslim women in Southern Thailand shed light on the phenomenon of self-management as an entrepreneur, wherein individuals seize an opportunity and address the gender gap prevalent not only locally but also globally. Muslim women in this study often turn to small business ownership due to a lack of job opportunities or limited knowledge about the halal business industry. According to Von Mizes (1998), entrepreneurship requires no specific education because entrepreneurs cannot be trained. Instead, an entrepreneur actively shapes the market and reinvents oneself by developing human capital rather than passively reacting to external forces. This chapter focuses on the everyday experiences of these women, uncovering rich insights into significant social phenomena. Using fieldwork for data collection was appropriate for this study as it allowed me to explore various practices across different research sites, allowing for a more nuanced representation.

I particularly focused on two research sites within contemporary Thai society: the Upper South and Deep South, specifically in a coffee shop and food booth. These locations represent religiously and socially bound spaces where the use of the headscarf intersects with the broader political economy. My methodology consisted of ethnographic observation—including regular visits to Phuket and Pattani between March 2020 and August 2022—as the main approach to this qualitative study. The fieldwork provided me with a broader picture of the re-Islamization processes in these areas. During my fieldwork, I spent extended periods with locals and conducted informal interviews with eight southern Thai Muslim women who run micro enterprises. The topics of these interviews were derived from my conversations with the participants. Specifically, they were prompted to discuss how their religious beliefs influence and are influenced by entrepreneurship, particularly within contexts shaped by restrictive cultural practices, and the impact of the COVID-19 pandemic on their businesses. Through a reflexive analysis of the data, I found that women strategically leverage their religious identity and social networks as marketable tools to expand their businesses.

Two of the women I spoke with were Muslim women residing in my hometown, Ao-Makham Bay and Panwa Cape, Phuket. They speak the southern dialect and live in popular tourist destinations where halal businesses thrive. Entrepreneurs in Phuket's food and beverage industry have embraced technology to expand online commercial activities and resegment their customer base (Kris 2022). Muslims living in the upper south provinces such as Phuket, Krabi and Phang Nga—often called Andaman Muslims—are heavily engaged in the tourism industry. Studies show that these provinces are attractive tourist destinations, including Muslim and non-Muslim international visitors, due to their halal-friendly amenities (Pimphun 2021). They offer community-based halal tourism experiences, such as health and sports tourism, which generate income for locals and enhance the local economy. The other six participants were Malay-speaking women from Pattani, an area in the far south of Thailand which has been conflict-ridden since January 2004. At the time of my research, these women were members of civil society organizations.

Contextual Meaning of Halal and *Hijab*

The term halal is derived from Arabic and translates to "permissible" or "lawful". This is in contrast to the term "haram", which means "forbidden" or "unlawful". Both terms are central to Islamic dietary requirements according to which certain products, including blood, carrion, and pork are prohibited. To be considered halal, meat must be sourced from an animal slaughtered according to Islamic regulations (de Araújo 2019). The halal designation also signifies that the food products have been produced and handled with strict adherence to these regulations (Mohd Syaifulzafni 2020). However, the interpretation of halal can vary, leading to contestation and disagreement. As a site of politics and cultural negotiation, the concept of halal encompasses debates over belonging and exclusion (Mukherjee 2014). Controversial areas include industrialized meat production, automatic slaughter, and the permissibility of slaughter performed by individuals of other faiths, such as Jews or Christians. These disputes have contributed to a broad and sometimes conflicting array of halal standards and regulations, reflecting the complexity of interpreting and applying this essential aspect of Islamic practice.

Halal certification in Thailand dates back to before 1949 when the halal status of products and services was determined solely by religious leaders, without any formal authentication or certification process. Between 1949 and 1997, the Sheikhul Islam Office of Thailand was responsible for issuing halal certificates. In 2002, the Halal Standard Institute of Thailand was launched, operating under the administration of the CICOT. This institute succeeded in convincing the government to establish a halal food hub in the south, marking a significant development. By 2016, further progression was made with the launch of the codex-based Halal Standard Institute, aligning with General Prayut Chan-ocha's government's (2014–23) strategy to promote halal products and services. The institute earned the trust of Muslims within Thai society and gained the authority to approve halal centres in Bangkok and later Pattani, the southernmost province of Thailand, where Muslims are the dominant population.

Halal accreditation is given upon inspection by CICOT, and this is certified by the halal logo. The halal logo, indicative of halal certification and a mark of commercialization, became prominent from 2017 onwards (Mohd Saiful Anwar et al. 2017). The CICOT also allocates funds to develop the halal Hazard Analysis and Critical Control (HACCP) or assurance system for halal quality. Additionally, the government has actively supported small and micro community enterprises (SMCEs), particularly in the five southern border provinces that have played an important role in the halal industry since 2009 (Buncha, Wiphada, and Prawat 2015). This commitment was cemented in Thailand's development plans from 2009 to 2012, including the government's approval of an industrial base for halal food production. Furthermore, Prince of Songkhla University's Pattani campus has been key in establishing the Halal Institute to bolster halal food development in the region.

The Thai government recently launched a programme to transform the southern border provinces, historically marked by conflict space, into a hub known as the "World Halal Kitchens". Studies on halal food and products within Thailand indicate that these items often face challenges in market domination, overshadowed by other brands with the advantage of legacy and earlier market entry (Pimphun 2021). However, Thailand's international acclaim as one of the top ten tourist destinations, celebrated for its rich cultural attractions and welcoming atmosphere, creates unique opportunities. This reputation attracts Muslim travellers and visitors, opening doors for halal tourism—a niche market catering to a growing Muslim population that seeks halal-certified food. To capitalize on this potential, businesses within the tourism industry must ensure that both the manufacturing processes and facilities adhere to halal food standards and possess halal certifications. Recognizing the importance of this sector, the Thai government has allocated funds to the Halal Standard Institute of Thailand to promote the halal food industry as the "Kitchen of the World". In this sense, halal standardization and certification have emerged as key government strategies. By aligning with global halal standards, Thailand aims to facilitate tourism marketing, enhance the allure of its food, and ultimately improve performance in these areas.

Within the context of Thai history, the *hijab*, worn by Muslim women, serves as a conspicuous marker of their Muslim identity. More than just a religious garment, the *hijab*'s presence has political and social ramifications, especially in how it has shaped educational opportunities for Muslim women. This dynamic was particularly evident during the Muslim women's movement of the 1990s, a hallmark period that championed the protection of Muslim women's identity within the broader Islamic reform movement. Many Muslim scholars and activists in Thailand trace Thailand's *hijab* narrative back to a pivotal event known as the "Yala Teacher Training College Incident" (1987–88), colloquially referred to as the *hijab* crisis in Yala (Chaiwat 1994). This incident in Yala province played a crucial role in catalysing the *hijab* movement in the country. Since then, wearing the *hijab* has gained visibility in Thai society, symbolizing Muslim women's courage to represent Islam publicly. The Muslim women's movement became a stage for grappling with identity issues and played out within the broader context of problems surrounding the modern Thai polity (Romdon 2012). It also illustrated how gender and public piety played a role in participatory political culture (Amporn 2016).

In the 2000s, the *hijab* evolved into a symbol of growing Islamic assertiveness, particularly among women who leveraged religious platforms to reinforce Islamic doctrines and rational interpretations. As a result, wearing the *hijab* became a means for Muslim women to articulate their religiosity through adherence to religious rituals. Within Thai religious and political discourse, the *hijab* has overcome feelings of exclusion as a result of ethnic and religious discrimination and has found prominence in academic and religious texts and daily conversations among educated Thai Muslims. Nowadays, the *hijab* is not only an expression of cultural identity but has also become a fashion industry of its own.

The study of global halal as spiritual capital connects halal issues with the *hijab* (Mukherjee 2014). The literature posits that the *hijab* is more than an article of clothing. Similarly, halal extends beyond mere dietary peculiarities within Muslim culinary practices. Both subjects give rise to political and spiritual debate. In this paper, I explore the intertwining of economic activity and religious identity among Thai Muslim women, focusing on their presence in everyday settings such as halal breakfast booths, cafés and home garden coffee shops. The women in this study did not seek halal certification for their micro businesses, primarily due to limited financial resources and their products' domestic orientation. Although halal certification has the potential to enhance business recognition and facilitate market expansion, it was not necessary for the women in this study. Instead, they reached out to other Muslim consumers and locals through alternative means, specifically using the *hijab*.

The anthropology of food and eating (Mintz and Du Bois 2002) has attracted the attention of ethnographers, particularly concerning the interplay between the cuisine of specific cultures and factors such as gender identity and social values. Furthermore, this field of study recognizes that food consumption is more than an act of sustenance; it is a socially constructed phenomenon. Ethnographic studies have analysed food as an expression of ethnic, racial or national identity (Caplan 1997). In my anthropological investigation, I have mostly focused on the dynamic nature of cultural change, emphasizing how the concept of halal permeates daily life and intersects with political economy. I closely look at local commercialization patterns arising from beliefs and cultures. Food anthropologists have confirmed the relationship between halal and global standards. These standards are comprehensive, encompassing not just the raw materials and ingredients but also the standards which involve the entire process of handling the halal products—including utensils and facilities—before being consumed by Muslims. Therefore, this handling process must align with the provisions of Islamic principles and customs, reflecting the consumption habits of specific ethnic groups.

Hijabi Vendor

The *hijab* represents the intersection of political economy and individual agency in a way that leads to ideological debates on everyday practices. For Muslim women, wearing the *hijab* is the most visible symbol of Islam and a constant reminder of their faith and devotion. Reducing the *hijab* to a sign of Islamism or religious piety fails to consider the ever-shifting meanings of this object across time and space.

Through my fieldwork, the differences within and between the everyday sites in southern Thailand revealed that Muslim food and products are intimately connected with women's identity. My experiences as a *hijabi*, travelling to these research sites, and purchasing local halal products from the participants in the areas, provided me with unique insights into their lives. Specifically, I engaged with the narratives of a Muslim woman entrepreneur residing and operating in the conflict zone of Pattani. Her narrative reflects the challenges she faced in the complex environment of Thailand's Deep South and her role in influencing entrepreneurial behaviour and contributing to cultural change.

I spoke with Nora, who operates a café on the outskirts of Pattani town. We first met online during a consultation programme for women living in conflict areas, but we felt it best to speak in person. She appeared in a modern Malay Muslim woman's outfit when I met her. She wore a Malay-styled floral tunic *hijab* with a jeans dress. Under the *hijab*, she used a bonnet to ensure no strand of her hair was shown, and she used pins to secure her headscarf. She also had a traditional religious upbringing. Pattani people—especially members of civil society organizations—recognize her as the daughter of a respected traditional Malay Muslim scholar.

Nora has a university degree and wishes to be an artist. In line with her involvement in ENOUGH, an international campaign dedicated to empowering women and promoting gender equality and non-violence, she also sought to reshape the perception of women in conflict zones and enhance women's capacities. Thus, together with her relatives, she set up a small cosy café on the city's outskirts and intended for it to be a place where Malay Muslim women could gather to discuss their roles as women living in a conflict zone. She even provides support for her two assistants, who were domestic abuse survivors. These two women participated in an economic empowerment programme operated by an international non-government organization (NGO). Nora generally invites the women who patronize her café to engage in entrepreneurship. In order to do so, she always shares the story of the wife of the Prophet Muhammad, Khadijah, an honourable woman in Islamic history who was a successful entrepreneur. For Nora, women's voice and participation in society and public life constructs and contributes to narratives that reflect equal opportunities, choices, and access to resources.

In addition to her café, Nora extends her influence online, using her Facebook page to showcase her business. There, she shares not only pictures of food but also highlights halal products provided by Wanita, a local women's collective of various villages in Pattani. Through both her physical establishment and online presence, Nora constructs narratives that champion equal opportunities, choices and access to resources. Her involvement in ENOUGH in Pattani specifically addresses harmful social norms towards women, demonstrating her unwavering commitment to fostering a community where women's voices are heard and celebrated.

Wanita, a community enterprise, produces a variety of domestic halal products such as fish crackers (*keropok*), crispy bananas, fried durian chips, and (Pa)tani batik. These are featured offerings within the One Tambon One Product (OTOP) initiative, a government-backed economic empowerment programme tailored to support SMCEs in the region. Launched during Thaksin Shinawatra's administration (2001–6), OTOP was conceived as a policy to boost economic growth and mitigate rural poverty. Thaksin's government designed this policy as part of a broader strategy to appeal to the rural majority of voters. Alongside OTOP, his government instituted a village-managed microcredit development fund and a rural SME development initiative. These policies aimed to strengthen economic transition by supporting community enterprises utilizing traditional knowledge in tandem with current knowledge to raise product quality and help businesses gain market access (McCargo and Ukrist 2005).

As with many other small businesses, Nora's café struggled to remain open as the COVID-19 pandemic worsened, managing to operate only for a few months. This effort was crucial to ensure that Nora's family maintained an income source, especially following the loss of her father in 2020 during the second decade of violent conflicts in the region. Nora observed that in her area, women were more inclined than men to become home-based entrepreneurs. This phenomenon, resonating with trends in other conflict zones (Bullough and Renko 2017), reveals the unique challenges faced by women. Typically, women face more significant challenges than men due to social injustices, loss, trauma, restricted mobility, marginalization and gender-based violence (Amporn 2017; Vilasinee 2014). Additionally, the roles of women and men are typically redefined during conflicts, with women frequently assuming responsibilities traditionally held by men, requiring women to generate income for their families.

Nora exemplifies a new generation of Malay Muslim women in southern Thailand who, while adhering to their religion and traditional family norms, also assert their independence, sometimes even in rebellious ways. In Nora's opinion, the *hijab* is an object of material culture representing religious piety. To her, the *hijab* can often be perceived as a distilled, material representation of Islam. Her awareness of the symbolism of the *hijab* was sharpened during her involvement with the ENOUGH campaign, about a year before she started her halal coffee shop at home. While working in the market, she noticed women owners of small food stalls were wearing what she considered a "proper" *hijab*. This style of using the *hijab* differed from the traditional Malay *kain lepas*, an unstitched cloth used by ordinary people in the past, especially when working at home. Nora shared a conversation with a woman who spoke about the traditional *kain lepas*, saying it is

> something which does not look right to wear in the market. Because it slips off sometimes, then the hair and neck are revealed. The customers here may not appreciate the way I dress as such. It can affect consumer attitudes and perceptions toward the purchase of halal food products.

In the market, women wear the *hijab* to cover their hair down to their forehead. The scarf comes under the chin to conceal the neck and falls over the chest and back. In this context, women wearing what is considered "proper" *hijab* are implicitly communicating the rhetoric of the *hijab* in public. By dressing modestly while working outside the village in a Muslim-dominated area, these women demonstrate that they are embracing their faith and role as entrepreneurs. This thus illustrates the *hijab*'s dynamism as an object with cultural and economic implications.

Nowadays, Nora supports a group of women struggling with domestic violence and the death of their husbands as a result of violent conflict. She advocates for their economic empowerment and independence, guiding them to generate income and attain greater autonomy in family and personal consumption decisions. Nora felt socially obliged to assist other women in the community who may not see themselves as modern entrepreneurs. She invited women in the campaign to her coffee shop and demonstrated how their local products can be integrated into a modern café setting. Her concerns resonate with the local Malay-Muslim community's lifestyle needs and untapped market potential. These women represent a demographic that could be attracted to a business that caters to their needs. Meanwhile, Muslims living in suburban Pattani are concerned with more pressing and immediate concerns, such as finding adequate halal food and looking at how the vendors cope with religious life. If the locals found that the business owners were non-Muslims or non-practising Muslims, they would not patronize the business.

Given this context, modern cafés in small, suburban areas of Pattani, which are often perceived as unpopular and unsuitable gathering places for young people, act as spaces where local *hijabi* activists gather to conduct dialogues with national and international NGO staff members. Rather than displaying a halal certificate from CICOT on the wall, as is common in other restaurants and cafés in the city, Nora emphasizes the halal and shariah-compliant aspect of her business through more subtle means, such as through her products and the specific clientele of *hijabi* women who frequent her café. She uses her artistic sensibilities, using a corner of her café as a gallery wall adorned with an array of traditional and rural women's scarves of various designs, including floral patterns and colourful *kain lepas*.

In the late nineteenth century, the café served as a third space for men to meet, and coffeehouses were known as places of political discourse and informal business in many parts of the world (Benhabib 1998). In many big cities, bourgeois citizens spent their spare time frequenting coffee shops where they came to discuss contemporary issues with one another. It then led to the rise of the public sphere in which public conversations were discursive. Cafés gradually evolved into more inclusive and accessible spaces facilitated by social and technological change. This same process is relevant to Pattani. In the olden days, many traditional coffee shops in Pattani were only patronized by men (Muhammad Arafat 2007 and Pawita 2020). Not many women were part of the public sphere. Today, the cafés in contemporary Pattani, such as the ones owned by Nora and her associates, are popular sites for women to have social gatherings.

Nora's case therefore provides women with a space to assert their entrepreneurial spirit, which not only contributes to economic and social development but also plays a vital role in women's empowerment to achieve their personal goals and ambitions (Parker and Dales 2014). Research reveals that women's entrepreneurial activities significantly contribute to the development of communities (Rahanee 2021). Nora expressed that the café, owned and operated by Muslim women, has evolved from being a place of consumption to a site of contestation. This is because many women recognize that structured spaces, such as the Provincial Islamic Hall, mosques and Islamic schools, have rules and regulations that people must follow. Nora therefore envisions her café as a space for women to exercise their right to lead businesses.

Halal Micro-Scale Landscape

This section focuses on the ethnographic examination of Muslim daily economic activities in the local halal food industry in Phuket, where both traditional and modern approaches are employed. I explore various villages, specifically highlighting the experience of Hasnah and her cousin, Maimune, who run their businesses. Many home-based and micro-halal Muslim entrepreneurs display the word "halal" on self-made logos and labels written in Thai, Arabic and English. Hasnah and Maimune's enterprises, which experience a low volume of sales, also lack official halal logos or certificates. For Hasnah, the absence of such certification raises questions of trust in the food and the provider, elements she identifies as essential to driving purchases. In other words, cultivating trust is a significant factor that can positively influence the retention of Muslim travellers.

As mentioned earlier, local Muslims operating micro halal food businesses in this study typically refrain from the official halal certification process, and the reasons for this vary. For some, halal certification is considered voluntary and not compulsory, especially for those dealing with foods such as meat, where the product actually necessitates halal certification. The halal label can be a competitive advantage for SMEs (Tri Ratnasari et al. 2019), micro halal businesses, and home-based food and beverage businesses. The reluctance to pursue certification often stems from factors such as the lack of knowledge of the procedure, the associated costs, and the complexity of the process, which requires both time and money (Sudarmiatin, Khoirul Anam, and Wafaretta 2020). Among the study's participants, particularly Muslim women entrepreneurs, the most frequently cited barrier is cost and the complex and demanding requirements for halal certification submission.

During my fieldwork, most participants identified with their religious identity by wearing the *hijab*. Interestingly, one of the main reasons they chose not to pursue halal certification was that consumers rarely inquired about the halal status of the food they were buying. Instead, consumers seemed to respond with confidence and trust, especially if the seller displayed Islamic attributes during business hours. My analysis of Hasnah's perspectives and Nora's views towards women with *hijab* revealed that everyday life practices and personal appearances are vital in shaping the narratives that reflect the participants' negotiations and decisions (Certeau, Giard, and Mayo 1998) and how these factors impact their entrepreneurial expressions.

Muslims constitute approximately 35 per cent of Phuket's population, primarily inhabiting specific areas around Phuket city and surrounding villages where migrant Malays, Indians and Pakistanis initially settled (Anderson 2010). These communities coexist harmoniously with other religious and ethnic groups. As a Muslim woman observing my community, I have noted an increase in Muslim women entrepreneurs who have launched local businesses to support their families financially. This includes women who are mothers of young children seeking ways to balance work and childcare. For example, Hasnah and Maimune took unpaid parental leave before the outbreak of the COVID-19 pandemic. They found themselves unable to return to their pre-pandemic employment status due to income loss and subsequent unemployment. Consequently, they started small businesses in their villages, aiming to generate an income and maintain a work-family balance.

Hasnah always wakes up at 4:00 a.m. to prepare *mee thai*, stir-fried rice noodles with tofu, which is popular among local Chinese and Muslims in Phuket. An hour later, she gets ready and puts the *hijab* on before riding her motorcycle with a basket of *mee thai* boxes to sell at her mother's food stall. Conveniently located next to the main road, the halal breakfast stall attracts passers-by looking for affordable local halal breakfast options. Hasnah revealed that she was unable to secure suitable employment before the COVID-19 outbreak, a situation that remains unchanged. As a mother of two sons bearing financial burdens, Hasnah has been compelled to adapt her daily schedule to align with available halal business opportunities.

Maimune started a small halal food business with limited capital, showcasing innovation by using social media. She always posts about local snacks produced in Phuket and various foods on her Facebook page. At her home garden coffee shop, Maimune's appearance fluctuates between wearing a *hijab* and choosing not to, depending on her preference and feelings at the time. She explains, "Home is my space. Women are not necessary to cover their heads at home. I rather invite guests and customers to come and have local taste." For Maimune, donning Islamic dress is reserved for specific occasions, such as participating in religious activities at the mosque or making monthly donations at Islamic village schools.

Serving coffee and local snacks at the home garden coffee shop has emerged as a strategy to utilize and enhance resources for economically disadvantaged families. This practice has the potential to generate income and improve household economic welfare, promote entrepreneurship, and support small businesses. Tracing its origins to 2019, this alternative café model can be linked to the subsistence production systems that began in small garden plots around the household, cultivating products such as coconut, lemongrass, and peppermint. Maimune continues to play an essential role in providing food and income for her family, relatives, friends, and villagers who were laid off and could not start a small business independently.

The inception of the home garden café has made extensive contributions to the local community, shaping definitions of local food characteristics. These establishments allow local Muslims to attain cultural relevance and invite visitors from Phuket City and beyond to engage with this innovative business model. The café's unique character aligns with Phuket's promotion as a part of Andaman's cultural capital. Maimune revealed that the local government should be concerned about the proliferation of creative women entrepreneurs across the villages and conduct emerging studies on the knowledge of Muslims and other ethnic minorities. The micro and small-scale business villagers could continue to represent a notion of the local entrepreneur in terms of being able to take risks, self-determine and innovate. This entrepreneurial spirit aligns with universal Islamic values, adding another layer to its cultural significance. In addition, locally owned businesses run by villagers can give communities unique character and role models with risk-taking courage, self-determination and creativity. As a result, they can inspire young Muslims and non-Muslims to become entrepreneurs in their areas. Maimune stated at the end of our conversations that

> indeed, it can be said that the pervasive values of mixed local products and knowledge can combine within the model of international entrepreneurialism if the government has eyes.

In her view, this represents a new trend where halal norms are aligned with broader entrepreneurial opportunities, allowing local entrepreneurs to engage religiously and culturally within a market-driven society. From

Maimune's perspective, halal certification may not entail merely religion and science, but the essence of halal can be coordinated with current industry structures, especially during economic instability. To illustrate her point, she refers to Indonesia, the world's largest Muslim country, where halal certification for micro businesses is minimal. Drawing from her travel experiences before the pandemic, she noted that certified halal documentation was rarely found in micro and small business sectors.

In the context of global tourism and the halal industry, Hasnah and Maimune have carved out a unique economic development path in their specific locales. By aligning religious perspectives with economic practices, they have developed a concept for small-scale halal businesses targeting lower-middle-class Muslim women. Their efforts reveal a connection between the meanings of Islam and consumerism, defining a cultural sphere in spatial terms.

Despite their successes, women entrepreneurs still face significant challenges, especially in securing the necessary working capital. In the current economic climate, women are reluctant to dedicate and contribute to the area of entrepreneurship. Women-owned businesses remain small and often lack robust economic support and social capital to make significant business growth. Through conversations with Hasnah and Maimune, who live with their families, I learnt that extended family members play an important role in supporting their small businesses. This indicates the connections between Muslim women's day-to-day lives and "economic globalization from below" (Ribeiro 2006).

Gender differences and the performance of women-owned businesses (Brush and Hisrich 2000) show aspects that could affect satisfaction and achievement. In some Muslim regions, women's roles may be shaped by specific patriarchal cultural norms (Roomi and Harrison 2010). For example, the *hijab* can be both a symbol of negotiation and an instrument of gender segregation. This study creates a competitive advantage for micro halal businesses. Moreover, women's activities existed both inside and outside of the home. Within the scope of this study, the *hijab* is also a symbol of the marketization of religion (McAlexander et al. 2014) for ordinary people in everyday life practice.

In Phuket, halal tourism is sought after by Muslim tourists and has emerged as a significant aspect of the halal food business. Halal compliance can advance the tourism industry, especially when supported and promoted through national and local government policies. The villagers engage in halal food-related businesses directly and indirectly because of limited opportunities and investment capacity. Hasnah and Maimune realized that

Muslims in local areas have little knowledge on tourist destinations which are compatible with the needs of foreign Muslim travellers.

As such, it is difficult for home-based businesses to reach out to international Muslim travellers and visitors. However, Hasnah and Maimune agreed on the benefits of halal tourism and halal certification. Nonetheless, the halal landscape has gradually evolved and has shaped economic activities and cultures in the public domain. In turn, this forms Islam-inspired social spaces, in which economic and religious dimensions are intertwined with formal and informal norms as well as regulations.

Conclusion

Much of the existing research on Muslims in Thai society concentrates on the southernmost region, marked by a long history of political tension between the Thai government and the rulers of Patani. Meanwhile, there is a dearth of research on Muslims in the upper south of the western coast, especially regarding the contested concept of halal. Within the socio-cultural and political economy, Muslim women like Nora can negotiate the boundaries of its classical ideology in their everyday lives. Nevertheless, drawing on notions of halal, businesses must consider the complexities surrounding a conflict-ridden field site's disorderliness in researching women's food space. Key reflections focus on women activists in Pattani who have focused on communicating through the site and online fora, particularly during the pandemic. The existence of halal coffee shops that are locally owned and operated in a conflict-ridden area has shed light on the importance of empowering entrepreneurs and creating employment in the conflict area. It is an alternative space to support the victims of violent conflict and gender-based violence.

History attests to the fact that Muslim women as leaders are not new and can be traced back to times when women were prominent merchandisers alongside men. The proliferation of women entrepreneurs can enhance economic development domestically and regionally. A central insight of this paper is how it illuminates Muslim women's beliefs and practices within specific cultural and social contexts. The consumption of halal products, adherence to shariah during business hours, and other practices are significant expressions of Islamic identity. The intersectionality of low- and middle-income Southern Thai Muslim women's consumption and business style along with halal food and products can be closely analysed in the association between the use of the *hijab* and food halalization. They have utilized the *hijab*, a visible identity marker, to gain more acceptance for their halal food-related businesses. The practice of halalization has expanded across secular and non-secular markets as entrepreneurs respond to the Thai government's establishment of halal regulatory bodies to supervise halal certification. This reflects a complex interplay where neither structural conditions nor individual actors operate in isolation.

Contextually, analysing religious discourse alone is not sufficient to comprehend ongoing changes. To understand changes, social relations and economics must be taken into consideration. Through a close ethnographic description of actions, it is worthwhile to mention the different lifestyles of Muslims in these two areas. Religious ideas and practices have brought in various dimensions of political identity foundation as opposed to Muslims living in conflict-ridden areas in the southernmost provinces.

Yet, it is important to note that not all Muslim village women have found success in becoming entrepreneurs. Muslim women's contributions to negotiating and navigating the multiplicity of local halalization have brought attention to the often-invisible aspects of halal food culture. To disassemble halal culture in Muslim minority contexts can reflect ways of looking at the world. The argument that the *hijab* serves as an identity marker for Muslim women, shaped by religious practice, calls for recognizing the role of state investment in political and economic development programmes across various contexts. This point is crucial for rethinking cooperation, not the opposition of consumerism and the way religion has political significance. The *hijab* issue is, after all, about the perceived insertion of Islam into space and therefore depends on the already achieved reconceptualizing of the material spaces and contemporaneous commercialization associated with everyday life in Southern Thailand. Consequently, it becomes impossible to speak of clearly delineated and uniformly present divisions between consumption and Islam, which have led to the building of trust.

This chapter has demonstrated that matters of halal food are much more complicated. To show the ever-shifting constellation of practices and objects—akin to the conceptualization of place— the women discussed in this chapter have a direct bearing on women's lives. In Pattani, I argue that the differences within and between these everyday suburb sites' complexities have become more accentuated, often contradictory, and discontinuous in relation to the geographies of ethnic norms, secular values and Islamic virtues that have led to an understanding of gender power relations from local, secular and religious perspectives. This chapter thus reveals that religious beliefs attempt to delineate clearly bounded spaces, subjects, and ideologies that have become vital to this modern society and representations.

References

Amporn Marddent. 2016. "Gender Piety of Muslim Women in Thailand". PhD dissertation, Johann Wolfgang Goethe University.

———. 2017. "Women Political Participation in Peacebuilding in Southern Thailand". *AL ALBAB* 6, no. 2: 229–46.

Anderson, Wanni W. 2010. *Mapping Thai Muslims: Community Dynamics and Change on the Andaman Coast*. Chiang Mai: Silkworm Books.

Baum, Tom, and Nguyen Thi Thanh Hai. 2020. "Hospitality, Tourism, Human Rights and the Impact of COVID-19". *International Journal of Contemporary Hospitality Management* 32, no. 7: 2397–407.

Benhabib, Seyla. 1998. "Models of Public Space: Hannah Arendt, the Liberal Tradition, and Jurgen Habermas". In *Feminism: The Public and the Private Realm*, edited by Joan B. Landes, pp. 65–99. Oxford: Oxford University Press.

Brush, Candida G., and Robert D. Hisrich. 2000. "Women-Owned Businesses: An Exploratory Study Comparing Factors Affecting Performance". *Research Institute for Small & Emerging Business* (RISE), Working Paper 00-02, Washington, DC.

Bullough, Amanda and Maija Renko. 2017. "A Different Frame of Reference: Entrepreneurship and Gender Differences in the Perception of Danger". *Academy of Management Discoveries* 3, no. 1: 21–41.

Buncha Somboonsuke, Wiphada Wettayaprasit, and Prawat Wettayapraait. 2015. "Micro Halal Community Enterprise Database System: Case Study in Pattani and Songkhla Provinces". *Kasetsart Journal (Soc. Sci)* 36, no. 1: 568–76.

Caplan, Pat. 1997. "Approaches to the Study of Food, Health and Identity". In *Food, Health and Identity*, edited by Pat Caplan, pp. 1–31. London and New York: Routledge.

Certeau, Michel de, Luce Giard, and Pierre Mayo. 1998. *The Practice of Everyday Life: Living and Cooking*, vol. 2, translated by Timothy J. Tomasik. Minneapolis: University of Minnesota Press.

Chaiwat Satha-Anand. 1994. "Hijab and Moments of Legitimation: Islamic Resurgence in Thai Society". In *Asian Visions of Authority: Religion and the Modern States of East and Southeast Asia*, edited by Charles F. Keyes, Laurel Kendall, and Helen Hardacre, pp. 279–300. Honolulu: University of Hawaii Press.

de Araújo, Shadia Husseini. 2019. "Assembling Halal Meat and Poultry Production in Brazil: Agents, Practices, Power and Sites". *Geoforum* 100, no. 1: 220–28.

Fischer, Johan. 2005. "Feeding Secularism: Consuming Halal among the Malays in London". *Diaspora*, 14, no. 2/3: 275–97.

Kris Sincharoenkul. 2022. "COVID-19 Management and the Effectiveness of Government Support of the Tourism SMEs in Phuket". *Journal of International Studies, Prince of Songkla University* 12, no. 2: 93–128.

Marcus, George. 1995. "Ethnography in/of the World System: The Emergence of Multi-Sited Ethnography". *Annual Review in Anthropology* 24, no. 1: 95–117.

McAlexander, James H., Beth Leavenworth Dufault, Diane M. Martin, John W. Schouten. 2014. "The Marketization of Religion: Field, Capital, and Consumer Identity". *Journal of Consumer Research*, 41, no. 3: 858–75.

McCargo, Duncan, and Ukrist Pathmanand. 2005. *The Thaksinization of Thailand*. Copenhagen: NIAS Press.

Mintz, Sidney, and Christine Du Bois. 2002. "The Anthropology of Food and Eating". *Annual Review of Anthropology* 31, no. 1: 99–119.

Mohd Saiful Anwar Mohd Nawawi, Che Wan Jasimah Wan Mohamed Radzi, Mohd Zufri Mamat, Maisarah Hasbullah, Mohd Istajib Mokhtar, Hashem Salarzadeh Jenatabadi, Saadan Man, Azmah Haji Othman, Suzana Ariff Azizan, and Norhidayah Pauzi. 2017. "Halal Food Industry in Thailand: History, Prospects, and Challenges". International Halal Management Conference 2017, Sejong University, Seoul, South Korea.

Mohd Syaifulzafni Abdul Aziz. 2020. "Halal Certification in Malaysia and Singapore: Culinary Infrastructure at the Intersection of Religion and Politics". Master's thesis, University of Tasmania.

Muhammad Arafat bin Mohamad. 2007. "Memories of Martyrdom and Landscape of Terror: Fear and Resistance among the Malays of Southern Thailand". Master's thesis, National University of Singapore.

Mukherjee, S. Romi. 2014. "Global Halal: Meat, Money, and Religion". *Religion* 5, no. 1: 22–75.

National Economic and Social Development Council (NESDC). 2019. "Gross Regional and Provincial Product Chain". Volume Measure 2019 Edition. https://www.nesdc.go.th/nesdb_en/more_news.php?cid=156&filename=index (accessed 28 March 2023).

Parker, Lyn, and Laura Dales. 2014. "Introduction: The Everyday Agency of Women in Asia". *Asian Studies Review* 38, no. 2: 164–67.

Pawita Jamklai. 2020. ร้านน้ำชาชายแดนใต้ พื้นที่สร้างความสัมพันธ์ในความขัดแย้ง [Southern Border Tea Shop, Conflict Relations Area]. *Social Issue in Nisit Naksuksa*. https://nisitjournal.press/2020/01/02/tea-shop-thailand/ (accessed 28 April 2023).

Pimphun Sujarinphong. 2021. "Muslim Tourism Promotion in Thailand: Investigation and Evaluation on Tourism Activities and Routes". *Manutsayasart Wichakan* 28, no. 2: 28–54.

Rahanee Da-oh. 2021. เมาะเยาะ หญิงผู้โอบอุ้มครอบครัว และความหวังในการสืบสานอาหารพื้นบ้านชายแดนใต้ [Mak Yoh: A Breadwinner with Hope for Local Food Preservation along the Southern Border]. United Nations Development Programme. https://www.undp.org/sites/g/files/zskgke326/files/migration/th/UNDP_TH_Neomind_Thai.pdf (accessed 28 April 2023).

Ribeiro, Gustavo Lins. 2006. "Economic Globalisation from Below". *Etnográfica* 10, no. 2: 233–49.

Rinallo, Diego, Linda Scott, and Pauline Maclaran. 2012. "When Sacred Objects Go B*A(N)D: Fashion Rosaries and the Contemporary Linkage of Religion and Commerciality". *Consumption and Spirituality*, pp. 29–40.

Romdon Panjor. 2012. "ประท้วงฮิญาบที่ยะลา: ความทรงจำของการต่อรอง/Pratuang hijab thi yala: Kwam songjam khong karn torong" [Hijab Demonstrations in Yala: Memories of Negotiation]. *Rusamilae* 33, no. 1: 18–34.

Roomi, Muhammade Azam, and Pegram Harrison. 2010. "Behind the Veil: Women Only Entrepreneurship Training in Pakistan". *International Journal of Gender and Entrepreneurship* 2, no. 2: 150-72.
Sudarmiatin, Suparti, Faris Khoirul Anam, and Vega Wafaretta. 2020. "The Intention of Halal Certification by Micro Business". In International Conference on Islam, Economy, and Halal Industry, *KnE Social Sciences*, pp. 141-55.
Tri Ratnasari, Ririn, Sri Gunawan, Bayu Taufiq Possumah, Sylva Alif Rusmita, Tika Widiastuti, Sri Herianingrum. 2019. "Halal Food Certification for Improving the Competitiveness of Small and Medium Enterprise". *Opción* 35, no. 22: 510-25.
Vickers, Adrian. 2004. "'Malay Identity': Modernity, Invented Tradition and Forms of Knowledge". In *Contesting Malayness: Malay Identity Across Boundaries*, edited by Timothy P. Barnard, pp. 25-55. Singapore: National University of Singapore Press.
Vilasinee Sukka. 2014. "Gender, Women's Livelihood in Conflict Area: A Case Study of Pattani Province, Deep South of Thailand". Mekong Institute, Research Working Paper Series 2014, no. 2, Khon Kaen, Thailand.
von Mizes, Ludwig. 1998. *Human Action: A Treatise in Economics*. Auburn, Alabama: Ludwig von Mizes Institute.
Wannaphong Durongkaveroj. 2013. "An Economic Impact of Development Project: Case of Phuket International Airport in Thailand". Munich: Munich Personal RePEc Archive.
Wannasiri Wannasupchue, Mohhidin Oothman, Ungku Fatimah Ungku Zainal Abidin, Farah Adibah Che Ishak, and Siti Fatimah Mohamad. 2019. "Current Trends and Opportunities for Halal Restaurants in Thailand: A Conceptual Framework". *International Journal of Academic Research in Business and Social Sciences* 9, no. 1: 235-47.

Index

A
A&W, 133
Abdi Hersi, 18–19
Abdul Hadi W.M., 91
Abdul Halim Abdul Kadir, 22
Abdul Latip Talib, 91
Abdul Somad, 106
Abdullah Ahmad Badawi, 31, 33
Abdullahi an Naim, 90
Abdurrahman Wahid (Gus Dur), 54–55, 87–88
ABIM (Angkatan Belia Islam Malaysia), 84–85
Active Pharmaceutical Ingredients (APIs), 40
Adi Hidayat, 111
Adian Husaini, 90
Administration of Muslim Law Act (AMLA), 136
adulterated meat, 15–17
adultery, 107
Aemi Syazwani Abdul Keyon, 16, 23
Agricultural Resource Authority of Yemen, 19
Agromedia group, 110
Ahlulbayt TV, 22
Ahmadiyah community, 50
AJ Biologics of Aljomaih Group, 41
AJ Pharma, 38, 40–41
Al-Arqam, 85
Al-Azhar University, 103, 135
Al-Hiqma Souq, 163
Al-Quran Tagging.Sg, 163
Al Sheikh Ahmad Hujji al Kurdi, 21

"Alcohol Free Kg Glam Conservation Area", 170
Ali Shariati, 134
American Muslim Consumer Consortium (AMCC), 11, 22–23
Andaman Muslims, 202
Anglo-Siamese Treaty, 63
anti-halal movement, 28
anti-Islam, 57, 87, 91
anti-Muslim sentiments, 177
Anwar Ibrahim, 84–85
aqidah (belief), 48
Arab-Israeli conflict, 83
Arab Spring, 117
Arab traders, and spread of Islam, 63
Arabization, 133, 167
Arie Untung, 111
arranged marriages, 98
Asatizah Recognition Scheme (ARS) certification, 145
ASEAN, 5, 9, 15–16, 21, 149
Ashaari Mohammad, 85
Asian Financial Crisis, 66
Asian Lives Matter, 115
Assessment Institute for Foods, Drugs and Cosmetics of Indonesian Ulama Council, *see* LPPOM MUI
Association of Islamic Economic Experts (IAEI), 52
Association of Muslim Travel Agents, Singapore (AMTAS), 137
Ayat-Ayat Cinta 1, 103
Ayat-Ayat Cinta 2, 103
Ayatollah Khomeini, 83, 132

B
Baitul Mal wa Tamwil (BMT), 51
BaitulJannah, dating site, 30
Bandung Institute of Technology, see ITB
Bank for Agriculture and Agricultural Cooperatives (BAAC), 67–68
Bank Indonesia, 52
Bank Islam Malaysia Berhad, 66
Bank Islam Muamalat (BMI), 51
Bank Negara Malaysia, 41
Bank Syariah Indonesia (BSI), 52–53, 105
Bassam Tibi, 90
Best Buy, retailer, 11
betel leaf, 20
betel nut, 20, 23
Big Tech, 178
Black Lives Matter, 115
Black Twitter, 115
blasphemy, 56–57
blockchain system, 16, 23
Bon Odori, 90
Bourdieu, Pierre, 194
BPJPH (Badan Penyelenggara Jaminan Produk Halal), 55–57
Brand Islam, 178, 182, 186–87, 192–93, 195
British East India Company, 151
Broadcasting Act, 124
Brunei
 communal surveillance in, 118–21
 Muslim practices and digital presence in, 117–18
Bukalapak Syariah, 106
Bujang Lapok, movie, 1, 3
Bursa Malaysia, 43
Buya Syafii, 87, 88

C
caffeine products, 18
cancel culture, 120, 123
capitalism, 4, 96, 135–36, 178, 189, 195, 200

Central Islamic Committee of Thailand (CICOT), 200, 203, 209
Central Islamic Council of Thailand, 77
Centre of Alliance of Labour and Human Rights, 180
Chemical Company of Malaysia (CCM), 39–40, 43
Chicken Soup for the Soul, 103
Child Online Protection National Strategy Framework, 124
China, and halal market, 12
Christian evangelism, 87
Cinta Suci Zahrana (Pure Love of Zahrana), 104
civet cat coffee bean, see *kopi luwak*
civil society organizations (CSOs), 85, 87, 202
Coca-Cola, 18
Cold War, 83
College of Islamic Studies, 76
colonialism, 132, 176
commodification
 of piety, 175, 178, 185–89, 192, 195
 of religion, 138, 143–44, 162, 169, 187–88
Computer Misuse Act, 124
consumerism, 77, 182, 195, 213, 215
Cooperative Auditing Department (CAD), 66, 68, 76
Cooperative Promotion Department (CPD), 66, 68, 76
corruption, 81–82, 123
COVID-19 pandemic, 137, 199, 202, 207, 211
Culson, NJ, 88
Cyber Ummah community, 115

D
Dakwah 2.0, 117
dakwah movement, 2, 82, 88, 99, 101–2, 132, 146, 184–86, 188–89, 191–92

Dalam Mihrab Cinta (Inside the Mihrab of Love), 104
Dancow milk product, 53
DAOL-Islamic, 68
DAOL (Thailand) PCL, 68
DBP (Dewan Bahasa dan Pustaka), 90
DDII (Dewan Da'wah Islamiyah Indonesia), 58, 99
Deen Dunya, 162, 183–88
Defamation Act, 124
Den Tomina, 66, 76
Department of Islamic Development in Malaysia, *see* JAKIM
Department of Standards Malaysia (DOSM), 32, 34
Department of Veterinary Services, 36
Derwish Turkish Restaurant, 168
digital activism, 117
digital vigilantism, 123
Dolce & Gabanna, 29
Douglas, Heather, 18
doxa, 194
DPR (Dewan Perwakilan Rakyat), 50
DPS (Dewan Pengawas Syariah), 51, 57
DSN (Dewan Syariah Nasional), 48–49, 51–52, 57
dUCk cosmetics, 117

E
Emha Ainun Nadjib, 91
ENOUGH, campaign, 206–8
enzyme-linked immunosorbent assay (ELISA), 16
Era Adicitra Intermedia, 103
Erick Thohir, 52
E-Ummah community, 115
Evi Effendi, 106

F
Facebook, 97, 104–6, 110, 207
fake halal meat, 15

Fatin Afika, 183–88
fatwa (legal opinions), 4, 17–18, 27, 47–48, 50, 53, 56–57, 59, 87
Fazlur Rahman, 90
Federation of Malaysian Manufacturers, 38
"feel-good Islam", 184–89
Felix Siauw, 106, 111
feminism, 88, 115
"Fight COVID Gift Pack", 159
Finansa Life Assurance PCL, 69
fiqh (jurisprudential), 33, 36, 43, 90
food industry, 153–56
Food Safety According to Hazard Analysis and Critical Control Points, 33
Food Safety and Quality Division, 36
FPI (Front Pembela Islam), 46
fraudulent marketing, 9–10, 14–17, 22
Free Trade Zone, Johor, 37

G
Gema Insani Press, 102
genetically modified food, 15
genetically modified organisms, 30
global halal food market, 9, 33
"global halal hub", 31
Global Halal Standards, 36
Global Islamic Economic Indicator (GIEI), 30
Global Islamic Economy Report, 16
Global Muslim travel index, 140
Global South, 87, 92, 176, 180
globalization, 87
glonggong, 16–17
Goldziher, Ignaz, 88
"good Muslim", 85
Google, 108
Government Savings Bank (GSB), 66–67
greenwashing, 180
Gucci, 29
Guntur Soeharjanto, 103

Gus Dur (Abdurrahman Wahid),
    54–55, 87–88
gutka, 20, 23

H
H&M, 178–83
Habibburahman El-Shirazi, 103–4
hadith, 19, 51, 158, 161–62
Hady Mirza, 144
Hafiz M. Ahmed, 12
haj, as an industry, 133–35
Haji Sulong, 66
Hajj, 134
halal
    activism, 4, 116
    branding, 167
    contextual meaning of, 203–6
    economy, 4, 30, 41–42, 116, 175, 201
    industry, 2, 13, 15–16, 22, 27, 29–32, 34–35, 37–38, 41–42, 53–55, 104–6, 109, 145, 204
    laboratory, 38
    lifestyle, 2–3, 10, 12, 27–29, 105–6, 115–18, 123
    logo, 13, 143, 203, 210
    matchmaking, 30, 99, 102, 105, 107, 109
    parks, 37–38
    pharmaceuticals, 38–41
    products, range of, 10
    standards, 32–35
    status, disputes regarding, 17–22
    tourism, 13, 31, 42, 133, 140, 146, 200, 202, 204, 213–14
    vaccines, 30, 39
Halal Auditor Institute, *see* LPH
halal certification
    accreditation, 16, 200, 203
    campaign against, 28
    confidence in, 15, 22
    core concepts for, 12
    eyeglasses, and, 167
    introduction of, 35–37
    investing in, 11
    mandatory, 30, 39, 56
    restaurants, and, 56
    standard procedures, and, 13, 22, 34, 145, 206
    universal agreement, and, 9–10
    voluntary, 54
Halal Ecosystem Solutions, 37
Halal Food and Islamic Consumer
    Products Committee, 32
"halal gap", 117
halal-haram police, 121
Halal Hub, 35–36, 38
Halal Industry Development
    Corporation (HDC), 31
Halal Industry Master Plan 2030, 41
"Halal National Mark", 22
Halal Product Assurance Law, 30, 39, 50, 57
Halal Standard Institute of Thailand, 200, 203–4
Halal Times, 12
halalan toyibban principle, 17
HalalBooking.com, 133
"halalization", 201, 214–15
Hamid Basalamah, 106
Hamka, 91, 93
Hanan Attaki, 106, 111
Handy Bonny, 111
Hanung Bramantyo, 103
haram status, disputes regarding, 17–22
Haryani Ismail, 144
Hasan Al-Banna, 100
Hasan Hanafi, 90
Hassan Basri, 54
Haw Chinese Muslims, 63
Hawaya, dating site, 110
Hawks, Lisa Svac, 11
Hazard Analysis and Critical Control
    (HACCP), 203
"heritage site", 152

H. Hartono Ahmad Jaiz, 90
hijab, 27, 28, 117–18, 150, 174, 179–80, 199–201
  contextual meaning of, 203–6, 208, 213
hijrah, 30, 98, 105–6, 109–10, 134, 137
Hijrah Taaruf, matchmaking app, 105, 110
Himpunan Perbankan Syari'ah, 4
Hizbut Tahrir Indonesia (HTI), 46, 97, 102
Hollywings, 56
hudud law, 46, 132
human capital, 201
Human Development Index (HDI), 64
human rights, 87
humanism, 4, 86–88
Hussein Bulhan, 176
hygiene and personal care, 156, 158–61

I
Ibank, 68–71, 75–76
IBM technologies, 16
Ichan Sam, 59
ICMI (Ikatan Cendekiawan Muslim Indonesia), 51
identity politics, 93
Ikhwanul Muslimin, *see* Muslim Brotherhood
IKIM (Institut Kefahaman Islam Malaysia), 84, 88
Indonesia
  halal certifier in, 28, 30
  Islamic lifestyle in, 105–6
"Indonesia Islamic Economic Masterplan 2019–24", 105
Indonesia-Malaysia-Thailand Triangle (IMT-GT), 67
Indonesia Tanpa Pacaran, dating site, 30, 106, 11
Indonesian Council of Ulama, *see* MUI
Indonesian Islamic Propagation Council, *see* DDII

influencer, 4, 119–22, 124–25, 144, 177–80, 182–83, 188–89
Instagram, 105–10, 119, 178–79, 183, 185, 188–89, 191
Institute for Islam and Social Studies, *see* LKiS
Institute of Language and Literature, *see* DBP
insurance, 48–49, 51, 62, 69–70, 150
Internal Halal Audit Committee, 36
International Halal Accreditation Board, 37
International Halal Authority Board (IHAB), 34
International Halal Certification, 37
International Islamic University of Malaysia (IIUM), 84
Internet Code of Practice, 124
Iran, and halal market, 12–13, 22
Iranian Revolution, 2, 83, 132
Ishqr, dating site, 110
Iskandar Halal Park (IHP), 37
Islam
  Arab traders, and spread of, 63
  commercialization of, 10
  hatred towards, 57
  pillar of, 134, 166
Islam and Secularism, 87
"Islam as a way of life", 2
"Islam Liberal", 88, 90
Islamic
  banking, 2, 51, 57, 62, 65–68, 71, 84, 150, 189–90
  cooperative, 66, 68–72
  finance, 4, 30, 41, 48–49, 62, 67, 70–73, 75–77, 145, 195
  identity, 97, 103, 180, 214
  law, 18, 34, 36, 71, 83, 93
  lifestyle, 5, 99, 150, 152, 155–56, 161, 165, 168–69
  loan, 72–73
  pawnbroking, 73
  populism, 97

products, 153–67
publishing, 102–3
resurgence, 2–3, 82–83, 130–32
revivalism, 2, 81–85, 132
values, 122, 212
Islamic Affairs Executive, 36
Islamic Bank Act, 67
Islamic Bank of Thailand Act, 67
"Islamic capitalist ideology", 70–71
Islamic Cooperatives Network, 68, 75
Islamic Defender Front, *see* FPI
Islamic Equity Account, 68
Islamic Financial Institution (IFI), 62, 65–67, 69–73, 75–77
"Islamic Lifestyle Store", 162
Islamic Party of Malaysia (PAS), 84
Islamic Private Fund, 68
Islamic Religious Council of Singapore, *see* MUIS
Islamic Smart Algo, 68
Islamic Youth Movement of Malaysia, *see* ABIM
Islamization, 42, 81–82, 84–88, 90–93, 109, 202
Islamophobia, 5, 11, 174–78, 183, 187, 193, 195
Ismail Sabri Yaakob, 41–42
Israel, and war with Palestine, 11, 83, 137
ITB (Institut Teknologi Bandung), 99

J
Jakarta Charter, 46, 59
JAKIM (Jabatan Kemajuan Islam Malaysia), 21, 31–32, 34–37, 39, 84, 87
Jamaat Tabligh, 102
Jamal Kazura Aromatics, 153
Jejak Rasul tours, 138–39
jihadism, 167
Johor Biotechnology & Biodiversity Corporation (J-Biotech), 37
Johor State investment company, 37
Joko Widodo (Jokowi), 52, 59

K
Kaabah, 134–35, 137–38, 165, 186
"Kaabah Bricks", 165–66, 168
"*kafir*", 86
KAMMI (Kesatuan Aksi Mahasiswa Muslim Indonesia), 99
Kampong Gelam, 150–53, 168–70
Kassim Ahmad, 91
kebab shops, ban on, 28
Kembali ke Akar, 91
Kembali ke Sumber: Jejak-Jejak Pengumulan Kesusastraan Islam di Nusantara, 91
Ketika Cinta Bertasbih (When Love Praises God), 104
Ketika Cinta Bertasbih II (When Love Praises God II), 104
KFC, 133
Khadijah, 207
khalwat, 107
khat, evergreen shrub, 18–19, 23
Kingdom of Sukhothai, 63
"Kitchen of the World", 204
KNEKS (Komite Nasional Ekonomi dan Keuangan Syariah), 105
KNKS (Komite Nasional Ekonomi dan Keuangan Syariah), 53
Kompas Gramedia Group (KKG), 103
kopi luwak, 21–22
kosher, 11, 15
Krung Thai Bank, 67
Krung Thai Shariah, 67
KTBST Holding PCL, 68
"KTBST-Islamic", 68
Kuntowijoyo, 91
Kuwait Finance House, 30
Kuwait National Fatwa Committee, 21
Kyai Sahal Mahfudh, 59

L
La Ode Munafar, 106
Layanan Syariah, 106
"liberal" Muslims, 2, 85

Lina Mukherjee, 56
Line, 106
Lingkar Pena Publishing House, 103
LinkAja, 106
Lisa Surihani, 189
Liyana Musfirah, 144
LKiS (Lembaga Kajian Islam dan Sosial), 102–3
LoveHabibi, dating site, 110
LPH (Lembaga Pemeriksa Halal), 57
LPPOM MUI (Lembaga Pengkajian Pangan, Obatan-obatan dan Kosmetika Majelis Ulama Indonesia), 28, 48, 53–55, 57
see also MUI
LTF-RMF, 68

M
madhhab (school of thought), 34, 42
Mahathir Mohamad, 83, 85, 132
Majelis Suro (Suro Assembly), 101–2
Majmūʿat al-Rasāil (*Collection of Treatises*), 100
Maklumat Sastra Profetik, 91
makruh (discouraged), 19
MalArab cuisine, 156–57
Malay-Muslim identity, 88, 146, 200
Malay Muslims, 63
Malay publishing industry, 90
Malay royal family, 150–51
Malayan Banking Berhad (Maybank), 189–90
Malaysia
 cartel, 15
 halal industry in, 13, 16, 31–32
Malaysia External Trade Development Corporation (MATRADE), 31, 38
Malaysia Games, 167
Malaysia Halal Analysis Centre (MyHAC), 38
Malaysia International Halal Authorities and Bodies System (MYIHAB), 36
Malaysia International Halal Show Case (MIHAS), 31
Malaysian Coat of Arms, 163
Malaysian Communication and Multimedia Commission, 87
Malaysian Halal Council (MHC), 34
Malaysian Institute of Islamic Understanding, *see* IKIM
Malaysian Ulama Association, *see* PUM
Malaysia's Halal Standards (MS), 32–33
Maqasid Al-Shariʿah, 40, 125–26
marhaenism, 86, 93
Marriage Conference, dating site, 30
Maʾruf Amin, 49, 52, 55, 58–59
Masturah Khalid, 178–83
Mat & Minah, dating site, 30
Maybank Islamic, 188–93
McDonald's, 133
Media Taaruf-Jodoh Islami, matchmaking app, 105, 110
Melayu Islam Beraja (Malay Islamic Monarchy, MIB), 116, 118, 120, 122–25
Menuju Taaruf dan Poligami, 105, 111
MES (Masyarakat Ekonomi Syariah), 52
Meta, 178
meta colonialism, 176
MFC Asset Management Company Limited, 68
"MFC Islamic Fund", 68
microcelebrity, 177–79, 183–84, 188
Midamar Corporation, 15
middle class, 2, 5, 10, 84, 130–31, 133, 139, 143, 149–50, 168, 175, 177, 182
Minder, dating site, 30, 110
Ministry of Agriculture and Cooperatives (MOAC), Thailand, 66, 68, 76
Ministry of Finance, Thailand, 68
Ministry of Health, Malaysia, 36
Ministry of Home Affairs Malaysia (KDN), 163–64

Ministry of Interior, Thailand, 64
Ministry of International Trade and Industry, Malaysia, 31
Ministry of National Development Planning (Bappenas), Indonesia, 105
Ministry of Science, Technology and Innovation, Malaysia, 32
Mixue, ice cream franchise, 56
Mizan, publisher, 102–3
Mizi Wahid, 188–93
modest fashion, 29, 143–44, 176, 179–80, 182, 185, 208
Mohamad Abdalla, 19
Mohamed Arkoun, 90
Mohammad Hashim Kamali, 133
Monetary Authority, *see* OJK
money laundering, 107
MS 1500-2009: Halal Food—Production, Preparation, Handling and Storage—General Guidelines, 33
MS2424: 2012 Halal Pharmaceuticals General Guideline, 39
mudarabah, 69–70, 77, 190
Muhammad, Prophet, 10, 106, 137, 152–53, 155, 158, 169, 191–92, 207
Muhammadiyah, 46–47, 53–55, 58–59
MUI (Majelis Ulama Indonesia), 4, 18, 21, 28, 46, 51, 56–60, 87
  shariah initiative, and, 47–50
  see also LPPOM MUI
MUIS (Majlis Ugama Islam Singapura), 136–38, 143, 145
multiculturalism, 4, 6, 87–90
murabahah, 69, 72–73, 190
Muscat Municipality of Oman, 152
musharakah, 69, 77
Muslim Brotherhood, 2, 97, 99–100, 167
Muslim consumer market, 3
Muslim identity, 27, 204

"Muslim market", 175–76
Muslim "pop" preachers, 10–11
Muslim population, 9, 13, 28–29
Muslim United network, 106
Mustafa Kamal Ataturk: Penegak Agenda Yahudi, 91
Mutawwif of Southeast Asian Pilgrims (Muasassah), 136
Muzmatch, dating site, 30, 96
myQuran.com, 105

N
Nahdlatul Ulama (NU), 46–47, 53–55, 59
Nata Reza, 111
National Agricultural Policy, 37
National Census, Thailand, 63
National Committees of Shariah Economy and Finance, *see* KNKS
National Economic and Islamic Finance Committee, *see* KNEKS
National Fatwa Council, 87
National Front of Indonesian Muslim Students, *see* KAMMI
National Pharmaceutical Regulatory Agency (NPRA), 39
National Shariah Board, *see* DSN
National Statistical Office, Thailand, 63–65
Neelofa, 117, 189
Negara Zikir (Zikir Nation), 116, 125–26
neoliberalism, 5, 87, 175–78, 183, 187, 193–95
New Order, 47–48, 51
nicotine, 23
Nik Aziz Nik Mat, 84
Nike, 29, 174, 176
non-government organization (NGO), 207, 209
non-*ribawi* (non-usury-based) system, 51
Normala binti Abdul Samad, 40

"Nothing Artificial, Ever", advertising claim, 15
Nurazmi Kuntum, 91
Nurcholish Madjid (Cak Nur), 87–88, 135

O
Office of the National Economic and Social Development Council (NESDC), Thailand, 64, 200
OJK (Otoritas Jasa Keuangan), 57
Oki Setiana Dewi, 111
"One Company, Two Systems", 69
One Tambon One Product (OTOP), 207
online dating, 3, 96–105
 see also matchmaking under halal
organic food, 14–15
Organization of Islamic Cooperation (OIC), 30, 139–42
Ottoman caliphate, 83
oud (agarwood) scent, 153

P
paan bahar, 20, 23
paan leaves, 19–20
Palestine, and war with Israel, 11, 83, 137
Pancasila, 46, 48–49, 55, 58–59
pan masala, 20, 23
Partai Keadilan (Justice Party), 101
Pattani Islamic Savings Cooperative Limited, 62, 66, 76
Pattani Provincial Islamic Council, 66
perfume industry, 153
Persatuan Islam (Persis), 47, 58
Pharmaniaga, 38
Philippines' Department of Trade and Industry (DTI), 13
Phillipe Life Assurance PCL, 69
PKS (Partai Keadilan Sejahtera), 99, 101–2

pluralism, 4, 87–90
Polemik Sastera Islam, 91
political Islam, 82
polymerase chain reaction (PCR), 16
pornography, 49, 50, 122
poverty, 64, 76, 207
P. Ramlee, 1
Prayut Chan-ocha, 103
Presidential Advisory Council (Wantimpres), 55
Prince of Songkla University, 66, 76, 204
Pro Hijab, 174
Prosperous Justice Party, *see* PKS
Pro-U Media, 103
Provincial Islamic Committees, Thailand, 200
PTS Litera, 90–91
Public Entertainment Act, 124
Pulau Indah Industrial Park, 37
PUM (Persatuan Ulama Malaysia), 22

Q
Quanta-Elez Media Komputindo, 110
Qultum Media, 110
Quraish tribe, 106
Quran, 19, 83, 100, 139, 162–65, 168–69, 185

R
racial riot, 84
racism, 115
Reddit, 116
religious commodification, 138, 143–44, 162, 169, 187–88
Republika, 110
Research Center for the Islamic Affairs Division, 35
"Revealed Knowledge", 86
rumahtaaruf.com, 105
Runtuhnya Islam Andalusia: Pelengkap Kemasyhuran Ratu Isabella, 91
Russia, and halal market, 12–13

S

sadaqah house (charitable house), 69, 73
"*Sadaqah* Removes Difficulties", 191
Sahal Mahfudh, 49
Salaam Gateway, 40
Salaam Swipe, dating site, 30, 96
Salafi-Wahhabism, 2, 83, 97, 132, 167
Samsina Abd. Rahman, 91
Sastera Islam (Islamic Literature), 4, 86–88, 91, 93
Sastera Melayu Islam: Konsep, Teori dan Aplikasi, 91
Sastra dan Religiositas, 91
Sastra yang Membebaskan: Sikap Terhadap Struktur dan Anutan Seni Moderen Indonesia, 91
Sayyed-Mohammad-Al Musawi, 22
Schacht, Joseph, 88
Second Industrial Master Plan, 37
Second World War, 83
secularism, 18, 87–88, 90
Securities Commission, 41
Sedition Act, 124
Selangor State Fatwa Committee, 87
self-censorship, 116, 121–23
Senior Council of Ulama, 18
September 11 (9/11) terrorist attacks, 9, 177
Shah of Iran, 83, 132
Shahnon Ahmad, 91
shariah
 banking, 47, 49, 51–53
 contracts, 69
 economy, 48, 51–53, 57–58
 governance, 70–71
 law, 2, 28, 32, 34–35, 46
 legislation, 49–50
shariah-compliant
 animal slaughter, 34
 financial system, 51–52, 68–69
 lifestyle, 55–57, 98, 115–16
 literature, 91, 93

social media content, 123–26
 tourism, 138–46
Shariah Economic Society, *see* MES
Shariah Supervisory Council, *see* DPS
shariahtization, 5, 46–49, 51, 53–55, 58–59
Sheikhul Islam Office of Thailand, 203
Shi'a, 83, 85, 132, 140
Shi'ism's *vilayet-e-faqeh*, 2
Shopee Barakah, 106
sidr honey, 155
SimplySiti, 117
Singapore
 colonization of, 150
 haj and *umrah* industry in, 130, 131, 135–37, 143–45
 halal hub, as, 15, 140
 Muslim middle class in, 131, 133, 149–50
 population, 130, 149
Singapore Tourism Board, 140
Singlemuslim, dating site, 30, 110
"Sipilis", 87
Sisters in Islam (SIS), 87
Slamet Effendy Yusuf, 59
small and medium industries (SMEs), 31, 36, 200, 207, 210
small and micro community enterprises (SMCEs), 203, 207
social custom, role of, 27
social media, 115–19, 121–22
 regulation, 124
 selective policing in, 120, 124
 shariah-compliant, 123–26
socio-cultural Islamism, 82, 85
Solahuddin Press, 102
Southeast Asia, 2, 9, 28–30
Sri Mulyani, 52
Sri Nakhon Bank, 66
Standards of Malaysia Act, 32
State Agency of Halal Product Assurance, *see* BPJPH
State Law on Job Creation, 57

State Law on Pornography legislation, 49–50
State of the Global Islamic Economy Report, 16, 39, 105, 175
Straits Times, 149
Suharto, 28, 47–48, 50–51, 53–54, 58, 83, 102–3, 132
Sukarno, 93
Sukuk, 68
Sulawesi Muslims, 63
Sunnah, 83
Sunni, 58, 83, 85, 132, 140
"surveillance capitalism", 178
Survey on Conditions of Society, Culture and Mental Health, Thailand, 63
Suryadharma Ali, 55
Susilo Bambang Yudhoyono (SBY), 28, 52, 55
Sweet Rose Couture, 185
Swing Muslim Lifestyle Store, 161–64, 169
Syahadat Cinta, 91
Syed Hussein Alatas, 92
Syed Muhammad Naquib Al-Attas, 87
Syed Sheikh Al-Hadi, 93, 135, 136

T
ta'aruf, 96, 98, 101–10
  concept of, 99–100
  various applications, 107–9
Taaruf ID, matchmaking app, 105, 110
Taaruf Islam Online, 105
Taaruf Lalu Nikah, matchmaking app, 105, 110
Ta'aruf Online Indonesia (TOI), 99, 104–5, 107–11
Taaruf Siap Nikah Islam International, 105, 111
tarbiyah movement, 2, 98–103, 106, 109–10
Tasyari (Taaruf Syar'i), matchmaking app, 105, 110

Taufiq Rahman Al-Azizy, 91
tawṣiyya (recommendations), 47–48
Tenggelamnya Kapal Van Der Wijck, 91
Teori dan Pemikiran Sastera Islam di Malaysia, 91
terrorism, 11, 28
Thailand
  Deep South, 63, 65, 72, 202, 206
  halal certification in, 203
  Islamic finance in, 62, 65–77
  mosques in, 64
  Muslims socio-economic status in, and, 63–65
  population, 63–64
  poverty in, 64, 76, 207
  tourism sector in, 199–200
  unemployment in, 65
Thaksin Shinawatra, 207
TikTok, 109, 116
Tinder, 107–9
Tokopedia Salam, 106
Trade Description Act of Malaysia, 35
Tri Susanto, 53
TudungPeople, 185
"Tun Abdullah Badawi's Lecture on Halal Economy" 41
TV3, 138
Twitter, 104

U
ulama (religious scholars), 9–10, 47, 54, 58, 81, 84
  government approved, 18
  halal/haram status, and disputes regarding, 17–22
  political governance, and, 132
ummah (Muslim community), 48, 88, 103, 115
Undesirable Publications Act, 124
unemployment, 64–65, 76, 199, 211
United Malayan Land Berhad (UM Land), 37

United Malays National Organization
(UMNO), 83–85
University of Brawijaya, 53
Urban Redevelopment Authority, 152
US Food and Drug Administration
(FDA), 159

V
vegetarian lifestyle, 11
Veil, dating site, 110

W
wadi'ah, 69
Wanita, women's collective, 207
waqf institution (endowment), 69, 73
war on terror, 176
Wawasan 2035, 125
Western Orientalists, 88
Western values, 28
WhatsApp, 106

Whole Foods Market, 14–15
women's rights, 115
World Halal Forum (WHF), 31
"World Halal Kitchens", 204

X
xenophobic, 11

Y
Yaacob Ibrahim, 149
"Yala Teacher Training College
Incident", 204
Y.B. Mangunwijaya, 91
youth activism, 116, 123
"youth bulge", 28
YouTube, 106, 109

Z
zakat (tithe) institution, 69, 73
Zalora, 182

www.ingramcontent.com/pod-product-compliance
Lightning Source LLC
Chambersburg PA
CBHW042225010526
44111CB00044B/2946